PracticePlanners®

Arthur E. Jongsma, Jr., Series Editor

The Intellectual and Developmental Disability Treatment Planner, with DSM-5 Updates

Kellye Slaggert

Arthur E. Jongsma, Jr.

WILEY

This book is printed on acid-free paper. ♾

Copyright © 2015 by John Wiley & Sons. All rights reserved.

Published simultaneously in Canada.

All references to diagnostic codes and the entire content of Appendix B are reprinted with permission from the *Diagnostic and Statistical Manual of Mental Disorders, Fourth Edition.* Copyright 1994. American Psychiatric Association.

No part of this publication may be reproduced, stored in a retrieval system or transmitted in any form or by any means, electronic, mechanical, photocopying, recording, scanning or otherwise, except as permitted under Sections 107 or 108 of the 1976 United States Copyright Act, without either the prior written permission of the Publisher, or authorization through payment of the appropriate per-copy fee to the Copyright Clearance Center, 222 Rosewood Drive, Danvers, MA 01923, (978) 750-8400, fax (978) 750-4744. Requests to the Publisher for permission should be addressed to the Permissions Department, John Wiley & Sons, Inc., 605 Third Avenue, New York, NY 10158-0012, (212) 850-6011, fax (212) 850-6008, E-Mail: PERMREQ @ WILEY.COM.

This publication is designed to provide accurate and authoritative information in regard to the subject matter covered. It is sold with the understanding that the publisher is not engaged in rendering professional services. If legal, accounting, medical, psychological or any other expert assistance is required, the services of a competent professional person should be sought.

Designations used by companies to distinguish their products are often claimed as trademarks. In all instances where John Wiley & Sons, Inc. is aware of a claim, the product names appear in initial capital or all capital letters. Readers, however, should contact the appropriate companies for more complete information regarding trademarks and registration.

Note about Photocopy Rights

The publisher grants purchasers permission to reproduce handouts from this book for professional use with their clients.

Library of Congress Cataloging-in-Publication Data:

Slaggert, Kellye.
The intellectual and developmental disability treatment planner / Kellye Slaggert, Arthur E. Jongsma, Jr.
p. ; cm. — (Practice planners series)
9781119073307 ePub 9781119075073 ePDF 9781119075066
1. Mental retardation—Treatment—Planning—Handbooks, manuals, etc. 2. Developmental disabilities—Treatment—Planning—Handbooks, manuals, etc. 3. Psychotherapy—Planning—Handbooks, manuals, etc. I. Jongsma, Arthur E., 1943– II. Title. III. Practice planners.
[DNLM: 1. Mental Retardation—therapy—Handbooks. 2. Patient Care Planning—Handbooks. 3. Developmental Disabilities—therapy—Handbooks. 4. Psychiatry—organization & administration—Handbooks. 5. Psychotherapy—methods—Handbooks. WM 34 D6295m 2000]
RC570.2 .S59 2000
616.85'8806—dc21

00-023875

Printed in the United States of America.

To Jeff, Tyler, Casey, Mitchell, and Danielle for their unyielding and constant support while I spent countless hours in front of the computer. This book truly was a family effort.

—Kellye Slaggert

To all those parents and family members who have advocated for, loved, and supported their fellow family member who is developmentally disabled. They have taught us selfless service.

—Arthur E. Jongsma, Jr.

CONTENTS

PRACTICE*PLANNERS*® SERIES PREFACE

Accountability is an important dimension of the practice of psychotherapy. Treatment programs, public agencies, clinics, and practitioners must justify and document their treatment plans to outside review entities in order to be reimbursed for services. The books in the Practice*Planners*® series are designed to help practitioners fulfill these documentation requirements efficiently and professionally.

The Practice*Planners*® series includes a wide array of treatment planning books including not only the original *Complete Adult Psychotherapy Treatment Planner*, *Child Psychotherapy Treatment Planner*, and *Adolescent Psychotherapy Treatment Planner*, all now in their fifth editions, but also *Treatment Planners* targeted to specialty areas of practice, including:

- Addictions
- Co-occurring disorders
- Behavioral medicine
- College students
- Couples therapy
- Crisis counseling
- Early childhood education
- Employee assistance
- Family therapy
- Gays and lesbians
- Group therapy
- Juvenile justice and residential care
- Intellectual and developmental disability
- Neuropsychology
- Older adults
- Parenting skills
- Pastoral counseling
- Personality disorders

- Probation and parole
- Psychopharmacology
- Rehabilitation psychology
- School counseling and school social work
- Severe and persistent mental illness
- Sexual abuse victims and offenders
- Social work and human services
- Special education
- Speech-language pathology
- Suicide and homicide risk assessment
- Veterans and active military duty
- Women's issues

In addition, there are three branches of companion books that can be used in conjunction with the *Treatment Planners*, or on their own:

- ***Progress Notes Planners*** provide a menu of progress statements that elaborate on the client's symptom presentation and the provider's therapeutic intervention. Each *Progress Notes Planner* statement is directly integrated with the behavioral definitions and therapeutic interventions from its companion *Treatment Planner*.
- ***Homework Planners*** include homework assignments designed around each presenting problem (such as anxiety, depression, substance use, anger control problems, eating disorders, or panic disorder) that is the focus of a chapter in its corresponding *Treatment Planner.*
- ***Client Education Handout Planners*** provide brochures and handouts to help educate and inform clients on presenting problems and mental health issues, as well as life skills techniques. The handouts are included on CD-ROMs for easy printing from your computer and are ideal for use in waiting rooms, at presentations, as newsletters, or as information for clients struggling with mental illness issues. The topics covered by these handouts correspond to the presenting problems in the *Treatment Planners*.

The series also includes adjunctive books, such as *The Psychotherapy Documentation Primer* and *The Clinical Documentation Sourcebook*, contain forms and resources to aid the clinician in mental health practice management.

The goal of our series is to provide practitioners with the resources they need in order to provide high-quality care in the era of accountability. To put it simply: We seek to help you spend more time on patients, and less time on paperwork.

ARTHUR E. JONGSMA, JR.
Grand Rapids, Michigan

PREFACE

Many powerful lessons have been learned in working with clients with developmental disabilities, some lessons far more powerful than any formal education. This book is enhanced by our having learned these lessons and by our having had the privilege of working with developmentally disabled clients. It is our hope that this Planner will make a significant contribution to improving the quality and consistency of care provided to people with developmental disabilities.

Examining the needs of this population yields a vast array of abilities and needs. Each person with a developmental disability is unique. Addressing the vast range of intellectual and adaptive abilities and the interactive effect of each creates a myriad of unique combinations. This book aims for comprehensive coverage of the needs of clients with developmental disabilities in a concise manner with thorough content.

Readers should use this book guided by what is important to the individual client and his/her family, letting them pursue their own dreams and goals. Empowering the client with decision making places the agency in a position of responding to the needs of the clients. This is a major shift away from making the client fit into the system. This requires listening to the client regarding what he/she needs to have a good life. Use of treatment plan suggestions in this book should be guided by the client's vision and dreams for his/her own life.

By promoting choices, independent decision making, positive community participation, and individual competencies, agencies can lay the foundation for a person's life plan. Program goals and objectives should be client focused and crafted to ensure that activities are age appropriate, functional, and community referenced.

Skill acquisition chapters should be used as guiding points, building upon the person's strengths and existing capacities. When skill building is not feasible, supports need to be provided to the client. Support networks, resources, and personnel, both formal and informal, need to be geared toward meaningful community involvement.

As we were writing this book, a companion book was being written by David Berghuis and Arthur Jongsma, the *Severe and Persistent Mental Illness*

Treatment Planner. The authors shared ideas and insights during the development of the two manuscripts; therefore, these two books should be viewed as complementing one another. The companion books are intended to be useful to clinicians in community mental health settings or elsewhere who serve clients with developmental disabilities, severe and persistent mental illness, or both conditions.

We are deeply indebted to the people and agencies that permitted access to their libraries—Steve Goodman from the Ottawa Area Intermediate District, Al Hoogewind at Hope Network, the Pine Rest Center for Developmental Disabilities, Ottawa County Community Mental Health, and the local offices of the Association of Retarded Citizens. From each library, valuable sources of information contributing to this book were obtained.

Special thanks goes to the individuals who offered insightful suggestions from their respective specialties—Dale Drooger, Karen Becker, and Susan Karpinski from Ottawa County Community Mental Health.

We are grateful to Jen Byrne for her assistance and support with preparing the manuscript and her patience and flexibility with some of the technical difficulties encountered during the scope of this book. She organized the innumerable details that are part of a completed manuscript.

David Berghuis and his wife Barbara, both community mental health professionals, spent numerous hours in reviewing chapters, improving wording, and offering critical review and helpful suggestions to enhance the contents of the chapters. Their fresh and objective ideas, coupled with their years of experience in working with clients with developmental disabilities, aided in bringing this book to completion. We would also like to recognize the able leadership of our editor at John Wiley & Sons, Kelly Franklin. She has worked tirelessly to make the Practice Planners a high-quality and successful series. Thank you again, Kelly.

Finally, at the completion of this project, we take time out to thank those who have granted us the time to spend writing, our spouses Jeff Slaggert and Judy Jongsma. Your support was invaluable.

—Arthur E. Jongsma, Jr.
—Kellye Slaggert

The Intellectual and Developmental Disability Treatment Planner, with DSM-5 Updates

INTRODUCTION

Since the 1960s, formalized treatment planning has gradually become a vital aspect of the entire health care delivery system, whether it is treatment related to physical health, mental health, child welfare, or substance abuse. What started in the medical sector in the 1960s spread into the mental health sector in the 1970s as clinics, psychiatric hospitals, agencies, and so on, began to seek accreditation from bodies such as the Joint Commission on Accreditation of Healthcare Organizations (JCAHO) to qualify for third-party reimbursements. To achieve accreditation, most treatment providers had to begin developing and strengthening their documentation skills in the area of treatment planning. Previously, most mental health and substance abuse treatment providers had, at best, a "bare-bones" plan that looked similar for most of the individuals they treated. As a result, clients and third-party payers were uncertain about the direction of mental health treatment. Goals were vague, objectives were nonexistent, and interventions were not specific to individual clients. Outcome data were not measurable, and neither the treatment provider nor the client know exactly when treatment was complete. The initial development of rudimentary treatment plans made inroads toward addressing some of these issues.

With the advent of managed care in the 1980s, treatment planning has taken on even more importance. Managed care systems *insist* that clinicians move rapidly from assessment of the problem to the formulation and implementation of the treatment plan. Medicaid managed care plans now require person-centered planning. Professional staff assist in the planning and delivery of treatment along with the planning and delivery of support systems needed by clients. Treatment and support provided must be designed to promote maximal independence, community involvement, and quality of life. This is a departure from Medicaid requirements and other regulatory standards of the past, which governed the treatment process each client received. The goal of most managed care companies is to expedite the treatment process by prompting the client and treatment provider to focus on identifying and changing behavioral problems as quickly as possible. Treatment plans must be specific as to the problems and interventions, individualized to meet the client's needs and goals, and measurable in terms of setting milestones that can be used to chart the client's progress. Pressure from third-party payers, accrediting agencies, and other outside parties has therefore increased the need for clinicians to produce effective, high-quality treatment plans in a short time frame. However, many mental health providers have little experience in treatment plan development. Our purpose in writing this book is to clarify, simplify, and accelerate the treatment planning process.

TREATMENT PLAN UTILITY

Detailed written treatment plans can benefit not only the client, therapist, treatment team, insurance community, and treatment agency, but also the overall mental health profession. The client is served by a written plan because it stipulates the issues that are the focus of the treatment process. It is very easy for both provider and client to lose sight of what the issues were that brought the client to seek services. The treatment plan is a guide that clarifies and structures the focus of the treatment needs. Since issues can change as clinical services progress, the treatment plan must be viewed as a dynamic document that can and must be updated to reflect any major change of problem, definition, goal, objective, or intervention.

Treatment plans for clients with developmental disabilities should be person centered. The person-centered planning process dictates that the client directs the planning process with a focus on what he/she wants and needs. This necessitates facilitating a support system for the client to live successfully in the community. This is different from the traditional treatment modality, which states that the client has a problem and will get better with treatment. A person experiencing developmental disabilities has a condition that requires support and assistance from others to live independently. The developmental disability cannot be cured with treatments.

Clients and clinicians benefit from the treatment plan, which forces both to think about clinical service outcomes. Behaviorally stated, measurable objectives clearly focus the treatment endeavor. Clients clearly understand the purpose of clinical services. Clear objectives also allow the client and care providers to channel their efforts into specific changes that will lead to the long-term goal of increased independence in identified areas. Both client and clinician are concentrating on specifically stated objectives using specific interventions.

Providers are aided by treatment plans because they are forced to think analytically and critically about therapeutic interventions that are best suited for objective attainment for the client. The formalized plan guides the treatment process. The clinician must give advance attention to the particular approaches and techniques that will form the basis for the interventions.

Clinicians benefit from clear documentation of treatment because it provides a measure of added protection from possible client litigation. Malpractice suits are increasing in frequency, and insurance premiums are soaring. The first line of defense against allegations of malpractice is a complete clinical record detailing the treatment process. A written, individualized, formal treatment plan that is the guideline for the therapeutic process, that has been reviewed and signed by the client, and that is coupled with problem-oriented progress notes is a powerful defense against exaggerated or false claims.

A well-crafted treatment plan that clearly stipulates identified needs and intervention strategies facilitates the treatment process carried out by team members in inpatient, residential, or intensive outpatient settings. Good communication between team members about what approach is being implemented and who is responsible for which intervention is critical. Team meetings to discuss client treatment used to be the only source of interaction between providers; often, therapeutic conclusions or assignment were not recorded. Now, a thorough treatment plan stipulates in writing the details of objectives and the varied interventions (pharmacological, milieu, group therapy, family therapy, recreational, individual therapy, and so on) and who will implement them.

Every treatment agency or institution is constantly looking for ways to increase the quality and uniformity of the documentation in the clinical record. A standardized, written treatment plan with problem definitions, goals, objectives, and interventions in every client's file enhances that uniformity of documentation. This uniformity eases the task of record reviewers inside and outside the agency. Outside reviewers, such as JCAHO, insist on documentation that clearly outlines assessment, treatment, progress, and discharge status.

The demand for accountability from third-party payers and health maintenance organizations (HMOs) is partially satisfied by a written treatment plan and complete progress notes. More and more managed care systems are demanding a structured therapeutic contract that has measurable objectives and explicit interventions. Clinicians cannot avoid this move toward being accountable to those outside the treatment process.

The mental health profession stands to benefit from the use of more precise, measurable objectives to evaluate success in mental health treatment. With the advent of detailed treatment plans, outcome data can be more easily collected to document that interventions are effective in achieving specific goals.

HOW TO DEVELOP A TREATMENT PLAN

The process of developing a treatment plan involves a logical series of steps that build on each other. The foundation of any effective treatment plan is the data gathered in a comprehensive assessment. As the client presents himself or herself for services, the clinician must sensitively listen in order to understand the client's needs, desires, current stressors, emotional status, social network, physical health, coping skills, interpersonal conflicts, self-esteem, and so on.

Assessment data may be gathered from a social history, physical exam, clinical interview, psychological testing, behavioral analysis, or contact with the client's significant others. The integration of the data by the clinician or the multidisciplinary treatment team members is critical for understanding the client, as is an awareness of the basis of the client's needs. We have identified six specific steps for developing an effective treatment plan based on the assessment data.

Step One: Need Selection

This Planner presents 28 common habilitative and mental health needs of persons with developmental disabilities. It is important to start with a thorough review of all the client's records followed by obtaining the client's and caretaker's view of his or her needs and long-term goals. The clinician must ferret out the most significant needs on which to focus the treatment process. Usually a *primary* need will surface, and *secondary* needs may also be evident. Some *other* needs may have to be set aside as insufficiently urgent to require treatment at this time. An effective treatment plan can only deal with a few selected needs, or clinical services will lose their direction.

As the clinical needs become clear to the clinician or the treatment team, it is important to include opinions from the client as to his or her prioritization of issues for which services are being sought. A client's motivation to participate in and cooperate with the treatment process depends, to some extent, on the degree to which treatment addresses his or her greatest needs.

Step Two: Need Definition

Each individual client presents with unique nuances as to how clinical needs behaviorally reveal themselves in his or her life. Therefore, each problem that is selected for a psychological treatment focus requires a specific definition about how it is evidenced in the particular client. The clinically based needs chapters have *Diagnostic and Statistical Manual of Mental Disorders, Fifth Edition* (*DSM-5*) criteria associated with the client's signs and symptoms of mental illness. The symptom pattern should be associated with diagnostic criteria and codes such as those found in the *DSM-5* or the *International Classification of Diseases.* (However, note that some third-party payers may require that the presenting medical diagnosis remain the primary diagnosis of record). This Planner, following the pattern established by *DSM-5,* offers such behaviorally specific definition statements to choose from or to serve as a model for your own personally crafted statements.

Step Three: Goal Development

The next step in treatment plan development is that of setting broad goals for the procurement of identified needs. These statements need not be crafted in measurable terms but can be global, long-term goals that indicate a desired positive outcome to the treatment procedures. This Planner suggests several possible goal statements associated with each chapter, but one statement is usually all that is required in a treatment plan.

Step Four: Objective Construction

In contrast to long-term goals, objectives must be stated in behaviorally measurable language. It must be clear when the client has achieved the established objectives; therefore, vague, subjective objectives are not acceptable. Review agencies (e.g., JCAHO), HMOs, and managed care organizations insist that mental health treatment outcome be measurable. The objectives presented in this Planner are designed to meet this demand for accountability. Numerous alternatives are presented to allow construction of a variety of treatment plan possibilities for the same identified needs. The clinician must exercise professional judgment as to which objectives are most appropriate for a given client.

Each objective should be developed as a step toward attaining the broad treatment goal. In essence, objectives can be thought of as a series of steps that, when completed, will result in the achievement of the long-term goal. There should be at least two objectives for each problem, but the clinician may construct as many as are necessary for goal achievement. Target attainment dates may be listed for each objective. New objectives should be added to the plan as the individual's treatment progresses. When all the necessary objectives have been achieved, the client should have demonstrated progress with skill deficits or improvements in Axis I symptomatology.

Step Five: Intervention Creation

Interventions are the actions of the clinician designed to help the client complete the objectives. There should be at least one intervention for every objective. If the client does not accomplish the objective after the initial intervention, extended time frames or new interventions should be added to the plan.

Interventions should be selected on the basis of the client's needs and desires and the treatment provider's full therapeutic repertoire. This Planner contains interventions from a broad range of therapeutic approaches, including cognitive, dynamic, behavioral, pharmacologic, family-oriented, and solution-focused brief therapy. The underlying focus across the range of interventions centers on helping clients obtain maximal independence and functioning. Other interventions may be written by the provider to reflect his or her own training and experience. The addition of new problems, definitions, goals, objectives, and interventions to those found in the Planner is encouraged because doing so adds to the database for future reference and use.

Some suggested interventions listed in this Planner refer to specific books that can be assigned to the client for adjunctive bibliotherapy. Appendix A contains a full bibliographic reference list of these materials. The books, videos, and skill-promoting aides are arranged under each chapter for which they are appropriate as assigned reading or viewing for clients. When a bibliotherapy source is used as part of an intervention plan, it should be reviewed with the client after it is read, enhancing the application of the content of the book to the specific client's circumstances. For further information about self-help books, mental health professionals may wish to consult *The Authoritative Guide to Self-Help Books* (1994) by Santrock, Minnett, and Campbell (available from The Guilford Press, New York). The Internet is also a rich source for locating information and self-help books, especially for recent publications (e.g., www.amazon.com or www.barnesandnoble.com).

Assigning an intervention to a specific provider is most relevant if the client is being treated by a multidisciplinary team (e.g., nurse, physical therapist, occupational therapist, psychologist, and psychiatrist) in an inpatient, residential, or intensive outpatient setting. Within these settings, personnel other than the primary clinician may be responsible for implementing a specific intervention. Review agencies may require that the responsible provider's name be stipulated for every intervention.

Step Six: Diagnosis Determination

The determination of an appropriate psychological diagnosis is based on an evaluation of the client's complete clinical presentation. The clinician must compare the behavioral, cognitive, emotional, and interpersonal symptoms that the client presents to the criteria for diagnosis of a mental illness condition as described in *DSM-5*. The issue of differential diagnosis is admittedly a difficult one that research has shown to have rather low interrater reliability. Psychologists have also been trained to think more in terms of maladaptive behavior than in terms of disease labels. In spite of these factors, diagnosis is a reality that exists in the world of mental health care, and it is a necessity for third-party reimbursement. (However, recently, managed care agencies are more interested in behavioral indices that are exhibited by the client than in the actual diagnosis.) It is the clinician's thorough knowledge of *DSM-5* criteria and a complete understanding of the client assessment data that contribute to the most reliable, valid diagnosis. An accurate assessment of behavioral indicators will also contribute to more effective treatment planning.

HOW TO USE THIS PLANNER

Our experience has taught us that learning the skills of effective treatment plan writing can be a tedious and difficult process for many clinicians. It is more stressful to try to develop this expertise when under the pressure of increased client load and short time frames placed on clinicians today by managed care systems. The documentation demands can be overwhelming when we must move quickly from assessment to treatment plan to progress notes. In the process, we must be very specific about how and when objectives can be achieved, and how progress is exhibited in each client. *The Intellectual and Developmental Disability Treatment Planner* was developed as a tool to aid clinicians in writing a treatment plan in a rapid manner that is clear, specific, and highly individualized according to the following progression:

1. Based on referral information, caregiver insight, and client self-reporting, identify the client's clinical/habilitative need (Step One). Locate the corresponding page number for that problem (or a closely related problem) in the Planner's table of contents.
2. Select two or three of the listed behavioral definitions (Step Two) and record them in the appropriate section on your treatment plan form. Feel free to add your own defining statement if you determine that your client's behavioral manifestation of the identified clinical/habilitative need is not listed.
3. Select a single long-term goal (Step Three) and again write the selection, exactly as it is written in the Planner or in some appropriately modified form, in the corresponding area of your own form.
4. Review the listed objectives for this problem and select the ones that you judge to be clinically indicated for your client (Step Four). Remember, it is recommended that you select at least two objectives

for each problem. You may add a target date or the number of sessions allocated for the attainment of each objective.

5. Choose relevant interventions (Step Five). The Planner offers suggested interventions related to each objective in the parentheses following the objective statement. But do not limit yourself to those interventions. The entire list is eclectic and may offer options that are more tailored to your theoretical approach or preferred way of working with clients. Also, just as with definitions, goals, and objectives, there is space allowed for you to enter your own interventions into the Planner. This allows you to refer to these entries when you create a plan around this problem in the future. You may assign responsibility to a specific person for implementation of each intervention if the treatment is being carried out by a multidisciplinary team.
6. Several *DSM-5* diagnoses are listed at the end of each chapter that are commonly associated with clients who have this type of problem. These diagnoses are meant to be suggestions for clinical consideration. Select a listed diagnosis or assign a more appropriate choice from the *DSM-5* (Step Six).

   Note: To accommodate those practitioners who tend to plan treatment in terms of diagnostic labels rather than presenting problems, Appendix B lists all the *DSM-5* diagnoses that have been presented in the various presenting problem chapters as suggestions for consideration. Each diagnosis is followed by the presenting problem that has been associated with that diagnosis. The provider may look up the presenting problems for a selected diagnosis to review definitions, goals, objectives, and interventions that may be appropriate for clients with that diagnosis.

Congratulations! You should now have a complete, individualized treatment plan that is ready for immediate implementation and presentation to the client. It should resemble the format of the sample plan presented at the end of this introduction.

A FINAL NOTE

One important aspect of effective treatment planning is that each plan should be tailored to the individual client's problems and needs. Treatment plans should not be mass-produced, even if clients have similar problems. The individual's strengths and weaknesses, unique stressors, social network, family circumstances, and symptom patterns *must* be considered in developing a treatment strategy. Drawing upon our own years of clinical experience, we have put together a variety of treatment choices. These statements can be combined in thousands of permutations to develop detailed treatment plans. Relying on their own good judgement, clinicians can easily select the statements that are appropriate for the individuals they are treating. In addition, we encourage readers to add their own definitions, goals, objectives, and interventions to the existing samples. It is our hope that *The Intellectual and Developmental Disability Treatment Planner* will promote effective, creative, treatment planning—a process that will ultimately benefit the client, clinician, and mental health community.

SAMPLE TREATMENT PLAN

Problem: SOCIAL SKILLS

Definitions: Strained interpersonal relationships resulting from inappropriate or exaggerated emotional responses.

Lack of skills to be assertive in making peer choices to avoid problem social situations.

Goals: Learn and implement social skills that allow for controlled, appropriate expression of emotions.

Short-Term Objectives	Therapeutic Interventions
1. Participate in an assessment of social skills.	1. Arrange for an assessment of the client's social skills to establish a baseline of the client's ability and to gain insight into his/her strengths and weaknesses.
	2. Ask family members or care givers to complete the Social Performance Survey Schedule (Matson, Helsel, Bellack, and Sanatore) prior to and after treatment.
	3. Provide direct feedback to the client, family members, and caregivers on the results of an assessment.
2. Adhere to training recommenda-	1. Obtain consensus from the

(Continued)

tions made from social skills evaluation.	client, family members, school officials, and caregivers regarding suitable social skills training programs or interventions that build on the client's strengths and compensate for his/her weaknesses; make referral to the selected program.
3. Maximize social skills acquisition by participating in social skills training exercises.	1. Encourage parents, caregivers, and teachers to model social skills that the client can imitate.
	2. Develop a specific plan regarding social skills to be taught, modalities to be used, and the number of sessions needed.
4. Implement basic social interaction skills.	1. Present social skills of benefit to the client (e.g., basic conversational skills, self-assertion, honesty, truthfulness, and how to handle teasing), identifying critical components, while providing positive and negative role-playing to the client for each skill; reward progress using a predetermined schedule of reinforcement.
	2. Assess the client's comprehension of presented skills by requesting that he/she verbalize or role-play social skills.
	3. Assess the client's ability to conform his/her behavior to acquired knowledge of social skills through spontaneous role-playing, self-reports, and reports from caregivers or supervisors.
5. Identify labels for and trigger events of strong emotions.	1. Teach the client about the different emotions and how to identify the triggering event of an emotion (e.g., "I am angry

(Continued)

because I was not considered for a job").

2. Request that the client identify his/her own problematic emotions and the situations that elicit those problematic emotions.

6. Demonstrate the ability to control and express strong emotions in a socially acceptable manner.

1. Assist the client in listing potential rewards that can be used to reinforce behavioral progress in social skills training.
2. Assist the client in identifying healthy ways to control and express problematic emotions, role-playing his/her identified strategies. Utilize role-reversal techniques to teach the impact of his/her negative behavior on others.
3. Provide the client with a written or pictorial form of his/her problematic emotions, triggers, and healthy responses so this can be referred to in the future.

DIAGNOSIS

F84.0	Autism spectrum disorder
F71	Moderate Intellectual Disability

Note: The numbers in parentheses accompanying the short-term objectives in each chapter correspond to the list of suggested therapeutic interventions in that chapter. Each objective has specific interventions that have been designed to assist the client in attaining that objective. Clinical judgment should determine the exact intervention to be used, including any outside of those suggested.

ACTIVITIES OF DAILY LIVING (ADL)

BEHAVIORAL DEFINITIONS

1. Lack of independence with self-feeding, as evidenced by not opening the mouth in response to stimulation or not eating independently with proper utensils.
2. Assistance needed with dressing, as evidenced by not selecting appropriate attire, failure to physically put clothes on, or inability to manipulate fasteners.
3. Impaired identification of hygienic needs and/or initiation of response to hygienic needs, as evidenced by deficiencies in caring for a runny nose, toileting needs, bathing, washing hands, and brushing teeth, resulting in poor hygiene.
4. Lower than expected eating, dressing, toileting, and/or hygiene skills resulting from overprotection of client by caregiver.
5. Absence of initiating activities of personal interest.
6. Failure to complete required tasks.
7. Failure to seek assistance when needed.
8. Lack of initiative to resolve problems.
9. Absence of self-assertion and self-advocacy.
10. Difficulties in comprehending requests, emotions, greetings, comments, protests, or rejection due to limitations in receptive communication.
11. Difficulties in expressing requests, emotions, greetings, comments, protests, or rejection due to limitations in expressive communication.
12. Poor interaction skills characterized by limited eye contact, insufficient attending, and awkward social responses.

__. ____

____

__. ____

____

__. ____

____

LONG-TERM GOALS

1. Strengthen existing ADL skills and develop independence with new ADL skills.
2. Develop and maintain appropriate eating habits that promote independence.
3. Develop and maintain skills for maintaining proper hygiene and personal cleanliness to promote good health.
4. Develop and maintain skills of dressing self to create greater autonomy from caregivers.
5. Maximize independence in all ADL areas.
6. Use adaptive equipment and training modalities that support independent functioning.
7. Reduce the frequency and severity of maladaptive behaviors that interfere with ADLs.
8. Caregivers and client reach a consensus on client's identified goals.
9. Caregivers provide adequate supervision and assistance to ensure client's safe treatment within a supportive learning environment.
10. Maximize the client's choices and preferences whenever possible.
11. Caregivers reinforce all steps toward independence with ADL skill acquisition.

__. ____

____

__. ____

____

__. ____

____

SHORT-TERM OBJECTIVES

1. Participate in a psychological assessment of adaptive and/or intellectual abilities. (1, 2, 3, 4)

THERAPEUTIC INTERVENTIONS

1. Arrange for or conduct a comprehensive intellectual and adaptive assessment to establish a baseline of the client's

2. Complete neuropsychological testing to assess contribution of organic factors contributing to behavioral deficits. (4, 5)
3. Accept and adhere to recommendations made by the interdisciplinary team regarding appropriate interventions. (5)
4. Cooperate with a physical and occupational therapy assessment to facilitate ADL skill acquisition. (6, 7)
5. Cooperate with a speech/language evaluation. (8)
6. Cooperate with nurse's monitoring of physical and medical conditions. (9)
7. Cooperate with a physician's examination for annual check up and/or treatment of acute medical problems. (10)
8. Take medications as prescribed by physician to maintain physical health. (11)
9. Cooperate with dental examination to promote healthy teeth and gums. (12)
10. Cooperate with visual examination to ensure adequate vision for ADL tasks. (13)
11. Cooperate with psychiatric examination to assess the need for psychotropic medications. (14)
12. Parents communicate with caregivers regarding psychiatric symptoms. (15)

ability and gain insight into his/her strengths and weaknesses.

2. Attend person-centered planning (PCP) meeting with client, family, client advocate, school officials, and caregivers to determine educational, vocational, recreational, communicative, ADL, and health goals along with eligibility for special services.
3. Consult with client, family, school officials, and caregivers to obtain an overview of all multidisciplinary treatments wanted by the client.
4. Arrange for or conduct a neurological exam and/or neuropsychological testing to identify sensory modalities best suited for the client's learning style.
5. Provide feedback to client, family, and staff on the results of intellectual, adaptive, psychological, behavioral, and neuropsychological testing.
6. Refer the client to a physical therapist to determine his/her level of motor functioning and whether ongoing physical therapy services are needed.
7. Refer the client to an occupational therapist for evaluation to determine what ADL skills training would be most appropriate.

13. Accept and follow dietician's recommendations. (16)
14. Accept placement in appropriate residential setting. (17)
15. Accept placement in an appropriate day program or school setting for rehabilitation and/or vocational training. (18)
16. Attend physical therapy sessions designed to maintain and/or enhance range of motion. (19, 20, 21, 22)
17. Use relevant adaptive equipment to promote independence in ADLs. (22)
18. Participate in occupational therapy sessions designed to maximize independence via ADL skills acquisition. (23, 24, 25)
19. Take bath or shower, comb hair, brush teeth, and apply deodorant daily. (23, 24, 38)
20. Eat and drink to fullest capability of independence. (23, 24, 25, 28)
21. Attend speech therapy sessions to improve functional communication. (26)
22. Utilize augmentative speech materials to improve functional communication. (27)
23. Increase the frequency of unprompted expressive statements. (28, 38)
24. Use expressive/receptive language skills when interacting

8. Refer the client to a speech therapist to determine the client's communicative strengths and weaknesses along with mode of communication best suited for him/her.
9. Refer the client to a nurse for ongoing monitoring of basic health, medical concerns, and medication management.
10. Arrange an appointment for an annual physical exam along with any follow-up or specialist care that is indicated.
11. Monitor the procedures for the administration of medications that have been prescribed for the client.
12. Arrange for biannual dental examinations and cleanings.
13. Arrange for yearly vision examinations.
14. Arrange for psychiatric evaluation to determine if a concomitant Axis I disorder may be contributing to poor ADLs and whether psychotropic medication may be helpful.
15. Enlist the help of family members and caregivers to monitor signs and symptoms of the client's psychiatric condition to provide accurate information to the psychiatrist.
16. Facilitate the client's obtaining dietician-approved

with others. (28, 29, 30, 38)

25. Initiate and respond to social greetings and smiles and make eye contact when involved in social situations. (30)
26. Begin to demonstrate and initiate independence by making all possible choices in daily events as evidenced by choosing clothing, food, leisure interests, and peer group. (30, 31)
27. Comply with prescriptive behavioral plan. (32, 33, 34)
28. Increase frequency of incompatible adaptive behaviors that compete with maladaptive behaviors. (35, 36, 37, 38)
29. Identify various emotions and their triggering events. (39)
30. Verbalize positive self-talk that reduces the level of frustration and anger. (40)
31. Parent increases positive feedback to the client. (41, 42)
32. Parents and caregivers develop realistic expectations of the client's ADL abilities. (43, 44)
33. Parents increase and/or maintain involvement with their son/daughter and his/her treatment. (45, 46, 47)
34. Caretakers reduce the frequency of speaking for the client and/or performing activ-

foods and meals that he/she enjoys.

17. Consult with client, family, school officials, and assigned clinicians on different residential options (e.g., adult foster care home, group home, supported living environments, apartments, or community treatment homes) before making an appropriate referral.
18. Refer the client to a suitable program site, a day program with habilitative training, community based instruction, a sheltered workshop, enclave work, or vocational training that has vocational opportunities that are of interest to the client.
19. Coordinate follow-through on physical therapy to provide range of motion exercises to prevent contractures.
20. Assign the client suitable gross motor activities that will increase independence with ADL skills.
21. Seek advice and recommendations from a physical therapist regarding suitable positioning for the client.
22. Arrange for the client to obtain necessary adaptive and/or physical therapy equipment.
23. Develop a skills acquisition program designed to teach feeding, bathing, grooming, and/or dressing skills.

ities that the client is capable of doing independently. (48, 49, 50)

35. Client indicates comfort and enjoyment in his/her activities through verbal and nonverbal behaviors, as evidenced by verbalizing positive statements, smiling often, relaxes posture, approaching caregivers freely and decrease in amount of time withdrawing. (51, 52, 60)

36. Caretakers verbalize the degree of the emotional strain related to providing service to the client. (53)

37. Caretakers utilize relaxation skills and respite care to relieve stress. (54, 55, 56)

38. Participate in stress-relieving activities. (57, 58)

39. Increase participation in extracurricular activities and outings. (58, 59, 60, 61, 62)

—. ______________________________
____

—. ______________________________
____

—. ______________________________
____

24. Specify suitable prompting levels for ADL skills acquisition programs (e.g., verbal prompts, physical prompts, or hand-over-hand guidance).

25. Assign the client suitable fine motor activities that will increase independence with ADL skills.

26. Provide or arrange for training in the client's recommended form of communication (e.g., sign language, picture symbols, computerized device, or picture board).

27. Arrange for the client to obtain recommended augmentative speech materials, and provide for ongoing training using augmentative speed materials.

28. Expand the client's receptive language by modeling pointing to body parts, objects, foods, clothing, animals, and responding to directions.

29. Expand the client's expressive language by demonstrating naming objects, body parts, food, clothing, animals, and verbs; personal identification; and linking nouns and verbs together.

30. Teach the client effective basic communication skills (i.e., noninterruptive listening, good eye contact, asserting self with "I" statements,

and responding to greetings) to improve his/her ability to express thoughts, feelings, and needs more clearly.

31. Present situations such that the client is required to make a choice between two to three options, and reinforce independent choices.
32. Using behavioral analysis, determine motivating variables for the client's maladaptive behaviors.
33. Identify several reinforcers that can be used to reward adaptive behaviors that are incompatible with maladaptive behaviors.
34. Assess ecological factors contributing to the maintenance of maladaptive behavior.
35. Design and implement a behavioral plan that reinforces desired behaviors coupled with behavioral techniques to decrease or eliminate maladaptive behaviors (e.g., shaping, fading, extinction, or differential reinforcement of other [DRO] behavior).
36. Conduct an in-service session with all caregivers on the client's behavioral treatment program to ensure effective implementation of treatment to strengthen desirable, prosocial behavior.
37. Obtain approval from the client's guardian and the

agency oversight committee for any restrictive or aversive programming.

38. Design a reward system to motivate the client to improve ADL, communication, and social skills.
39. Teach the client about the different emotions and how to identify the triggering event of an emotion (e.g., "I am angry because I was viewed as different").
40. Teach the client positive self-talk that will help him/her accept and positively cope with his/her ADL difficulties.
41. Monitor the client's progress at specified intervals and report information to client, family, and caregivers.
42. Encourage family members and caregivers to provide frequent and immediate positive feedback to the client for progress in ADL skills training.
43. Educate family members and caregivers on expected time frames of ADL skills training along with potential obstacles the client may face.
44. Assist family members and caregivers in developing realistic expectations of the client's adaptive functioning.
45. Arrange for family members to read *The Special Need Reading List* (Sweeny) to provide information on

resources on general issues affecting lives of the disabled along with information on specific disabilities.

46. Encourage family members to maintain regular social contact with the client.
47. Encourage family members to maintain regular communication with involved clinicians regarding status of the client's ADL skills, health, and maladaptive behaviors.
48. Provide family members and caregivers with training and/or in-service sessions needed to support the client's advancement with ADL training.
49. Assess the client's strengths and weaknesses in self-determination by using *The ARC's Self-Determination Scale* (Wehmeyer) and use results to promote the client's involvement in planning future goals with the support of his/her family.
50. Encourage family members and caregivers to agree to promote lifelong learning opportunities and experiences for the client to promote his/her choice making, decision making, problem solving, goal setting, and attainment along with self-awareness and knowledge.
51. Monitor, acknowledge, and reinforce all signs of the client's pleasure, self-esteem,

confidence, and social comfort.

52. Contact a recipient rights representative if the client's rights have been violated.
53. Observe family members and caregivers for frustration, which may reduce their effectiveness to interact effectively with the client, and provide them with opportunities for venting feelings as necessary.
54. Teach deep muscle relaxation, abdominal breathing, and safe place imagery to caregivers to alleviate the stress of the many demands of caring for a person with ADL deficits.
55. Arrange for respite care for family members and caregivers.
56. Recommend that family members read *The Resourceful Caregiver: Helping Family Caregivers Help Themselves* (National Family Caregivers Association).
57. Teach the client stress reduction techniques (e.g., deep muscle relaxation, abdominal breathing and safe place imagery) to alleviate stressors encountered.
58. Refer the client to a recreational therapist to determine possible leisure and community activities available to the client.

59. Encourage the client's participation in Special Olympics.
60. Assess the client's and/or family members' interest in faith-based activities and provide access to church ministry as indicated.
61. Refer family members and caregivers to *Dimensions of Faith and Congregational Ministries with Persons with Developmental Disabilities and Their Families* (Gavanta) to obtain information on many different faith-based books, videos, and programs available for persons with developmental disabilities and their families.
62. Observe the client for obvious and subtle signs of likes and dislikes and provide all possible enjoyable situations.

__. ______________________________
____

__. ______________________________
____

__. ______________________________
____

DIAGNOSTIC SUGGESTIONS:

ICD-9-CM	*ICD-10-CM*	*DSM-5* Disorder, Condition, or Problem
299.00	F84.0	Autism Spectrum Disorder
787.6	F98.1	Encopresis
307.6	F98	Enuresis
317	F70	Intellectual Disability, Mild
319	F71	Intellectual Disability, Moderate
319	F72	Intellectual Disability, Severe
319	F73	Intellectual Disability, Profound
319	F79	Unspecified Intellectual Disability
V62.89	R41.83	Borderline Intellectual Functioning
_____	_____	______________________________
_____	_____	______________________________

ANGER

BEHAVIORAL DEFINITIONS

1. Explosive, aggressive physical or verbal outbursts that are out of proportion to any precipitating stressors.
2. Swift and harsh judgment statements made to or about others.
3. Physical aggression toward self or others.
4. Property destruction and/or hostile opposition that occurs in response to correction, confrontation, or unwanted directives.
5. Body language characterized by tense muscles such as clenched fist or jaw, glaring looks, or refusal to make eye contact.
6. Use of verbally abusive language.
7. Hostile, threatening, and/or assaultive behavior in response to appropriate requests from others.
8. History of poor anger management resulting in significant impairments in family, social, and vocational relationships or opportunities.

—. ____

____

—. ____

____

—. ____

____

LONG-TERM GOALS

1. Reduce intensity and frequency of all types of angry behaviors.
2. Identify early warning signs of anger or hostility.
3. Implement prosocial ways of expressing anger, frustration, embarrassment, or impatience.

4. Avoid situations that produce feelings of anger, frustration, embarrassment, or impatience when possible.
5. Complete requested tasks without verbal or physical aggression.
6. Enjoy warm and caring relationships with family, friends, and caregivers.
7. Make choices and communicate preferences whenever possible.
8. Caregivers reinforce all steps toward managing anger.

__. ______________________________

__. ______________________________

__. ______________________________

SHORT-TERM OBJECTIVES

1. Participate in a psychological/neuropsychological assessment of anger problems, including developmental history, family history, and previous psychiatric involvement. (1, 2, 3, 4, 5)
2. Cooperate with medical examination to rule out medical etiologies for anger or aggression. (6, 7)
3. Cooperate with psychiatric examination to assess the need for psychotropic medications. (7, 8, 9)
4. Attend individual and/or group therapy sessions focused on resolving anger issues and teaching anger management skills. (10, 11)
5. Complete homework exercises that promote anger

THERAPEUTIC INTERVENTIONS

1. Arrange for a psychological assessment of the client's anger symptoms, including a developmental history, family history, and previous psychiatric involvement.
2. Refer the client for a neurological exam or neuropsychological testing.
3. Operationally define and collect data on behaviors related to anger.
4. Assess the severity of the client's anger/aggression through interviews, reports from caregivers, and rating scales such as the Reiss Screen for Maladaptive Behavior, Second Edition (Reiss) or the State-Trait Anger Expression inventory (Spielberger).

awareness and anger management. (12)

6. Correctly label and recognize emotions generated in self and others. (13, 14, 15)
7. Identify and list early signs of feeling and expressing frustration, annoyance, and anger. (13, 16, 17)
8. Identify personal triggers for anger. (13, 18)
9. Verbalize problem-solving techniques that will be used in future anger-arousing situations. (19, 20)
10. Carry written lists of problem-solving techniques to remind self of actions to implement in conflict situations. (21, 22)
11. Implement conflict coping strategies at early stages of anger arousal. (23, 24, 25)
12. List triggers for anger and alternate healthy responses to those triggers. (26)
13. Identify the negative impact uncontrolled anger expression has on others. (27)
14. Increase the usage of assertive responses to meet personal needs. (28, 29, 30)
15. Implement proper nutrition, increased exercise, and time management as means to reduce stress. (31)
16. Identify maladaptive responses to stress that create their own set of problems. (32)

5. Train family members and caregivers to monitor signs and symptoms of the client's psychiatric condition to provide accurate information to the psychiatrist and psychologist.
6. Arrange for the client to obtain a complete physical to rule out any biomedical causes for his/her anger/aggression symptoms (e.g., temporal epilepsy, diabetes, or brain tumor).
7. Follow up on recommendations from the evaluation, including additional lab work, medications, or special assessments.
8. Arrange for a psychiatric evaluation to determine whether psychotropic medications may be helpful.
9. Monitor the client for compliance, effectiveness, and side effects associated with prescribed medications.
10. Arrange for the client to receive individual therapy using a therapeutic model best suited for him/her (e.g., cognitive, behavioral, developmental cognitive, or psychoeducational).
11. Arrange for the client to participate in group therapy to learn anger management skills.
12. Assign homework exercises (e.g., problem-solving sheets, mood log, utilizing action plan, and/or asking for

17. Report success at implementing relaxation techniques. (23, 33)
18. Attend group sessions that focus on enhanced social skills. (34, 35)
19. Identify reinforcers for angry and calm behavior. (1, 36, 37, 38)
20. Increase positive management of anger through behavior modification procedures. (39, 40, 41)
21. Family members, caregivers, and client modify the environment to reduce stress. (42)
22. Identify irrational beliefs and negative self-talk that mediates anger. (43)
23. Verbalize positive self-talk that mediates calm. (44)
24. List positive, adaptive alternatives for expressing anger. (45, 46)
25. Demonstrate independence and initiative by making all possible choices in daily events, as evidenced by choosing clothing, food, leisure interests, and peer group. (47, 48)
26. Family members and caretakers assist and support the client in his/her attempts to make positive behavioral changes to manage anger. (49, 50)
27. Increase participation in extracurricular activities and outings. (51, 52)

assistance) from the *Anger Workbook* (Bilodeau) to promote anger management skills. Emphasize the client's choice and power to make good decisions in managing his/her anger.

13. Teach the client to be aware of, to be able to label, and to understand the universality of different emotions through the use of modeling, pictures, and intermittent testing.
14. Present verbal or pictorial scenarios of conflict between two people. Request that the client verbally describe what is happening from both parties' perspective and why each perspective is different.
15. Using real conflicts from the client's life, discuss the differences in perspective between self and the other in order to foster development of empathy toward and understanding of others.
16. Request that the client identify his/her early signs of feeling and expressing anger and frustration, soliciting input from others who know the client's anger expression patterns.
17. Request that the client verbally identify or demonstrate how our bodies change during anger (e.g., clenched fist and teeth, tense posture, narrowed eyes, or faster breathing); ask

—. ______________________________

____

—. ______________________________

____

—. ______________________________

____

the client to identify his/her own body cues.

18. Request that the client identify the situations and conditions under which he/she typically develops feelings of anger or frustration (e.g., "I am angry because my friend ignored me"). Direct the client to solicit input from others.
19. Teach the client problem-solving techniques (e.g., identifying the problem, listing possible solutions, selecting a solution, and evaluating the solution's outcome; see *Thinking It Through: Teaching a Problem-Solving Strategy for Community Living* [Foxx and Bittle]).
20. Role-play several problem situations for the client to solve, and provide feedback on the client's progress.
21. Provide the client with a notebook of problem-solving sheets (e.g., identifying the problem, listing possible solutions, selecting a solution, and evaluating the solution's outcome) to use as situations occur and use as a reference if problems repeatedly occur.
22. Create small cards with pictorial or written reminders of conflict resolution techniques. Provide these for the client and caregivers.

23. Discuss several activities that the client can do when beginning to feel angry in order to reduce tension (e.g., talk with others, go for a walk, listen to soothing music, write a letter, keep a mood log, practice progressive muscle relaxation, do deep breathing, and use thought-stopping techniques).
24. Reinforce the client's efforts to use healthy alternate activities to reduce tension and anger while emphasizing the importance of practice.
25. Read *Don't Pop Your Cork on Mondays!* (Moser) to the client (or request that he/she read or view it) in order to promote his/her understanding of the importance of controlling anger.
26. Assist the client in creating a master list of his/her anger triggers, angry responses, personal signs of anger, and identified prosocial alternate responses. Encourage the client to keep the list close at hand for easy reference.
27. Use role-playing and role-reversal techniques to teach the client the impact of his/her negative behavior on others.
28. Model assertive, passive, and aggressive responses to situations, and request that the client identify which of the three is most effective.

Request that the client role-play assertive, passive, and aggressive responses to identify his/her current response type.

29. Use an assertiveness questionnaire to query the client about situations in which he/she would like to be more assertive (see *The Relaxation and Stress Reduction Workbook* [Davis, Eshelman, and McKay]).
30. Using specific examples from the client's experience, request that he/she role-play assertive responses to a variety of situations. Provide feedback on the client's progress with role-playing, and encourage him/her to use assertive responses when needed.
31. Review lifestyle changes that can help in reducing stress (e.g., proper nutrition, regular exercise, and time management skills). Encourage the client to adopt these healthy lifestyle changes.
32. Assist the client in identifying nonproductive means of expressing anger (e.g., alcohol, drugs, aggression, and venting) and request that he/she identify why these are not effective responses.
33. Review the different types of relaxation techniques (e.g.,

deep breathing, progressive muscle relaxation, or imagery) and provide training in the various relaxation techniques. Encourage and reinforce use and practice.

34. Arrange for the client to obtain the necessary social skills training to foster good interpersonal relationships (see Social Skills in this Planner).
35. Refer the client to a support group for individuals with developmental disabilities.
36. Refer the client to a behavior specialist in order to determine the eliciting stimuli and maintaining reinforcers for his/her maladaptive expression of anger.
37. Assess the ecological factors contributing to the maintenance of the client's anger or aggression.
38. Identify several reinforcers that can be used to reward prosocial behaviors that are incompatible with anger outbursts. Request that the client identify or endorse desired reinforcers.
39. Refer the client to a behavioral specialist to design and implement a behavior plan that reinforces desired behaviors coupled with behavioral techniques (e.g., reinforcing low reactivity levels, reinforcing incompatible behaviors,

extinction, response cost, and overcorrection) to decrease or eliminate angry and aggressive behaviors.

40. Train all caregivers on the client's behavioral treatment program to ensure consistent, effective implementation and strengthening of desirable prosocial behaviors (see *Skills Training for Children with Behavioral Disorders* [Bloomquist] for a guide covering basic behavioral techniques).
41. Obtain approval from the client's guardian and the agency oversight committee for any use of restrictive or aversive programming.
42. Modify the client's environment to remove physical and psychological conditions not conducive to healthy behaviors (e.g., noisy conditions, hunger, crowding, or heat). Replace with conditions that encourage calm, relaxed behaviors.
43. Review a list of irrational beliefs (e.g., "Everybody always picks on me," "Nobody ever says anything nice to me," and "My parents do not love me") that are contributing to the client's anger. Using client-specific examples, present alternative self-talk to demonstrate the importance of changing irrational beliefs.

44. Facilitate the client's understanding that anger is due to how he/she perceives and interprets the situation rather than any external event, situation, or person. Model and role-play client-specific situations that demonstrate his/her control over the self-talk that governs how a problematic situation is perceived.
45. Request that the client read (or read to the client) *Don't Rant and Rave on Wednesdays!* (Moser) or *Dealing with Anger* (Johnston) to facilitate an understanding of the universality of anger and the optional positive behaviors for dealing with this powerful emotion.
46. Demonstrate different ways to release anger to the client, and process the selected activity with him/her (e.g., forgiving, letting go, writing or drawing about feelings, and using humor or symbolic activities).
47. Present multiple choices in a variety of situations such that the client is able to make a selection between the options.
48. Encourage the client's family to allow the client to make all possible choices and to demonstrate maximum independence in daily events.
49. Obtain the client's consent to enlist support for his/her

anger management efforts from clinicians, residential staff, family members, and vocational and educational staff.

50. Encourage family members and caregivers to increase the frequency of positive interactions with the client while modeling desirable conflict resolution behaviors, positive demeanor, and helpful attitudes. Model these behaviors to family members and caregivers in formal and informal situations.
51. Refer the client to a recreational therapist to determine possible leisure, social, and community activities available to the client.
52. Encourage the client's participation in Special Olympics or other athletic events.

__. ______________________________

__. ______________________________

__. ______________________________

DIAGNOSTIC SUGGESTIONS:

ICD-9-CM	*ICD-10-CM*	*DSM-5* Disorder, Condition, or Problem
312.34	F63.81	Intermittent Explosive Disorder
296.xx	F31.xx	Bipolar I Disorder
296.89	F31.81	Bipolar II Disorder
310.1	F07.0	Personality Change Due to another Medical Condition
309.81	F43.10	Posttraumatic Stress Disorder
294.11	F02.81	Probable Neurocognitive Disorder Due to Alzheimer's Disease, with Behavioral Disturbance
294.10	F02.80	Probable Neurocognitive Disorder Due to Alzheimer's Disease, without Behavioral Disturbance
294.10	F02.80	Major Neurocognitive Disorder Due to Traumatic Brain Injury, without Behavioral Disturbance
294.10	F02.81	Major Neurocognitive Disorder Due to Traumatic Brain Injury, with Behavioral Disturbance
294.8	R41.9	Unspecified Neurocognitive Disorder
299.00	F84.0	Autism Spectrum Disorder
317	F70	Intellectual Disability, Mild
319	F71	Intellectual Disability, Moderate
319	F72	Intellectual Disability, Severe
319	F73	Intellectual Disability, Profound
319	F79	Unspecified Intellectual Disability
V62.89	R41.83	Borderline Intellectual Functioning
______	______	____________________________
______	______	____________________________

ANXIETY

BEHAVIORAL DEFINITIONS

1. Feeling restless, keyed up, or on edge, as evidenced by increased motor activity, muscle tension, or shakiness.
2. Autonomic hyperactivity including dry mouth, nausea, diarrhea, shortness of breath, or rapid heartbeat.
3. Hypervigilance, as evidenced by difficulty in falling or staying asleep, difficulty with concentration, exaggerated startle response, or irritability.
4. Disorganization or agitated behaviors following exposure to a traumatic event.
5. Fears specific to a certain situation that interfere with daily life because of high levels of anxiety or avoidance of certain stimuli.
6. Excessive or unrealistic anxiety, worry, or apprehension.
7. Obsessions or compulsions that are time consuming, interfere with daily activities, and seem uncontrollable.

—. ____

____

—. ____

____

—. ____

____

LONG-TERM GOALS

1. Reduce or eliminate anxiety symptoms.
2. Develop skills and strategies to cope positively with stressors.
3. Implement behavioral and cognitive coping techniques to reduce anxiety.

4. Make choices and communicate preferences whenever possible.
5. Caregivers reinforce all steps toward anxiety reduction.

__. ____

____

__. ____

____

__. ____

____

SHORT-TERM OBJECTIVES

1. Participate in a psychological assessment of anxiety symptoms. (1, 2, 3, 4)
2. Cooperate with medical examination to rule out medical etiologies for anxiety symptoms. (5)
3. Cooperate with a psychiatric examination to assess the need for psychotropic medications. (6, 7)
4. Attend individual psychotherapy sessions focused on anxiety reduction. (8)
5. Attend group therapy sessions focused on teaching anxiety reduction techniques. (9)
6. Keep records of anxiety symptoms, precipitating events, and resolution methods. (10)
7. Verbalize realistic beliefs that challenge anxiety-inducing thoughts. (11, 12)
8. Report a reduction in phobic anxiety after participating in

THERAPEUTIC INTERVENTIONS

1. Arrange for psychological assessment of the client's anxiety symptoms, including developmental history, family history, and previous psychiatric involvement.
2. Operationally define and collect data on behaviors indicative of anxiety.
3. Assess the severity of the client's anxiety (e.g., consider using a rating scale such as the Diagnostic Assessment for the Severely Handicapped, Second Edition [DASH-II; Matson] or the Reiss Screen for Maladaptive Behavior, Second Edition [Reiss]).
4. Train family members and caregivers to monitor the client's signs and symptoms of anxiety to provide accurate information to the psychiatrist or psychologist.
5. Arrange for the client to obtain a complete physical to

systematic desensitization treatment. (13)

9. Increase frequency of relaxing, calm behaviors that compete with anxiety behaviors. (14, 15, 16)
10. Implement alternative activities that reduce agitation and anxiety at early stages of onset. (12, 17, 18)
11. Meet with a mentor regarding how to minimize problems between self and the environment. (19)
12. Attend a support group for individuals with developmental disabilities. (20)
13. Participate in social skills training to alleviate social anxiety. (21)
14. Implement environmental stress management techniques. (22)
15. Cooperate with recommendations from a speech therapist as to ways to improve communication. (23)
16. Family members and caregivers report increased understanding of the client's communication and problematic behaviors. (24, 25)
17. Utilize an activity board to keep self informed of the day's scheduled events in order to reduce confusion and ambiguity that could trigger anxiety. (26)
18. Identify reinforcers for nonanxious behaviors. (27, 28, 29)

rule out any biomedical causes for his/her anxiety symptomatology (e.g., substance abuse, medications, and hyperthyroidism).

6. Arrange for a psychiatric evaluation to determine whether psychotropic medications may be helpful.
7. Monitor the client for compliance, effectiveness, and side effects associated with prescribed antianxiety medications.
8. Arrange for the client to receive individual therapy using a therapeutic model best suited for him/her (e.g., cognitive-behavioral, behavioral, or psychoeducational) to facilitate changes in anxious feeling and thinking.
9. Arrange for the client to participate in group therapy to learn skills incompatible with his/her anxiety symptomatology (e.g., relaxation, visualization, and deep breathing).
10. Request that the client keep a daily mood record to better understand his/her anxiety patterns, precipitating events, and coping behaviors used.
11. Request that the client read (or read to the client) relevant portions of *SOS: Help for Emotions: Managing Anxiety, Anger, and Depression* (Clark) to help eliminate irrational beliefs that contribute to his/her anxiety.

19. Increase the frequency of calm and relaxed verbal, social, and motor behaviors. (30, 31, 32)
20. Family members and caregivers decrease the client's stress through the implementation of a quieter, more routine environment. (29, 33, 34, 35)
21. Demonstrate independence and initiative by making all possible choices in daily events, as evidenced by choosing clothing, food, leisure interests, and peer group. (36, 37)
22. Family members and caregivers express greater understanding of the client's emotional and developmental disorder. (38, 39, 40)
23. Family members and caretakers assist and support the client in his/her attempts to make positive behavioral changes to manage anxiety symptoms. (41, 42)
24. Increase participation in extracurricular activities and outings. (43, 44)

—. ______________________________
____

—. ______________________________
____

—. ______________________________
____

12. Instruct the client in cognitive restructuring techniques (e.g., replacing irrational, automatic thoughts with realistic self-talk that mediates calm confidence) to change his/her thoughts that perpetuate specific fears. Model these for the client and provide role-playing opportunities to facilitate mastery of the new skill.
13. Use systematic desensitization to assist the client in coping with his/her specific phobic responses. Construct a hierarchy of least-anxiety-provoking to greater-anxiety-provoking scenarios, gradually introducing each level until the client is anxiety free.
14. Request that the client generate a list of activities he/she enjoys and finds relaxing (e.g., listening to soothing music, taking baths, or going for walks) and request that the client specify times during the day to schedule calming activities.
15. Teach the client anxiety-reducing skills for managing anxiety symptoms (e.g., deep breathing, progressive muscle relaxation, or positive imagery). Model these for the client and provide him/her with practice opportunities to facilitate mastery of the new skill.

16. Prepare an audiotape of progressive muscle relaxation prompts or calm, soothing music for the client to use at early stages of anxiety. Provide a headset for the client.
17. Teach the client to recognize early signs of negative emotions and then to initiate alternative activities that will reduce expressed agitation (e.g., client's preferred activities, deep breathing, progressive muscle relaxation, or positive imagery).
18. Provide training and in-service sessions to family members and caregivers to promote their identification of early signs of the client's agitation. Direct family members to assist the client in utilizing distraction or coping techniques at low levels of agitation (e.g., deep breathing, relaxation, or positive self-talk).
19. Coordinate a mentor relationship with a volunteer or a peer who can assist in resolving conflicts between the client and his/her environment to promote more effective management of problems.
20. Refer the client to a support group for people with developmental disabilities.
21. Arrange for the client to participate in social skills training to reduce anxiety

experienced in social situations (see Social Skills in this Planner).

22. Teach the client relevant environmental stress reduction techniques to alleviate stressors (e.g., time management, exercise, or improved nutrition).

23. Refer the client to a speech therapist for suggestions or hardware to increase his/her communication ability.

24. Use modeling and role-playing to teach family members and caregivers to listen for the client's direct and indirect communications. Reinforce the client for cooperating with reasonable, routine requests.

25. Assist family members and caregivers in identifying what the client may be communicating through his/her problematic behavior (e.g., fear, helplessness, or frustration). Refer family members and caregivers to the *Parent Survival Manual* (Schopler) for examples of effective responses to the client's behavior problems.

26. Recommend that family members and caregivers use an activity board to display the client's schedule (written or pictorially) for the day, week, or month to minimize his/her anxiety related to uncertainty about what is upcoming.

27. Use behavioral analysis to identify reinforcers for the client's anxious behaviors.
28. Identify several reinforcers that can be used to reward behaviors that are incompatible with the client's anxiety behaviors. Ask the client to contribute to the list.
29. Assess ecological factors contributing to the maintenance of the client's anxiety behaviors.
30. Refer the client to a behavioral specialist to design and implement a behavioral plan that reinforces desired behaviors coupled with behavioral techniques (e.g., reinforcing low reactivity levels, reinforcing incompatible behaviors, extinction, response cost, and overcorrection) to decrease or eliminate anxious behaviors.
31. Train all caregivers on the client's behavioral treatment program to ensure effective implementation and strengthening of desirable nonanxious behaviors. (Consider using *Skills Training for Children with Behavioral Disorders: A Parent and Therapist Workbook* [Bloomquist] as a guide.)
32. Obtain approval from the client's guardian and the agency oversight committee for restrictive or aversive programming.

33. Modify the client's environment to remove physical and psychological conditions not conducive to low stress (e.g., noisy conditions, hunger, bright sunlight, and physical discomfort).
34. Recommend that family members and caregivers read *Helping People with Autism Manage Their Behavior* (Dalrymple) to learn how to create a structured, ordered environment that accommodates the client's needs and minimizes anxiety.
35. Recommend that family members and caregivers read the *Anxiety and Stress Self-Help Book* (Lark) or the *Anxiety and Phobia Workbook* (Bourne) to examine environmental changes that could reduce the client's anxiety and stress levels (e.g., dietary changes, physical exercise, and breathing exercises).
36. Present situations on a daily basis such that the client is required to make a choice between two to three options, and reinforce independent choices.
37. Encourage family members to allow the client to make all possible choices and to demonstrate maximum independence in daily events.
38. Obtain the client's consent to enlist support from clinicians, residential staff, family

members, and vocational and educational staff.

39. Provide specific information to client, family, and caregivers about the client's specific anxiety disorder (e.g., from the *Anxiety and Phobia Workbook* (Bourne) or from the National Institute of Mental Health Web site).
40. Recommend that caregivers read *The Psychiatric Tower of Babble* (Gabriel) to learn about the mental health needs of persons with developmental disabilities.
41. Arrange for family members and caregivers to spend time with the client doing only what the client expresses an interest in (e.g., planning a meal, playing a game, or watching a video) to promote unconditional, nondemanding interactions while the family members and caregivers Zprovide verbal attention to the client's activities.
42. Encourage family members and caregivers to increase the frequency of positive interactions with the client while modeling desirable behaviors, positive demeanor, and helpful attitudes. Model these behaviors to family members and caregivers in formal and informal situations.
43. Refer the client to a recreational therapist to determine

possible leisure, social, and community activities available to the client.

44. Encourage the client's participation in Special Olympics or other athletic events.

—. ____________________

—. ____________________

—. ____________________

DIAGNOSTIC SUGGESTIONS:

ICD-9-CM	*ICD-10-CM*	*DSM-5* Disorder, Condition, or Problem
300.02	F41.1	Generalized Anxiety Disorder
300.09	F41.8	Other Specified Anxiety Disorder
300.00	F41.9	Unspecified Anxiety Disorder
309.24	F43.22	Adjustment Disorder, With Anxiety
309.21	F93.0	Separation Anxiety Disorder
300.01	F41.0	Panic Disorder
300.22	F40.00	Agoraphobia
300.29	F40.xxx	Specific Phobia
300.23	F40.10	Social Anxiety Disorder (Social Phobia)
309.81	F43.10	Posttraumatic Stress Disorder
308.3	F43.0	Acute Stress Disorder
317	F70	Intellectual Disability, Mild
319	F71	Intellectual Disability, Moderate
319	F72	Intellectual Disability, Severe
319	F73	Intellectual Disability, Profound
319	F79	Unspecified Intellectual Disability
V62.89	R41.83	Borderline Intellectual Functioning
______	______	______________________________
______	______	______________________________

CHEMICAL DEPENDENCE

BEHAVIORAL DEFINITIONS

1. Consistent use of alcohol or other mood-altering drugs until high, intoxicated, or passed out.
2. Inability to stop or cut down use of mood-altering drugs once started, despite the verbalized desire to do so and negative consequences associated with continued use.
3. Difficulty understanding the concept of substance abuse and its problem despite direct feedback from spouse, relatives, friends, or employer that the use of the substance is negatively affecting them and others.
4. Marked change in behavior as evidenced by withdrawal from family or friends, loss of interest in activities, or sleep disturbances.
5. Unpredictable mood swings, irritability, tantrums, aggression, property destruction and self-injury resulting from substance use.
6. Continued drug and/or alcohol use despite experiencing persistent or recurring physical, legal, vocational, social or relationship problems that are directly caused by the drug/alcohol abuse, or the inability to foresee legal and personal consequences of behavior.
7. Gradual increase in the consumption of the mood-altering substance in larger amounts and for longer periods than intended, in order to attain the desired effect.
8. Physical symptoms, including shaking, seizures, nausea, headaches, sweating, anxiety, or insomnia when withdrawing from the substance.
9. Long periods of time spent at home with lack of challenging activities due to health problems or employment difficulties, resulting in increased substance use.
10. Typical daily activities affected by time spent obtaining the substance, using it, or recovering from its effect.
11. Continued use of mood-altering chemicals after being told that it potentiates the effects of existing medications and chronic medical conditions such as epilepsy, cerebral palsy, or mental illness.

12. Family members and caregivers reluctant to address substance use because they do not consider substance use problematic or wish to avoid another stigmatizing label.

__. ____
____
__. ____
____
__. ____
____

LONG-TERM GOALS

1. Accept chemical dependence and begin to actively participate in an integrated dual diagnosis recovery program.
2. Withdraw from mood-altering substance, stabilize physically and emotionally, and then establish a supportive recovery plan.
3. Gain an understanding of the negative impact of substance abuse on disability concerns and the effectiveness of prescribed medications.
4. Establish and maintain total abstinence while increasing knowledge of the disease and the process of an integrated recovery.
5. Identify and pursue relationships, groups, activities, and locations that will promote a healthy and satisfying lifestyle.

__. ____
____
__. ____
____
__. ____
____

SHORT-TERM OBJECTIVES

1. Describe the amount, frequency, and history of substance abuse. (1)

THERAPEUTIC INTERVENTIONS

1. Gather a complete drug and alcohol history including the type, amount, and pattern of use, as well as the negative life

2. Participate in a psychological assessment of adaptive and intellectual abilities and current stressors. (2, 3)
3. Review extended family's chemical dependence history and verbalize an acceptance of a genetic component to substance abuse. (4, 5)
4. Cooperate with a psychiatric examination to evaluate the need for psychotropic medications. (6, 7, 8, 9)
5. Participate in a medical examination to evaluate the effects of chemical dependence. (10, 11, 12)
6. Improve nutritional status relative to the effects of long-term substance abuse. (13, 14)
7. Begin the 12-step recovery process. (15, 16, 17, 18)
8. Cooperate with a supervised, medically supported detoxification program. (19, 20, 21, 22)
9. Implement the assertiveness and decision-making skills that promote a substance free lifestyle. (15, 23, 24, 25)
10. Identify the negative consequences of drug and/or alcohol abuse. (25, 26, 27)
11. Verbalize an understanding of the risks and the effects of substances on the mind and body. (25, 28, 29)
12. Identify the role substance abuse has played in meeting needs. (25, 30, 31, 32)

consequences resulting from substance use (e.g., social, legal familial, and vocational).

2. Assess the client's intellectual, personality, and cognitive functioning as they relate to his/her chemical dependence.
3. Explore situational stressors contributing to the client's substance misuse.
4. Explore the extended family's chemical dependence history. Utilize a genogram to pictorially display family relationships and substance abuse concerns.
5. Educate the client about his/her genetic predisposition to chemical dependence.
6. Arrange for a psychiatric evaluation to evaluate whether psychotropic medications may be helpful (see Anxiety and Depression in this Planner).
7. Monitor the client for compliance, effectiveness, and side effects associated with prescribed psychotropic medications.
8. Train family members and caregivers to monitor the client's signs and symptoms of mental illness to provide accurate information to the psychiatrist, psychologist, or other clinicians.
9. Emphasize to the client the difference between taking a prescribed medication for a

13. Verbalize an understanding of the risks associated with the use of mood-altering substances. (33, 34)
14. Eliminate denial behaviors and accept personal responsibility for substance use. (35, 36, 37, 38)
15. Accept legal consequences of behavior related to substance abuse. (39, 40, 41)
16. Verbalize increased knowledge of substance abuse and the process of recovery. (28, 42)
17. Verbalize an understanding of personality, social, and family factors that contribute to substance use. (3, 4, 25, 43)
18. Identify alternative coping behaviors to handle stressors. (25, 44, 45, 46)
19. Identify how sobriety could positively impact life. (47, 48)
20. Identify changes needed in social system and lifestyle to support recovery. (49, 50)
21. Increase number, duration, and intensity of social contacts. (16, 51)
22. Identify and alter living situation contributing to substance use. (52, 53, 54)
23. List recreational, social, and household activities that will replace substance abuse–related activities. (55, 56)

specific medical condition and the use of street drugs to achieve a high.

10. Arrange for the client to obtain a complete physical to determine the effects of his/her substance abuse.
11. Coordinate any follow-up to the physical examination, such as prescriptions, lab tests, or specialized assessments.
12. Coordinate with the physician to determine the safest way to decrease or eliminate the client's dependence on substances.
13. Review the client's eating habits and encourage the client to maintain healthy nutrition.
14. Refer the client to a dietician or nutritionist for assessment or recommendations regarding his/her dietary needs.
15. Review support groups available for persons with developmental disabilities experiencing difficulties with substance abuse (e.g., Alcoholics Anonymous [AA], Narcotics Anonymous [NA], community mental health agencies, drug detoxification centers, or support groups for persons with developmental disabilities). Refer the client to the most suitable programs.

24. Agree to make amends to significant others who have been hurt by the life dominated by substance abuse. (25, 57)
25. Write a goodbye letter to drug of choice telling it why it must go. (58)
26. Identify potential relapse triggers and develop strategies for constructively dealing with each trigger. (59, 60, 61, 62)

__. ____________________

__. ____________________

__. ____________________

16. Arrange for volunteers to take the client to AA or NA meetings.
17. Arrange for the client to receive training on the jargon and customs of AA meetings so he/she can avoid feeling lost and inadequate.
18. Teach the client social skills such as assertiveness, reciprocity, and courtesy to ensure that he/she can fit socially into support groups (see Social Skills in this Planner).
19. Advocate with the substance abuse treatment program for the client to be able to utilize existing prescription medications for medical conditions while in treatment.
20. Coordinate with the treatment program to extend the length of treatment, simplify information, provide information repetitively, and use behavioral techniques as needed by the client to ensure that he/she gets maximal benefits from program.
21. Provide substance abuse professionals with information regarding intellectual disability (e.g., this Treatment Planner) as well as substance abuse training for intellectual disability professionals (e.g., *The Chemical Dependence Treatment Planner* [Perkinson and Jongsma]).

22. Coordinate the development of a multidisciplinary, interagency team to provide integrated treatment.
23. Arrange for the client to receive individual, family, and/or group counseling to discuss substance use.
24. Use a variety of activities to promote self-exploration, handling peer pressure, and decision-making skills, (e.g., see *101 Support Group Activities: For Teenagers Recovering from Chemical Dependence* [Fleming]).
25. Assign appropriate homework assignments from the *Chemical Dependence Treatment Homework Planner* (Finley and Lenz). Modify the assignments as needed to meet the client's level of intellectual functioning.
26. Request that the client make a list of the ways substance abuse has negatively impacted his/her life and process it with the clinician.
27. Assign the client to meet with two or three people who are close to him/her to discuss how they see his/her chemical dependence negatively impacting their lives.
28. Provide the client with factual information in concrete terms on the effects of substance abuse on physical and mental health (e.g., see *The Addictions Workbook* [Fanning and O'Neill]).

29. Arrange for the client to view a video on his/her drug of choice (e.g., the *Gateway Drugs* series: *Binge Drinking Blowout, Tobacco X-Files,* or *Marijuana: The Gateway Drug* [Discover Films Video]).
30. Discuss with the client his/her needs, real and perceived, met through substance use. Assist the client in identifying alternate, constructive ways to meet these needs while remaining abstinent.
31. Ask the client about the physical cravings he/she has experienced for the substance of choice; discuss coping behaviors to replace substance abuse.
32. Request feedback from the client on the ways in which the drug or alcohol has been used as a social icebreaker; discuss alternate social and relaxation skills that could be used.
33. Educate the client on the effects of substance misuse (e.g., increased tolerance, altered judgment, and negative medication interactions). Stress this concept by using specific examples of how his/her quality of life can be improved by eliminating substance use.
34. Arrange for the client to view a video on the effects of substance misuse (e.g., the *Addiction and Recovery Series*

[American Institute for Learning]).

35. Acknowledge and reinforce all statements made by the client indicating his/her personal responsibility for the substance abuse. Provide reassurances to limit fear or shame that might cause undue guilt and anxiety.
36. Use specific examples to describe positive and negative choices about substance use, and how each choice results in vastly different consequences. Determine the client's interest in making positive future choices.
37. Model and reinforce statements made by the client indicating his/her understanding of the destructive consequences substance misuse has created for himself/herself and others.
38. Confront the client's use of defense mechanisms to justify or rationalize behavior.
39. With proper release, provide information to the police or prosecutor regarding the impact of the client's developmental disability on his/her behavior.
40. Facilitate the client's involvement with legal appointments, court dates, and so on. (See Legal Problems in this Planner.)
41. Obtain documentation from law enforcement personnel regarding the client's illegal

behaviors relative to substance abuse. Process with the client the role his/her use of addictive substances has had in illegal activities.

42. Modify educational materials (available from local substance abuse treatment agencies) to accommodate the client's individual learning requirements (e.g., orally review written materials on a one-to-one basis, or use simplified pictures or videos).
43. Question the client about his/her understanding of how triggers contribute to substance abuse. Reinforce knowledge or understanding of these relationships.
44. Assist the client in identifying healthy alternatives for coping with problems (e.g., physical exercise, increased socialization, talking to an identified support person or peer). Provide the client with a written or pictorial list of alternative behaviors for him/her to refer to as needed.
45. Help to identify the client's specific personal triggers for substance use (location, events, moods, thoughts, or peer group). Request that the client identify alternative healthy responses to each identified trigger.
46. Model and role-play with the client his/her identified

alternative responses until the client is able to do so independently and confidently.

47. Assist the client in identifying positive changes resulting from eliminating substance abuse (e.g., relationships, work, health, and home environment). Create a written or pictorial list of the positive changes.
48. Review the negative influence of continuing existing substance-related friendships (drinking buddies) and assist the client in making a plan to develop new substance-free friendships.
49. Discuss with the client life changes needed in order to maintain long-term substance-free living. Request that the client identify specific changes he/she believes are necessary. Contract with him/her to make the identified changes.
50. Practice a variety of social skills with the client (see Social Skills in this Planner).
51. Refer the client to drop-in centers, clubhouse programs, and community-based social programs.
52. Evaluate the role of the client's living situation in fostering a pattern of substance abuse.
53. Assign the client to make a list of negative influences for chemical dependence

inherent in his/her current living situation.

54. Encourage, support, and reinforce the client's desire to seek alternative living arrangements that will foster recovery.
55. Assist the client in planning social and recreational activities that are free from substance use (see Recreation/Leisure Activities in this Planner).
56. Request that the client identify household or work-related projects to fill the time previously spent using substances.
57. Discuss with the client the negative effects his/her substance abuse has had on family, friends, and work relationships, and encourage a plan to make amends for such hurt.
58. Request that the client write a goodbye letter to the drug of choice, read it, and process related feelings with the therapist.
59. Help the client develop an awareness of relapse triggers and alternative ways of effectively handling them.
60. Develop an abstinence contract with the client regarding the use of his/her drug of choice. Provide the client with a copy in a format that promotes frequent independent review (e.g., written or

pictorial chart, audiotape, or videotape). Process the emotional impact of this contract with the clinician.

61. Develop with the client a comprehensive aftercare plan to ensure maintenance of changes, including a support network, treatment alternatives, a plan for coping with triggers, and a safety plan.
62. Recommend that the client view *H.A.L.T.: A Relapse Prevention Guide* (Visions Video).

__. ______________________________

____

__. ______________________________

____

__. ______________________________

____

DIAGNOSTIC SUGGESTIONS:

ICD-9-CM	*ICD-10-CM*	*DSM-5* Disorder, Condition, or Problem
303.90	F10.20	Alcohol Use Disorder, Moderate or Severe
305.00	F10.10	Alcohol Use Disorder, Mild
304.30	F12.20	Cannabis Use Disorder, Moderate or Severe
305.20	F12.10	Cannabis Use Disorder, Mild
304.20	F14.20	Cocaine Use Disorder, Moderate or Severe
305.60	F14.10	Cocaine Use Disorder, Mild
305.70	F15.10	Amphetamine Use Disorder, Mild
304.40	F15.20	Amphetamine Use Disorder, Moderate or Severe
305.50	F11.10	Opioid Use Disorder, Mild
304.00	F11.20	Opioid Use Disorder, Moderate or Severe
305.90	F18.10	Inhalant Use Disorder, Mild
304.60	F18.20	Inhalant Use Disorder, Moderate or Severe
291.2	F10.27	Moderate or Severe Alcohol Use Disorder, with Alcohol-Induced Major Neurocognitive Disorder, Nonamnestic-Confabulatory Type
291.1	F10.26	Moderate or Severe Alcohol Use Disorder, with Alcohol-Induced Major Neurocognitive Disorder, Amnestic-Confabulatory Type
V71.01	Z72.811	Adult Antisocial Behavior
304.10	F13.20	Sedative, Hypnotic, or Anxiolytic Use Disorder, Moderate or Severe
299.00	F84.0	Autism Spectrum Disorder
301.7	F60.2	Antisocial Personality Disorder
317	F70	Intellectual Disability, Mild
319	F71	Intellectual Disability, Moderate
319	F72	Intellectual Disability, Severe
319	F73	Intellectual Disability, Profound
319	F79	Unspecified Intellectual Disability
V62.89	R41.83	Borderline Intellectual Functioning
______	______	______________________________
______	______	______________________________

COGNITIVE/EMOTIONAL DECOMPENSATION

BEHAVIORAL DEFINITIONS

1. Memory loss, resulting in disorientation, confusion, and/or inability to learn simple new tasks.
2. Changes in personality, as evidenced by increased emotional difficulties (e.g., paranoia, depression, anxiety, or emotional lability).
3. Previously learned tasks become increasingly more difficult to recall and perform.
4. Deterioration of personal, community, and household safety skills.
5. Decreased independence in the areas of self-care, hygiene, and continence.
6. Deterioration of receptive, expressive, and written-language skills.
7. Deterioration of physical health resulting from the aging process (e.g., circulatory problems, prostate concerns, or osteoporosis).
8. Gait imbalance, as evidenced by increased frequency of falling.
9. Nocturnal confusion, as evidenced by an increase in nighttime wakefulness.
10. Increase in psychotic episodes.

__. ____

____

__. ____

____

__. ____

____

LONG-TERM GOALS

1. Maintain existing activities of daily living (ADL) and instrumental activities of daily living (IADL) skills.
2. Use adaptive equipment and training modalities that support independent functioning.
3. Maintain optimal health.
4. Reduce the frequency and severity of maladaptive behaviors resulting from confusion and disorientation, or attempts to escape or avoid.
5. Identify long-term retirement plans.
6. Caregivers and client reach a consensus on identified goals for the client.
7. Maximize the client's choices and preferences whenever possible.
8. Caregivers reinforce all steps toward skill maintenance.

__. ____
____

__. ____
____

__. ____
____

SHORT-TERM OBJECTIVES

1. Participate in a psychological assessment of adaptive and intellectual abilities. (1, 2)
2. Complete neuropsychological testing to assess contribution of organic factors to behavioral deficits. (2, 3, 4, 5)
3. Accept and adhere to recommendations made by the interdisciplinary team regarding appropriate interventions. (2, 5, 6)

THERAPEUTIC INTERVENTIONS

1. Perform or arrange for a comprehensive intellectual and adaptive assessment to establish the baseline of the client's ability and to gain insight into his/her strengths and weaknesses.
2. Attend person-centered planning (PCP) meeting with client, family, client advocate, school officials, and caregivers to determine e ducational, vocational, recreational, communicative, IADL, and health goals

4. Cooperate with a physical and occupational therapy assessment to identify baseline skills to maintain. (2, 7, 8, 9)
5. Cooperate with a speech/language evaluation. (2, 10)
6. Cooperate with nurse's monitoring of physical and medical conditions. (2, 11, 12)
7. Cooperate with physical examination for periodic check-up and treatment of acute medical problems. (13, 14, 15)
8. Cooperate with psychiatric examination to stabilize Axis I concerns. (16, 17, 18, 19)
9. Cooperate with dental examinations to maintain teeth and gums. (20)
10. Cooperate with visual examination to ensure adequate vision for daily tasks. (21)
11. Implement a stable, healthy, and appealing diet. (22)
12. Verbalize acceptance of retirement plan. (23, 24, 25)
13. Accept placement in an appropriate residential setting and day program to meet leisure, habilitative, or vocational needs. (23, 25, 26, 27)
14. Family members, caregivers, and client verbalize an understanding of the effects of aging and resulting health changes. (28, 29)

along with eligibility for special services.

3. Arrange for a neurological exam and/or neuropsychological testing to identify the nature, severity, and causes of the client's cognitive/emotional decompensation.
4. Arrange for a screening for dementia (e.g., the Early Signs of Dementia Checklist [in Visser, Aldenkamp, and Van Huffelen] or the Dementia Rating Scale for Mentally Retarded Adults [Evenhuis, Kengen, and Eurlings]).
5. Consult with the client, family, school officials, and caregivers to obtain an overview of all multidisciplinary treatments wanted by the client.
6. Provide feedback to client, family, and staff on the results of intellectual, adaptive, psychological, behavioral, and neuropsychological testing and on recommendations based on those results.
7. Refer the client to a physical therapist to assess his/her current level of motor functioning and gait in order to determine if ongoing physical therapy services are needed to maintain motor skills.
8. Refer the client to an occupational therapist for an evaluation of current skill

15. Maintain all acquired self-care and social skills that support independent living. (30, 31)
16. Engage in a consistent evening sleep schedule. (32)
17. Display a regular schedule of continence. (33)
18. Verbalize appreciation of a quieter, more routine environment. (34)
19. Replace maladaptive behaviors with adaptive, goal-directed, socially compatible behaviors. (31, 35, 36, 37)
20. Identify and express feelings associated with deterioration of skill level. (38)
21. Implement positive self-talk to cope with skill loss. (39)
22. Family members increase positive feedback to client. (30, 40, 41)
23. Family members and caregivers develop realistic expectations of the client's overall abilities. (42)
24. Family members increase and/or maintain involvement with the client and his/her treatment. (43, 44)
25. Caretakers reduce the frequency of speaking for the client and/or performing activities that the client is capable of doing independently. (45, 46)
26. Verbally or nonverbally indicate comfort and enjoyment of activities as evidenced by verbalizing

levels and to develop strategies to maintain existing personal care and household skills.

9. Arrange for the client to obtain necessary adaptive or physical therapy equipment.
10. Refer the client to a speech therapist to determine the client's communicative strengths and weaknesses, and the mode of communication best suited for him/her.
11. Refer the client to a nurse for ongoing monitoring of basic health, medical concerns, and medication management.
12. Monitor the procedures for the administration of medications that have been prescribed for the client.
13. Arrange appointments for periodic physical exams and any follow-up or specialist care that is indicated.
14. Consult with the physician about the client's type of developmental disability (e.g., intellectual disability due to Down's Syndrome) and the expected health changes with aging (hearing loss, thyroid disease, sleep apnea, heart disease, and/or musculoskeletal problems).
15. Consult with the pharmacist to rule out current medications or polypharmacy as a causal variable in the client's declining abilities.

positive statements, smiling often, displaying a relaxed posture, approaching caregivers freely, and decreasing the amount of time spent withdrawing. (47)

27. Caretakers verbalize the degree of emotional strain related to providing service to the client. (48, 49)
28. Caretakers utilize relaxation skills, respite care, and other community resources to relieve stress. (50, 51)
29. Participate in stress-relieving activities. (52, 53)
30. Increase participation in leisure, extracurricular, and fitness activities. (53, 54, 55, 56, 57)
31. Caregivers reinforce all steps toward maintaining optimal functioning. (30, 58, 59, 60)

—. ______________________

____

—. ______________________

____

—. ______________________

____

16. Arrange for psychiatric evaluation to determine if a concomitant Axis I disorder may be contributing to the client's declining skills and whether psychotropic medication may be helpful.
17. Monitor the client for permanent side effects of neuroleptic medications (e.g., tardive dyskinesia, muscle rigidity, or dystonia).
18. Enlist the help of family members and caregivers to monitor signs and symptoms of the client's psychiatric condition in order to provide accurate information to a psychiatrist.
19. Provide family members and caregivers with forms and a data collection system to ensure reliable symptom data collection.
20. Arrange for biannual dental examinations and cleanings.
21. Arrange for yearly vision examinations.
22. Facilitate the client's obtaining dietician-approved foods and meals that he/she enjoys and that are adequate to maintain good health.
23. Determine with the client what his/her residential and day program preferences are for retirement (e.g., continued working/day program or reduced schedule). Determine

what options are available that match his/her interest.

24. Recommend that family members read *The Elderly Caregiver* (Roberto) or *The Life Planning Workbook* (Russell and Grant) to address concerns of elderly parents and caregivers and plan for the future care of the client.
25. Obtain family members' input regarding ideal retirement options for the client.
26. After consultation with client, family, vocational supervisors, staff, and assigned clinicians, make a referral to an appropriate residential option (e.g., adult foster care home, group home, supported living environments, apartments, community treatment homes, or nursing home).
27. Refer the client to a suitable program site or day program that has opportunities of interest to him/her.
28. Educate family members and the client on the normal aging process and how it relates to and differs in people with developmental disabilities (e.g., view a video such as *Aging People with Mental Retardation* [Kopp] or read *The Thirty-Six Hour Day* [Mace and Rabings]).
29. Recommend that family members read *Alzheimer's*

Disease and People with Mental Retardation (Association for Retarded Citizens [ARC]) to gain a better understanding of the signs, symptoms, and diagnosis of Alzheimer's disease, and where to obtain an evaluation for Alzheimer's.

30. Encourage family members and caretakers to continue promoting and reinforcing the client's independence in all tasks of which he/she is capable.
31. Design a reward system to motivate the client to maintain existing abilities (e.g., personal care, household skills, communication, and social skills). Use the reward system to promote behaviors that are incompatible with maladaptive behaviors.
32. Collect data on the client's sleep patterns to identify patterns in his/her periods of lengthy sleep to use as a foundation for developing a consistent sleep regime (see Sleep Disturbance in this Planner).
33. Request that family members and caregivers look for physical signs (pacing, crotch grabbing, and wiggling) that would indicate that the client is experiencing the urge to void. Develop a schedule for prompting the client to use the bathroom (see Enuresis/Encopresis in this Planner).

34. Generate several environmental modification strategies (e.g., consistent schedules or routines portrayed pictorially, reduction in noise levels, or creating a calm, relaxing environment) that family members and caretakers can employ to maximize the client's functioning while minimizing confusion and disorientation. Arrange for family members and caregivers to view the video *ABC's* (Teri).
35. Using behavioral analysis, determine motivating and maintaining reinforcers for the client's maladaptive behaviors.
36. Train all caregivers on the client's behavioral treatment program in order to ensure effective implementation and strengthening of desirable, prosocial behavior. Arrange for caregivers to view *Managing Aggressive Behaviors* (Teri) and *Managing Psychotic Behaviors* (Teri).
37. Obtain approval from the client's guardian and the agency oversight committee for any restrictive or aversive programming.
38. Request that the client discuss problematic emotions related to the deterioration of his/her abilities and how to identify the triggering event of an emotion (e.g., "I am angry because I am less

capable of performing various activities").

39. Teach the client positive self-talk (e.g., "With practice I can do this" or "It may take longer, but I can do it") that will help the client accept and positively cope with his/her ADL/IADL skill difficulties.
40. Monitor the client's progress at specified intervals and report information to client, family, and caregivers.
41. Encourage family members and caregivers to provide frequent and immediate positive feedback to the client for progress in ADL skills training and maintenance.
42. Educate family members and caregivers on expected time frames for ADL skills maintenance and potential obstacles the client may face, in order to promote realistic expectations of his/her adaptive functioning.
43. Encourage family members to maintain regular social contact with the client.
44. Encourage family members to maintain regular communication with involved clinicians regarding status of the client's ADL skills, health, and maladaptive behaviors.
45. Provide family members and caregivers with training needed to support the client's skills maintenance

(e.g., person-centered planning training or self-direction training).

46. Encourage family members and caregivers to agree to promote lifelong learning opportunities and experiences for the client in order to promote his/her choice making, decision making, problem solving, goal setting and attainment, along with self-awareness and knowledge.
47. Monitor, acknowledge, and reinforce all verbal and non-verbal signs of the client's pleasure, self-esteem, confidence, and social comfort.
48. Observe family members and caregivers for frustrations that may reduce their ability to interact effectively with the client. Provide opportunities for venting feelings.
49. Recommend that family members read *Taking Care of Caregivers* (Roberts), *The Alzheimer's Sourcebook for Caregivers* (Gray-Davidson), or *The Resourceful Caregiver* (National Family Caregivers Association) to generate positive coping strategies (e.g., stress management, communication strategies, identifying caregiver needs, and dealing with grief).
50. Teach deep muscle relaxation, abdominal breathing, and safe-place imagery to

caregivers to alleviate the stress of the many demands of caring for a person with ADL deficits.

51. Refer caregivers to community resources to facilitate coping with the supervision of an elderly person with developmental disabilities (e.g., respite care, skills training, or support groups).
52. Teach the client stress reduction techniques (e.g., deep muscle relaxation, abdominal breathing, and safe place imagery) to alleviate stressors encountered.
53. Refer the client to a recreational therapist to determine possible appropriate leisure and community activities available.
54. Encourage the client's participation in Special Olympics or other athletic activities.
55. Assess the client's and family members' interest in faith-based activities and provide access to church ministry if indicated.
56. Refer family members and caregivers to *Dimensions of Faith and Congregational Ministries with Persons with Developmental Disabilities and Their Families* (Gavanta) to obtain information on many different faith-based books, videos, and programs available for persons with

developmental disabilities and their families.

57. Observe the client for obvious and subtle signs of likes and dislikes and provide all possible enjoyable situations.
58. Urge and reinforce all independent choices exercised by the client and teach family members to do so also.
59. If the client is unable to express wants and desires, request that the person who knows the client best identify what he/she is likely to want.
60. Strengthen the client's alliances and natural supports through encouraging support, linking to support groups, and facilitating his/her natural support system's involvement.

—. ______________________________
____

—. ______________________________
____

—. ______________________________
____

DIAGNOSTIC SUGGESTIONS:

ICD-9-CM	*ICD-10-CM*	*DSM-5* Disorder, Condition, or Problem
299.00	F84.0	Autism Spectrum Disorder
294.11	F02.81	Probable Neurocognitive Disorder Due to Alzheimer's Disease, with Behavioral Disturbance
294.10	F02.80	Probable Neurocognitive Disorder Due to Alzheimer's Disease, without Behavioral Disturbance
294.10	F02.80	Major Neurocognitive Disorder Due to another Medical Condition, without Behavioral Disturbance
294.11	F02.81	Major Neurocognitive Disorder Due to another Medical Condition, with Behavioral Disturbance
294.10	F02.80	Major Neurocognitive Disorder Due to Traumatic Brain Injury, without Behavioral Disturbance
294.10	F02.81	Major Neurocognitive Disorder Due to Traumatic Brain Injury, with Behavioral Disturbance
294.8	R41.9	Unspecified Neurocognitive Disorder
309.0	F43.21	Adjustment Disorder, With Depressed Mood
317	F70	Intellectual Disability, Mild
319	F71	Intellectual Disability, Moderate
319	F72	Intellectual Disability, Severe
319	F73	Intellectual Disability, Profound
319	F79	Unspecified Intellectual Disability
V62.89	R41.83	Borderline Intellectual Functioning
_____	_____	____________________________
_____	_____	____________________________

COMMUNITY ACCESS

BEHAVIORAL DEFINITIONS

1. Limited independent community access to shopping, worship, park, libraries, theaters, and community business.
2. Difficulties in recognizing and understanding common public information signs.
3. Inability to effectively communicate address and phone number to others.
4. Lack of understanding on how to utilize public transportation services.
5. Lower than expected community access resulting from overprotection of client by caregiver.

__. ____

____

__. ____

____

__. ____

____

LONG-TERM GOALS

1. Strengthen existing community access skills and develop new community access skills.
2. Increase independence and community access skills acquisition.
3. Increase the frequency of community access.
4. Learn basic skills needed to access the community independently in a safe, supported, supervised environment.
5. Caregivers consistently reinforce all steps toward independence with community access skills acquisition.

—. ____

____

—. ____

____

—. ____

____

SHORT-TERM OBJECTIVES

1. Participate in an assessment of community access skills. (1, 2)
2. Participate in training sessions designed to maximize independence with community access training. (3, 4)
3. List potential reinforcers or rewards to be earned through progress in learning household safety skills. (5)
4. Demonstrate a knowledge of common community signs by verbally identifying specific signs when shown pictures of them. (4, 5, 6)
5. Identify, recognize, and locate common signs while out in the community. (5, 7, 8)
6. Demonstrate the ability to comprehend signs by displaying correct behavior after encountering a sign. (5, 8)
7. Display ability to communicate home address to others. (5, 9, 10, 11)

THERAPEUTIC INTERVENTIONS

1. Assess or arrange for an evaluation of the client's community access skills through direct observation and reports from caregivers to establish a baseline of the client's ability and gain insight into his/her strengths and weaknesses.
2. Provide direct feedback to client, family, and caregivers on the results of the evaluation.
3. Determine a safe training site in the community to provide the client with realistic training opportunities.
4. Provide direct instruction with frequent quizzing on common signs that provide community information (i.e., ask the client to name or point to railroad, bathroom, poison, walk/don't walk, and telephone signs).
5. Design and implement a reward system to motivate the client to improve his/her community access skills.

8. Appropriately use public transportation. (5, 12, 13, 14, 15, 17)
9. Seek assistance when needed while in the community. (16, 17, 18)
10. Navigate to desired locations in community. (19, 20, 21, 22)
11. Participate in extracurricular activities, outings, and community events. (23, 24, 25, 26)
12. Become familiar with using escalators and elevators in public buildings. (27, 28)
13. Caretakers monitor the client's progress and model needed skills while in the community. (6, 29, 30, 31)
14. Family members reduce the frequency of speaking for the client and/or performing activities that the client is capable of doing independently. 32, 33, 34)

—. ______________________________
____

—. ______________________________
____

—. ______________________________
____

6. Request that the client role-play proper reactions to signs.
7. Point out signs while in the community, asking the client to name the sign and interpret its meaning.
8. Observe the client's understanding of signs and ability to functionally use signs of direct behavior while in the community (e.g., identifying correct bathroom sign and using the correct bathroom independently).
9. Provide multiple repetitions of direct instruction to teach the client his/her home address and telephone number.
10. Assist the client in obtaining a state identification card or other picture identification.
11. Model the presentation of an identification card to communicate one's address or telephone number for the client.
12. Model the skills necessary to obtain public transportation, and have the client repeat these behaviors under supervision.
13. Show the client bus stop locations in community areas where he/she is likely to need bus service.
14. Teach the use of proper bus fare and request that the client independently produce the correct fare from his/her

wallet to have ready prior to boarding.

15. Ask the client where the desired destination is along the public transportation route and what landmarks will indicate the desired location.
16. Brainstorm possible sources of assistance available in the community.
17. Use role-playing, modeling, and behavior rehearsal to teach the client how to ask for assistance in finding a destination.
18. Prompt the client to identify two or more people who can provide him/her with information or help if needed.
19. Request that the client identify three or four sites in the community that he/she would like to access (e.g., library, sporting facilities, places of worship, theaters, and community businesses).
20. Assist the client in locating the proper location or room of a building.
21. Request that the client locate the building independently, while under supervision.
22. Review the utility and procedures of using basic maps to obtain a route to a location.
23. Refer the client to a recreational therapist to determine possible leisure and community

activities available to the client.

24. Encourage the client's participation in Special Olympics or other athletic events.
25. Assess the client's and/or family members' interest in faith-based activities and provide access to church ministry as indicated.
26. Refer family members and caregivers to *Dimensions of Faith and Congregational Ministries with Persons with Developmental Disabilities and Their Families* (Gavanta) to obtain information on many different faith-based books, videos, and programs available for persons with developmental disabilities and their families.
27. Demonstrate to the client how to properly use escalators and elevators.
28. Request that the client demonstrate the use of escalators and elevators under supervision, reinforcing appropriate actions.
29. Provide family members and caregivers with training needed to support the client's advancement in community access skills (e.g., how and when to reinforce, behaviors to increase, and client-specific teaching strategies).

30. Urge family members and caregivers to provide the client with a variety of supervised activities in the community to foster skills acquisition.
31. Request that parents, caregivers, and teachers model community access skills, requesting that the client imitate what is modeled.
32. Encourage family members and caregivers to promote the client's independence in the community to the full extent of his/her abilities while allowing for frequent and regular community access.
33. Encourage family members and caregivers to agree to promote lifelong learning opportunities and experiences for the client in order to promote his/her choice making, decision making, problem solving, goal setting, and attainment, along with self-awareness and knowledge.
34. Urge the client to make all reasonable choices in daily events in the practice of increased independence, and provide reinforcement for doing so.

__. ____________________________
____

__. ____________________________
____

__. ____________________________
____

DIAGNOSTIC SUGGESTIONS:

ICD-9-CM	*ICD-10-CM*	*DSM-5* Disorder, Condition, or Problem
299.00	F84.0	Autism Spectrum Disorder
317	F70	Intellectual Disability, Mild
319	F71	Intellectual Disability, Moderate
319	F72	Intellectual Disability, Severe
319	F73	Intellectual Disability, Profound
319	F79	Unspecified Intellectual Disability
V62.89	R41.83	Borderline Intellectual Functioning
______	______	______________________________
______	______	______________________________

COMMUNITY SAFETY SKILLS

BEHAVIORAL DEFINITIONS

1. Limited independent community access to shopping, worship, parks, libraries, theaters, and community businesses.
2. Lack of knowledge regarding community rules and laws.
3. Failure to use seat belt when riding in vehicles.
4. Limited knowledge of traffic laws.
5. Inability to adequately respond to emergency situations.
6. Lower than expected safety skills resulting from overprotection of client by caregiver.

—. ____
____

—. ____
____

—. ____
____

LONG-TERM GOALS

1. Increase level of independent functioning within the community at large.
2. Learn the importance and key components of community safety skills.
3. Increase frequency of community access.
4. Increase ability to respond to potential emergency situations.
5. Learn skills essential to protect self from potential harm.
6. Caregivers promote and reinforce the client's increased independence.

__. ____

____

__. ____

____

__. ____

____

SHORT-TERM OBJECTIVES

1. Participate in evaluation of community safety skills. (1, 2)
2. Adhere to recommendations made from evaluation regarding appropriate interventions. (3, 4)
3. Participate in training sessions designed to maximize independence by strengthening community safety skills. (5, 6)
4. Agree to receive training in community safety skills in a safe, supported environment to ensure safety while out in the community. (6, 7)
5. Increase participation in community-based activities, businesses, and institutions. (6, 8, 9)
6. Participate in Special Olympics activities. (6, 10)
7. Participate in faith-based activities. (6, 9, 11)
8. Demonstrate safe street crossing through training situations. (6, 12, 13, 14, 15)

THERAPEUTIC INTERVENTIONS

1. Assess or arrange for an evaluation of the client's community safety skills through direct observation and reports from caregivers to establish a baseline of the client's ability.
2. Identify the client's strengths that can be built on and weaknesses that must be considered in training for community safety.
3. Present a variety of options to client, family, caregivers, and school officials regarding programs for teaching the client community safety skills.
4. Obtain consensus from client, family, school officials, and caregivers regarding suitable learning programs or interventions that build on the client's strengths and compensate for his/her weaknesses.
5. Clients, parents, caregivers, and teachers model community skills to be taught, and

9. Identify essential street safety signs, pictorially and while out in the community. (6, 16, 17, 18)
10. Identify common danger signs pictorially and while out in the community. (6, 19, 20)
11. Use seat belts independently when riding in a vehicle. (6, 21, 22)
12. Practice necessary safety skills related to potentially dangerous animals. (6, 23, 24)
13. Caretakers reduce the frequency of speaking for the client and/or performing activities that the client is capable of doing independently. (25, 26, 27)

—. ______________________________

____

—. ______________________________

____

—. ______________________________

____

encourage the client to imitate what is modeled.

6. Design and implement a reward system to motivate the client to improve his/her safety skills acquisition.
7. Coordinate the training to be offered in a supervised, safe, supported environment to ensure maximum skills acquisition while maintaining safety.
8. Request that the client identify three or four different places in the community that he/she would like to access (e.g., library, sporting facilities, theaters, and community businesses).
9. Provide opportunities to go to community areas that the client has identified as desirable to visit.
10. Encourage the client's participation in Special Olympics or other athletic events.
11. Assess the client's and/or family members' interest in faith-based activities and provide access to church ministry as indicated.
12. Provide pictures of streets with crosswalks and encourage the client to indicate (verbally or by pointing) where safe crossing should occur.
13. Using a safe intersection, model proper street-crossing steps for the client.

14. Using a safe intersection and providing close supervision, encourage the client to cross the street in a safe manner.
15. After several supervised successful training sessions, encourage the client to independently cross the street.
16. Present color photographs of common street safety signs (e.g., walk/don't walk and stop), and encourage the client to correctly point to and/or verbally indicate the meaning of each sign.
17. Assess the client's ability to correctly identify street safety signs in the community by testing him/her in a variety of situations.
18. Assess the client's ability to follow and comprehend street safety signs by requesting him/her to explain what is meant by a variety of signs identified while in the community.
19. Present color pictures of danger signs or signals (e.g., RR Crossing, No Swimming, No Trespassing, High Voltage, and Keep Out) to the client while verbally identifying safety concepts, and encourage the client to correctly point to and/or verbally identify corresponding danger signs.
20. Assess the client's ability to observe danger signs and

conform his/her behavior accordingly by practicing in a safe community area or in session via role-playing.

21. Model the proper use of seat belts and encourage the client to repeat these demonstrations.

22. Instruct the client on the laws regarding seat belts and observe his/her use of seat belts when in vehicles.

23. Present color photographs of animals that can be dangerous (e.g., dogs, snakes, and cats) and have the client correctly point to and/or verbally identify each animal.

24. Teach family members and caregivers to ask the client to identify animals when they are seen in the community, noting those that are safe to approach and modeling steps to remain safely away from dangerous animals.

25. Provide family members and caregivers with training and/or in-service sessions needed to support the client's advancement in community safety skills.

26. Encourage family members and caregivers to agree to promote lifelong learning opportunities and experiences for the client in order to promote his/her choice making, decision making, problem solving, goal setting and attainment,

along with self-awareness and knowledge.

27. Urge the client to make all reasonable choices in daily events in the practice of increased independence, and provide reinforcement for doing so.

—. ______________________________
____

—. ______________________________
____

—. ______________________________
____

DIAGNOSTIC SUGGESTIONS:

ICD-9-CM	*ICD-10-CM*	*DSM-5* Disorder, Condition, or Problem
299.00	F84.0	Autism Spectrum Disorder
317	F70	Intellectual Disability, Mild
319	F71	Intellectual Disability, Moderate
319	F72	Intellectual Disability, Severe
319	F73	Intellectual Disability, Profound
319	F79	Unspecified Intellectual Disability
V62.89	R41.83	Borderline Intellectual Functioning
______	______	______________________________
______	______	______________________________

COOKING/HOUSEKEEPING SKILLS

BEHAVIORAL DEFINITIONS

1. Inability to properly and safely plan, prepare, cook, and clean up after a meal.
2. Poor understanding and initiation of necessary basic housekeeping tasks.
3. Limited ability to properly care for clothing (e.g., washing, drying, and putting away laundered clothes).
4. Failure to properly clean and put away dishes after a meal.
5. Inadequate knowledge of proper housekeeping cleaning tasks (e.g., dusting, sweeping, vacuuming, mopping, disinfecting kitchen and bath surfaces, and putting things away).
6. Limited comprehension of essential housekeeping skills that compromise home safety.
7. Failure to comply with housekeeping rules to ensure organization and safety.
8. Maladaptive behaviors that interfere with acquisition of housekeeping skills.
9. Lower than expected housekeeping skills resulting from overprotection of client by caregiver.

__. ____

____

__. ____

____

__. ____

____

LONG-TERM GOALS

1. Strengthen existing housekeeping skills and develop independence with new housekeeping skills.
2. Plan and safely prepare meals.
3. Develop and maintain skills for proper clothing care.
4. Develop and maintain skills for maintaining a clean household.
5. Reduce the frequency and severity of maladaptive behaviors that interfere with housekeeping skills.
6. Caregivers reinforce all steps toward independence with housekeeping skill acquisition.
7. Use adaptive equipment and training modalities to support independent functioning.

__. ____

____

__. ____

____

__. ____

____

SHORT-TERM OBJECTIVES

1. Participate in an assessment of housekeeping skills. (1, 2, 3)
2. Cooperate with psychiatric examination to assess the need for psychotropic medications. (4, 5)
3. Participate in training sessions designed to maximize independence via basic housekeeping skills acquisition. (6, 7, 8, 9)
4. Demonstrate proper care of clothing to maintain good hygiene. (9, 10, 11, 12, 13)
5. Implement proper meal preparation by selecting recipes and

THERAPEUTIC INTERVENTIONS

1. Arrange for an assessment to establish a baseline of the client's housekeeping skills and gain insight into his/her strengths and weaknesses.
2. Attend person-centered planning (PCP) meeting with client, family, client advocate, school officials, and caregivers to determine appropriate housekeeping skills and/or supports needed along with eligibility for special services.
3. Consult with client, family, school officials, and caregivers to obtain an overview

safely preparing meals. (9, 14, 15, 16)

6. Implement proper and safe use of household cooking appliances. (9, 17, 18)
7. Serve and prepare food in a sanitary manner and clean up following meals. (9, 19, 20, 21, 22)
8. Demonstrate basic skills to organize and clean a room. (9, 23, 24)
9. Implement skills to hygienically clean a bathroom. (9, 25)
10. Remove trash from house in a timely manner. (9, 26)
11. Perform the steps of removing dirty sheets in a timely fashion and placing clean linens on bed. (9, 27)
12. Adhere to scheduled routines that promote home safety, cleanliness, and organization. (9, 28, 29, 30)
13. Make independent choices regarding meals and housekeeping chores. (9, 31, 32, 33)
14. Respond to prescriptive behavioral plan with closer approximations of desired behaviors. (9, 33, 34, 35, 36)
15. Family members increase positive feedback to client. (37, 38)
16. Family members and caregivers develop realistic expectations of the client's housekeeping abilities. (39, 40)

of all multidisciplinary treatments wanted by the client.

4. Arrange for psychiatric assessment of the client to determine if a concomitant Axis I disorder may be contributing to poor housekeeping skills and whether psychotropic medication may be helpful.
5. Enlist the help of family members and caregivers to monitor signs and symptoms of psychiatric symptoms in order to provide accurate information to psychiatrist.
6. Refer the client to an occupational therapist for evaluation to determine what housekeeping skills training would be best suited to the client.
7. Arrange for the client to obtain necessary adaptive equipment to compensate for his/her disability.
8. Provide the client with a pictorial checklist of housekeeping chores that should be performed regularly (e.g., *The Housekeeping/Grooming Checklist* [Redmond]) to aid the client in organizing and help remind him/her of what should be done.
9. Identify several reinforcers that can be used to reward housekeeping skills acquisition along with other positive housekeeping behaviors that are incompatible with maladaptive behaviors.

17. Family members increase and/or maintain involvement with the client and his/her treatment. (41, 42)
18. Caregivers reduce the frequency of speaking for client and/or performing activities that the client is capable of doing independently. (42, 43, 44)
19. Indicate comfort and enjoyment in activities as evidenced by verbalizing positive statements, smiling often, displaying a relaxed posture, approaching caregivers freely, and decreasing the amount of time spent withdrawing. (45, 46)
20. Family members and caregivers verbalize the degree of the emotional strain related to providing service to the client. (47, 48)
21. Family members and caregivers utilize relaxation skills and respite care to relieve stress. (49, 50)
22. Participate in stress-relieving activities. (51, 52)

__. ____________________________
____

__. ____________________________
____

__. ____________________________
____

10. Utilize encouragement, prompts, and reinforcers while modeling collecting and sorting clothing, loading the washing machine, adding soap, and starting the machine for the client.
11. Provide a visual aid to assist the client in identifying correct settings on washing machine and dryer.
12. Provide encouragement, prompts, and reinforcers while modeling transferring clothing from the washing machine to the dryer and setting the proper drying cycle.
13. Demonstrate proper methods of folding various types of clothing and have the client repeat the demonstrations.
14. Provide the client with a pictorial recipe cookbook (e.g., *101 Pictures Cookbook* [Redmond]) and request that he/she select a recipe and identify the necessary ingredients.
15. Assist the client in obtaining all the necessary ingredients.
16. Model proper and safe cutting, measuring, and cooking techniques and encourage the client to repeat the demonstrations.
17. Provide verbal instruction along with pictorial examples of safe and unsafe behaviors

when operating the microwave, oven, stove, and toaster.

18. Model the proper and safe usage of cooking appliances and have the client repeat the demonstration.
19. Demonstrate safe and sanitary ways to cook and serve food and have the client repeat the demonstration.
20. Provide verbal prompts to the client on cleaning the table following the meal.
21. Provide verbal directions along with physical demonstrations of rinsing, washing, drying, and putting away dishes.
22. Provide verbal instructions and demonstrations of proper kitchen clean-up following meals and encourage the client to repeat the demonstrations.
23. Teach the client necessary floor-cleaning techniques (vacuuming, sweeping, mopping, and dusting) through educational information and physical demonstrations. Prompt the client to perform each technique.
24. Request that the client pick out all objects that are out of place in a room and identify the proper storage spot for each, while providing verbal assistance.
25. Provide verbal instructions and demonstrations of proper sanitation of all bathroom

surfaces and encourage the client to repeat each demonstration.

26. Teach the client through modeling and verbal instruction how and when to empty garbage cans and remove trash from the house.
27. Teach the client through modeling and verbal instruction how and when to strip sheets from a bed and how to remake the bed.
28. Provide written or pictorial reminders of housekeeping chores to the client.
29. Review the chores list and the rationale for each chore with the client periodically.
30. Assist the client in scheduling each housekeeping task.
31. Teach the client effective communication skills (e.g., noninterruptive listening, good eye contact, asserting self with "I" statements, and responding to greetings) to improve his/her ability to express thoughts, desires, feelings, and needs more clearly.
32. Present the client with situations that require him/her to make a choice between options (e.g., scheduling time for housekeeping tasks, choosing meals, choosing when to eat, and choosing tasks for which he/she will have primary responsibility). Reinforce independent choices.

33. Assess ecological factors contributing to the maintenance of the client's maladaptive behavior.
34. Design and implement a behavioral plan that reinforces desired housekeeping and meal preparation behaviors coupled with behavioral techniques to decrease or eliminate maladaptive behaviors (e.g., shaping, fading, and symptom replacement).
35. Train all caregivers on the client's behavioral treatment program to ensure effective reinforcement of desirable housekeeping and meal preparation behaviors.
36. Obtain approval from the client's guardian and the agency oversight committee for any restrictive or aversive programming.
37. Monitor the client's progress at specified intervals and report the information to client, family, and caregivers.
38. Encourage family members and caregivers to provide frequent and immediate positive feedback to the client for progress in housekeeping and meal preparation skills acquisition.
39. Educate family members and caregivers on expected time frames of housekeeping skills acquisition along with potential obstacles the client may face.

40. Assist family members and caregivers in developing realistic expectations of the client's housekeeping abilities.
41. Encourage family members to maintain regular social contact with the client.
42. Encourage family members to maintain regular contact with the involved clinicians regarding status of the client's housekeeping skills acquisition.
43. Provide family members and caregivers with training needed to support the client's advancement in housekeeping skills training.
44. Encourage family members and caregivers to agree to promote lifelong learning opportunities and experiences for the client in order to promote his/her choice making, decision making, problem solving, goal setting, and attainment, along with self-awareness and knowledge.
45. Monitor, acknowledge, and reinforce all signs of the client's pleasure, self-esteem, confidence, and social comfort.
46. Contact recipient rights representatives if the client's rights have been violated.
47. Observe family members and caregivers for frustrations that may reduce their effectiveness to interact effectively with the

client, providing them with opportunities for venting feelings as necessary.

48. Recommend that family members read *The Resourceful Caregiver: Helping Family Caregivers Help Themselves* (National Family Caregivers Association).
49. Teach deep muscle relaxation, abdominal breathing, and safe-place imagery to family members and caregivers to alleviate the stress of the many demands of caring for a person with housekeeping skill deficits.
50. Arrange for respite care for family members and caregivers.
51. Teach the client stress reduction techniques (e.g., deep muscle relaxation, abdominal breathing, and safe-place imagery) to alleviate stressors encountered.
52. Refer the client to a recreational therapist to determine possible leisure and community activities available to the client.

__. ______________________________

____

__. ______________________________

____

__. ______________________________

____

DIAGNOSTIC SUGGESTIONS:

ICD-9-CM	*ICD-10-CM*	*DSM-5* Disorder, Condition, or Problem
299.00	F84.0	Autism Spectrum Disorder
317	F70	Intellectual Disability, Mild
319	F71	Intellectual Disability, Moderate
319	F72	Intellectual Disability, Severe
319	F73	Intellectual Disability, Profound
319	F79	Unspecified Intellectual Disability
V62.89	R41.83	Borderline Intellectual Functioning
______	______	________________________________
______	______	________________________________

DEPRESSION

BEHAVIORAL DEFINITIONS

1. Mood disturbance characterized by sadness, withdrawal, agitation, or spontaneous crying.
2. Increase or decrease in sleep pattern.
3. Increase or decrease in eating patterns.
4. Onset of or increase in self-injurious behavior.
5. Psychomotor retardation and decreased activity level.
6. Social withdrawal and loss of interest in previously enjoyed activities or reinforcers.
7. Decrease in work performance.
8. Somatic complaints such as headache, abdominal pain, or vomiting.
9. Loss of daily living skills (e.g., onset of urinary incontinence).
10. Fearfulness or anxiety, as evidenced by excessive worry, motor tension, or hypervigilance.
11. Suicidal ideation, comments, gestures, or attempts.
12. Atypical behaviors such as regression with attention seeking, hysterical symptoms, negativism, robotic responsiveness, or elective mutism.
13. Increase in aggressiveness and temper tantrums.

__. ____

____

__. ____

____

__. ____

____

LONG-TERM GOALS

1. Reduce or eliminate depressive symptoms.
2. Develop skills and strategies to cope positively with stressors.
3. Improve work performance.
4. Increase social supports and activities.
5. Resume enjoyment of activities, reinforcers, and other positive life experiences.
6. Reduce or eliminate suicidal ideation, plans, or attempts.
7. Make choices and communicate preferences whenever possible.
8. Caregivers reinforce all steps toward skill maintenance.

__. ____
____

__. ____
____

__. ____
____

SHORT-TERM OBJECTIVES

1. Participate in psychological assessment of depressive symptoms. (1, 2, 3, 4, 5)
2. Cooperate with medical examination to rule out biomedical etiologies for depressive symptoms. (6)
3. Cooperate with psychiatric examination to assess the need for psychotropic medications. (4, 7, 8)
4. Participate in individual and/or group therapy focused on depression relief. (9, 10)
5. Increase frequency of nondepressive, pleasurable behaviors

THERAPEUTIC INTERVENTIONS

1. Arrange for psychological assessment of the client's depressive symptoms, including a developmental history, family history, and previous psychiatric involvement.
2. Refer the client for a neurological exam or neuropsychological testing.
3. Operationally define and collect data on behaviors indicative of depression.
4. Assess the severity of the client's depression through interviews, reports from caregivers, and rating scales such as the Beck Depression Inventory,

that compete with depressive behaviors. (10, 11)

6. Increase verbalization of thoughts and feelings while reducing acting-out or internalization of negative emotions. (12, 13, 14, 15)
7. Listen to and accept guidance from respected support network on how to minimize problems between self and the environment. (9, 16, 17)
8. Increase enjoyment in social activities by increasing social skills. (12, 13, 16, 18)
9. Implement anger-control techniques. (19)
10. Implement behavioral and cognitive stress reduction techniques. (20)
11. Share feelings of grief regarding the experience of a significant loss. (21, 22)
12. Implement alternative activities that reduce agitation at early stages of onset. (23, 24)
13. Report increased satisfaction with environment that has been modified to promote improvement in spirits. (25, 26, 27)
14. Cooperate with a behavior modification program designed to reinforce nondepressive verbal, social, and motor activity. (28, 29, 30, 31, 32)
15. Eat nutritious meals regularly. (7, 33)

Second Edition (Beck, Steer, and Brown) or the Diagnostic Assessment for the Severely Handicapped, Second Edition (DASH-II; Matson).

5. Train family members and caregivers to monitor signs and symptoms of the client's psychiatric condition in order to provide accurate information to the psychiatrist and psychologist.
6. Arrange for the client to obtain a complete physical to rule out any biomedical causes for his/her depressive symptoms.
7. Arrange for a psychiatric evaluation to determine if an Axis I disorder is present and whether psychotropic medications may be helpful.
8. Monitor the client for compliance, effectiveness, and side effects associated with prescribed antidepressant medications.
9. Arrange for the client to receive individual therapy using a therapeutic model best suited to facilitate changes in his/her feeling and thinking (e.g., directiveness, client-centered, developmental psychotherapeutic, or sensory-motor/communication reeducation activities).
10. Arrange for the client to participate in group therapy to teach skills incompatible with his/her depressive symptoms.

16. Adjust sleep hours to previous pattern of healthy, restful sleep. (7, 34)
17. Demonstrate independence and initiative by making all possible choices in daily events, as evidenced by choosing clothing, food, leisure interests, and peer group. (35, 36)
18. Family and caretakers assist and support client in his/her attempts to make positive behavioral changes to manage depressive symptoms. (36, 37, 38, 39, 40)
19. Increase participation in extracurricular activities and outings. (41, 42)

__. ____________________
____

__. ____________________
____

__. ____________________
____

11. Assist the client in generating a list of activities he/she enjoys and arrange for opportunities to participate in identified activities.
12. Teach the client by role-playing and role reversal how to express his/her emotions to others and avoid internalizing difficult emotions.
13. Teach the client effective basic communication skills (e.g., noninterruptive listening, good eye contact, asserting self with "I" statements, and responding to greetings) to improve his/her ability to express thoughts, feelings, and needs more clearly.
14. Arrange for the client to improve his/her communication skills through speech therapy, adaptive technologies, or skill training.
15. Encourage reciprocal interactions with family members and caregivers, such as listening to the client while teaching him/her to cooperate with reasonable, routine requests.
16. Refer the client to a support group for people with developmental disabilities.
17. Coordinate a mentor relationship with a volunteer or peer who can assist in resolving conflicts between the client and his/her environment

to promote more effective management of problems.

18. Arrange for the client to participate in social skills training (see Social Skills in this Planner).
19. Arrange for the client to participate in a stress management program (see Anger in this Planner).
20. Teach the client stress reduction techniques (e.g., deep muscle relaxation, abdominal breathing, and safe-place imagery) to alleviate stressors encountered.
21. Assist the client in accepting the reality of the loss of a relationship with a significant other, experiencing the pain of loss, adjusting to an environment without the lost relationship, and reinvesting emotional energy into other relationships.
22. Read a story to the client about grief and bereavement (e.g., *The Saddest Time* [Simon] or *When Someone Dies* [Greenlee]); process thoughts and feelings precipitated by this experience.
23. Teach the client to recognize early signs of negative emotions (e.g., butterflies in the stomach, tension in the neck, or a furrowed brow) through didactic lessons, role-playing, or stories. Encourage the client to self-initiate alternative

activities that will reduce expressed agitation (e.g., talking to staff, spending time alone, going for a walk, or listening to soothing music).

24. Provide training via modeling and role-playing to family members and caregivers in order to promote their identification of early signs of the client's agitation (e.g., pacing, tense facial expression, or new repetitive movements) and encourage them to learn early intervention strategies (e.g., redirecting the client, empathic listening, and prompting problem-solving behaviors).
25. Assess ecological factors contributing to the maintenance of the client's depressive behaviors.
26. Modify the client's environment to remove physical and psychological conditions not conducive to healthy behaviors (e.g., noisy conditions, hunger, and lack of sunlight) and replace with conditions that encourage appropriate prosocial behaviors.
27. Provide education to family members and caregivers (e.g., counseling and training) regarding the importance of providing stimulation and a positive physical and psychosocial environment for the client.

28. Using behavioral analysis, or by referral to a behavioral specialist, determine motivating variables for the client's maladaptive behaviors.
29. Identify several reinforcers that can be used to reward behaviors that are incompatible with the client's depressive behaviors.
30. Refer the client to a behavioral specialist to design and implement a behavioral plan that reinforces desired behaviors coupled with behavioral techniques (e.g., reinforcing low levels, reinforcing other behaviors, extinction, response cost, and overcorrection) to decrease or eliminate depressive behaviors (e.g., apathy tantrums and self-abuse).
31. Train all caregivers on the client's behavioral treatment program to ensure effective implementation and strengthening of desirable nondepressive behaviors. Use *Skills Training for Children with Behavioral Disorders* (Bloomquist) for an easy-to-read guide covering basic behavioral techniques.
32. Obtain approval from the client's guardian and the agency oversight committee for any use of restrictive or aversive programming.
33. Monitor and encourage the client's consumption of healthy foods.

34. Monitor the client's sleep patterns and the restfulness of his/her sleep.
35. Present multiple choices in a variety of situations such that the client is able to make a selection between the options.
36. Encourage family members and caregivers to use active listening techniques to support the client's interdependence, establishment of companionship, and value-centered interactions.
37. Encourage family members and caregivers to agree to promote lifelong learning opportunities and experiences for the client in order to promote his/her choice making, decision making, problem solving, goal setting, and attainment, along with self-awareness and knowledge.
38. Obtain the client's consent to enlist support from clinicians, residential staff, family members, and vocational and educational staff.
39. Arrange for family members or caregivers to spend time with the client doing only what the client expresses an interest in (e.g., planning a meal, playing a game, or watching a video) in order to promote unconditional, nondemanding interactions while the family members and caregivers provide

verbal attention to the client's activities.

40. Encourage family members and staff to increase the frequency of positive interactions with the client while modeling desirable behaviors, positive demeanor, and helpful attitudes. Model these behaviors to the family members and caregivers in formal and informal situations.
41. Refer the client to a recreational therapist to determine possible leisure, social, and community activities available to the client.
42. Encourage the client's participation in Special Olympics or other athletic events.

__. ________________________

____

__. ________________________

____

__. ________________________

____

DIAGNOSTIC SUGGESTIONS:

ICD-9-CM	*ICD-10-CM*	*DSM-5* Disorder, Condition, or Problem
300.4	F34.1	Persistent Depressive Disorder
296.xx	F32.x	Major Depressive Disorder, Single Episode
296.xx	F33.x	Major Depressive Disorder, Recurrent Episode
296.89	F31.81	Bipolar II Disorder
296.xx	F31.xx	Bipolar I Disorder
301.13	F34.0	Cyclothymic Disorder
309.0	F43.21	Adjustment Disorder, With Depressed Mood
310.1	F07.0	Personality Change Due to Another Medical Condition
311	F32.9	Unspecified Depressive Disorder
311	F32.8	Other Specified Depressive Disorder
V62.82	Z63.4	Uncomplicated Bereavement
299.00	F84.0	Autism Spectrum Disorder
317	F70	Intellectual Disability, Mild
319	F71	Intellectual Disability, Moderate
319	F72	Intellectual Disability, Severe
319	F73	Intellectual Disability, Profound
319	F79	Unspecified Intellectual Disability
V62.89	R41.83	Borderline Intellectual Functioning
______	______	______________________________
______	______	______________________________

EATING DISORDER

BEHAVIORAL DEFINITIONS

1. Excessive food consumption, as evidenced by obesity and/or bingeing.
2. History of ingestion of nonnutritive substances (e.g., paint chips, wood, or plastic) that creates significant health consequences (e.g., intestinal obstruction, parasitic infection, and poisoning).
3. Chewing and reswallowing of regurgitated stomach contents.
4. Rapid consumption of large quantities of food in a short time followed by self-induced vomiting and/or the use of laxatives due to the fear of weight gain.
5. Health risks such as dehydration, electrolyte imbalance, malnutrition, weight loss, upper respiratory distress, dental problems, aspiration, choking, and pneumonia.
6. Pattern of selective eating and/or food refusals during mealtimes, which may result in tantrums and other disruptive behaviors.
7. Pattern of oral-motor self-stimulatory behaviors such as mouthing objects.
8. Delay or difficulty in chewing, sucking, or swallowing food.
9. Nutritional deficiencies (e.g., of iron and zinc) that result from poor eating habits.
10. Eating difficulties resulting from medical condition such as neuromotor dysfunction, mechanical obstruction, or medical/genetic abnormality (e.g., gastroesophageal reflux, heart disease, or short-gut syndrome).
11. Systemic variables such as too many different people feeding the client, lack of consistency of feeding techniques, or environmental stressors that result in food refusal and inadequate nutrition.
12. Extreme weight loss (and amenorrhea in females) with refusal to maintain a minimal healthy weight.
13. Very limited ingestion of food and high frequency of secret, self-induced vomiting, inappropriate use of laxatives, and/or excessive strenuous exercise.

14. Persistent preoccupation with body image related to grossly inaccurate assessment of self as being overweight.

—. ____

____

—. ____

____

—. ____

____

LONG-TERM GOALS

1. Develop healthy eating habits by reducing or eliminating eating disorder.
2. Increase socially acceptable eating behaviors.
3. Improve health status by restoring electrolytes, weight, hydration, and dental condition.
4. Decrease negative system variables, resulting in increased food intake.
5. Caregivers provide consistent, proactive reinforcement of appropriate behaviors.
6. Resolve medical concerns or make accommodations to decrease adverse effects of medical concerns.

—. ____

____

—. ____

____

—. ____

____

SHORT-TERM OBJECTIVES

1. Participate in assessment of eating habits and history. (1, 2, 3, 4)
2. Cooperate with medical examination to rule out medical

THERAPEUTIC INTERVENTIONS

1. Arrange for a speech, occupational, or physical therapist to evaluate the client for oral-motor dysfunction.

etiologies for eating disorder. (5, 6)

3. Obtain a dietician-approved diet of food types and quantities. (5, 7)
4. Allow adequate time and space for eating, and maintain proper postural alignment during meals. (8, 9)
5. Use adaptive equipment as recommended. (1, 10)
6. Participate in oral stimulation activities. (11)
7. Change timing of food intake and food textures. (12, 13)
8. Cooperate with a behavior modification program designed to eliminate or reduce problematic eating behaviors. (2, 14, 15, 16, 17)
9. Discriminate between eating undigestible, nonnutritional items and nutritional, digestible items. (14, 15, 18)
10. Family members and caregivers modify environment to promote safe, stimulating conditions for client. (19, 20, 21)
11. Make all possible choices of menu items. (7, 22, 23)
12. Express emotional concerns (i.e., control issues) as a factor in anorectic or bulimic behaviors. (24, 25)

—. ______________________________

____

2. Refer the client to a behavioral specialist or conduct a behavioral assessment of the client's feeding history and habits in order to obtain a clear understanding of the onset and nature of problems, mealtime routines, and feeding concerns.
3. Identify variables contributing to the client's condition (e.g., parent or caregiver distress, financial problems, lack of knowledge about nutrition, or major life transitions).
4. Arrange for psychological assessment of the client to rule out depression, anxiety, or other emotional conditions that contribute to eating disorders.
5. Arrange for a medical examination to assess biomedical factors contributing to the client's eating dysfunction (e.g., iron deficiency anemia, anatomic defects, medical disorders, or oral-motor dysfunction).
6. Review the client's medications for side effects that would negatively impact swallowing or esophageal functioning (e.g., benzodiazepines and neuroleptics).
7. Consult with a dietician to evaluate the nutritional status of the client's diet.
8. Teach the client a healthy protocol for mealtimes, including adequate time and space

__. ______________________________
____

__. ______________________________
____

for the meal and calm periods directly after eating.

9. Determine the proper body positioning (e.g., supportive, stable postural alignment) that promotes the active participation of the client at mealtimes and minimizes the eating disorder.
10. Obtain any necessary adaptive equipment (seats, positioners, cups, or utensils) needed to promote healthy, active eating habits.
11. Provide alternative oral-motor stimulation (e.g., tactile, proprioceptive, gustatory, or olfactory) with which the client can replace the self-stimulatory aspect of the maladaptive eating behavior.
12. Recommend modified eating techniques to the client and family members, such as spaced eating (to reduce gastric volume) and separating solids and liquid intake by 3 to 4 hours (to minimize the occurrence of rumination or regurgitation).
13. Increase oral-motor stimulation during meals and snacks by providing the client with large quantities of food or by providing foods with specific textures or consistencies (e.g., milk shakes or peanut butter).
14. Identify several reinforcers that can be used to reward behaviors that are incompatible

with inappropriate eating behaviors. Request that the client identify or endorse desired reinforcers.

15. Refer the client to a behavioral specialist to design and implement a behavioral plan that reinforces desired behaviors (e.g., keeping ingested food in the stomach, eating only edibles, or eating independently) coupled with behavioral techniques (e.g., reinforcing low levels, reinforcing other behaviors, extinction, response cost, and overcorrection) to decrease or eliminate stereotypic behaviors.
16. Train all caregivers on the client's behavioral treatment program to ensure consistent, effective implementation and strengthening of desirable eating behaviors. Use *Skills Training for Children with Behavioral Disorders* (Bloomquist) for an easy-to-read guide covering basic behavioral techniques.
17. Obtain approval from the client's guardian or the agency oversight committee for any restrictive or aversive programming.
18. Refer the client to a behavioral treatment specialist to teach him/her the difference between edible and nonedible items through discrete training trials.

19. Make recommendations to family members and caregivers on essential safety steps to implement in the home relative to the client's eating disorder (e.g., removing lead objects from the floor or painted objects from the area and knowing basic first-aid techniques).
20. Stress with the family members and caregivers the importance of providing increased supervision to the client in order to implement a behavioral plan early in the onset of maladaptive eating behaviors.
21. Assist family members and caregivers in generating a list of enriched activities for the client to enjoy and participate in that are incompatible with disruptive eating habits.
22. Request that the client identify his/her favorite foods.
23. Observe the client's reactions to specific foods to determine his/her natural preferences and then increase the frequency of these items in his/her diet.
24. Evaluate the client's behavior and explore for the presence of anorexia or bulimia.
25. Refer the client to a psychotherapist for emotional concerns regarding anorectic or bulimic behaviors.

—. ______________________________
____

__. ______________________________

____

__. ______________________________

____

DIAGNOSTIC SUGGESTIONS

ICD-9-CM	*ICD-10-CM*	*DSM-5* Disorder, Condition, or Problem
307.52	F50.8	Pica, Adult
307.53	F98.21	Rumination Disorder
307.1	F50.02	Anorexia Nervosa, Binge-Eating/Purging Type
307.1	F50.01	Anorexia Nervosa, Restricting Type
307.51	F50.2	Bulimia Nervosa
307.51	F50.8	Binge-Eating Disorder
307.50	F50.9	Unspecified Feeding or Eating Disorder
299.00	F84.0	Autism Spectrum Disorder
317	F70	Intellectual Disability, Mild
319	F71	Intellectual Disability, Moderate
319	F72	Intellectual Disability, Severe
319	F73	Intellectual Disability, Profound
319	F79	Unspecified Intellectual Disability
V62.89	R41.83	Borderline Intellectual Functioning
______	______	______________________________
______	______	______________________________

ENURESIS/ENCOPRESIS

BEHAVIORAL DEFINITIONS

1. Repeated passage of bodily waste into inappropriate places (e.g., clothing, bed, or floor) either voluntarily or involuntarily after continence has been obtained.
2. Constipation, stool impaction, or leakage of fecal material or urine into clothing occurring on a frequent basis.
3. Pain associated with normal body elimination, resulting in a cycle of ignoring urges.
4. History of being verbally reprimanded and punished for toileting accidents.
5. Deliberate smearing of feces, eating fecal material, or stripping.
6. Limitation of vocational, social, and recreational opportunities, due to urinary or bowel incontinence.

—. ____

____

—. ____

____

—. ____

____

LONG-TERM GOALS

1. Eliminate all episodes of enuresis and/or encopresis.
2. Eliminate or reduce pain associated with urination and/or defecation.
3. Improve health status by resolving medical issues contributing to enuresis or encopresis.

4. Resolve the underlying core emotional conflicts contributing to the emergence of enuresis or encopresis.
5. Break the cycle of caregiver criticism of the client's enuresis or encopresis followed by the client angrily punishing caregivers with increased enuresis or encopresis.

__. ____

____

__. ____

____

__. ____

____

SHORT-TERM OBJECTIVES

1. Participate in an assessment of urination/defecation habits and history. (1, 2, 3)
2. Cooperate with medical examination to rule out medica l etiologies for enuresis or encopresis. (4, 5)
3. Adhere to dietary changes designed to promote regular, pain-free voiding of the bowel. (6, 7, 8)
4. Caregivers support the client's progress in continence. (1, 9, 10, 11)
5. Eliminate or reduce the frequency of enuresis or encopresis. (9, 12, 13, 14)
6. Develop independent toileting and continence. (15, 16, 17, 18)
7. Use a urine-alarm pad to attain nocturnal continence. (19, 20, 21)

THERAPEUTIC INTERVENTIONS

1. Coordinate a behavioral assessment of the client's elimination history and habits in order to obtain a clear understanding of the onset and nature of the problems, the client's toileting routines, and the client's motivation, as well as to identify variables contributing to the client's incontinence.
2. Refer the client for psychological testing to rule out serious underlying emotional problems contributing to incontinence.
3. Request that family members and caregivers collect baseline data on the frequency and type of the client's toileting accidents.
4. Arrange for medical examination of the client to assess biomedical factors contributing to incontinence

8. Articulate and assume responsibility for implementing self-monitoring and staying clean. (22, 23)
9. Verbalize the negative social consequences that may occur with peers if enuresis or encopresis continues. (24)
10. Verbally recognize the secondary gain that results from enuresis or encopresis. (1, 3, 25)
11. Appropriately express anger rather than channeling anger through enuresis or encopresis. (26, 27)
12. Overly critical family members and caregivers identify how rigid toileting practices or hostile remarks can contribute to the cycle of enuresis or encopresis. (9, 10, 28)
13. Caregivers and family members develop a more supportive role in assisting the client in decreasing encopresis or enuresis. (28, 29)

—. ______________________________
____

—. ______________________________
____

—. ______________________________
____

(e.g., enlarged colon, impaired elimination sensation, structural disease, neurological difficulties, or hypothyroidism).

5. Facilitate follow-through on recommendations from the medical evaluation, which may include further treatment or assessments.
6. Refer the client to a dietician for an assessment of dietary factors related to incontinence and/or constipation.
7. Facilitate the client's instituting recommended dietary modifications to promote bowel movements (e.g., increasing dietary fiber or drinking cr anberry juice).
8. Refer the client to a physician for stool softeners, enemas, or suppositories to promote regularity and ensure that no pain or discomfort is associated with bowel movements.
9. Counsel family members and caregivers on effective toilet-training practices and the use of positive reinforcement for continence appr oximations.
10. Explore caregiver–client interactions to assess whether the current toilet-training practices are excessively rigid.
11. Train family members and caregivers on the range of biomedical factors that can

disrupt bowel or bladder functioning in order to promote their understanding of conditions affecting the client's ability to obtain continence.

12. Stress to family members and caregivers the importance of prompting the client to use the bathroom regularly during the day. Focus the client on voiding with minimal bowel or bladder pressure versus initiating toileting only when intense bowel or bladder pressure is felt and accidents are more likely.
13. Establish with family members, caregivers, and client a schedule of toileting times for the client throughout the day. Stress the importance of family members and caregivers providing the client with reinforcement for accident-free intervals.
14. Ensure that the client has the requisite self-care skills (e.g., dressing and undressing) needed for independent toileting (see Activities of Daily Living [ADL] in this Planner).
15. Identify several reinforcers that can be used to reward the client's continence. Request that the client identify or endorse desired reinforcers.
16. Refer the client to a behavioral specialist to design and implement a behavioral plan that

reinforces the client's independent toileting and continence (e.g., verbal praise, edibles, or increased privileges). Add behavioral techniques to decrease or eliminate incontinence behaviors (e.g., shaping, positive practice, cleaning up accidents, or response cost).

17. Train all caregivers on the client's behavioral treatment program to ensure consistent and effective implementation and strengthening of desirable continence behaviors. Use *Skills Training for Children with Behavioral Disorders* (Bloomquist) for an easy-to-read guide covering basic behavioral techniques.
18. Obtain approval from the client's guardian and the agency oversight committee for any restrictive or aversive programming used in training continence behaviors.
19. Request that family members, caregivers, and client use urine-alarm pad to wake the client at the onset of urination while sleeping.
20. Provide family members and caregivers with verbal and written instructions to ensure proper use of the urine-alarm pad.
21. Set specific time frames and goal achievement indicators to identify when to

discontinue use of the urine-alarm pad.

22. Encourage and challenge the client to assume active responsibility in achieving bladder and bowel control through self-monitoring techniques (e.g., keep a record of wet and dry days, set an alarm clock for voiding times, clean soiled clothing and linens).
23. Challenge and confront the client's lack of motivation or compliance in following through with recommended therapeutic interventions.
24. To increase the client's motivation to master bladder and bowel control, request that he/she identify and discuss negative social consequences that he/she may experience from peers.
25. Assist the client, family members, and caregivers in developing insight into the secondary gain received from enuresis or encopresis (e.g., escape, avoidance, or increased attention).
26. Teach the client effective communication and assertiveness skills to improve his/her ability to express thoughts and feelings through appropriate verbalizations.
27. Teach the client appropriate physical outlets (e.g., power walking, shooting baskets, or hitting a pillow) that allow the expression of anger in a

constructive manner rather than channeling anger through inappropriate wetting or soiling.

28. Confront and challenge hostile, rigid caregivers or family members about remarks or practices that contribute to the client's low self-esteem and a dysfunctional cycle of repeated enuresis or encopresis.
29. Assist family members and caregivers in developing more supportive and esteem-building interactions with the client while reinforcing his/her progress in attaining continence.

__. ______________________________

____

__. ______________________________

____

__. ______________________________

____

DIAGNOSTIC SUGGESTIONS:

ICD-9-CM	*ICD-10-CM*	*DSM-5* Disorder, Condition, or Problem
787.6	F98.1	Encopresis
307.6	F98	Enuresis
299.00	F84.0	Autism Spectrum Disorder
317	F70	Intellectual Disability, Mild
319	F71	Intellectual Disability, Moderate
319	F72	Intellectual Disability, Severe
319	F73	Intellectual Disability, Profound
319	F79	Unspecified Intellectual Disability
V62.89	R41.83	Borderline Intellectual Functioning
______	______	______________________________
______	______	______________________________

FAMILY CONFLICT

BEHAVIORAL DEFINITIONS

1. Frequent arguing among family members.
2. Lack of communication among the client, family members, and caretakers.
3. Unresolved grief, blame, guilt, or denial among family members related to the client's condition.
4. Dependence fostered by overly controlling or overinvolved parents.
5. Frustration of family members due to the lack of opportunities, support and services available for their developmentally disabled family member.
6. Separation among family members by anxiety and anger over concerns related to the client's caretaking and/or medical issues.
7. Burnout of family members due to the stress of being the client's primary caregiver.
8. Inability of elderly family members to continue to care for the client and absence of future residential arrangements.
9. Discipline problems due to limited parenting skills.
10. Guilt among family members relative to prior institutionalization or other care decisions made on the client's behalf.

__. ____
____

__. ____
____

__. ____
____

LONG-TERM GOALS

1. Increase communication and resolve conflicts between family members.
2. Enable family members to resolve negative emotions related to the client's disability.
3. Enable family members to cope effectively with the physical, emotional, and financial burdens of caregiving while enjoying the rewards of the caregiving role.
4. Negotiate a way of living together that honors the parents and their needs while respecting the emerging independence of the client.
5. Maximize the parenting skills of the parent with developmental disabilities.
6. Develop support, respite, and guidance for the role of parenting.

—. ____

____

—. ____

____

—. ____

____

SHORT-TERM OBJECTIVES

1. All family members identify the family's strengths and capabilities. (1, 2)
2. Attend family therapy sessions focused on reducing conflict and increasing harmony and mutual respect. (3)
3. Family members accept the client for who he/she is, cherishing his/her unique personality characteristics. (4, 5)
4. Family members share their feelings regarding the client's disability. (6)

THERAPEUTIC INTERVENTIONS

1. In a family session, assess family strengths and capabilities by obtaining a thorough social and family history; point out the family's strengths that can be used as building blocks for increased harmony.
2. Develop a genogram to graphically display the client's family and the relationships between family members.
3. Refer the client and family members to a qualified family therapist who is

5. Family members report a reduction in negative emotions related to the client's disability and an increase in feelings of acceptance. (7)
6. Family members verbalize knowledge about community resources available and develop relationships with relevant support agencies. (8, 9, 10, 11)
7. Family members and client work together to develop long- and short-term goals regarding the client's care. (3, 12, 13)
8. Family members obtain information regarding giving proper care to the client. (14, 15, 16, 17)
9. Family members acknowledge and plan for their own health and well-being needs relative to the caretaking role. (3, 18, 19, 20)
10. Family members supplement daily care for the client with opportunities for their own pleasure and relaxation. (21, 22, 23)
11. Family members implement stress management techniques. (3, 24, 25, 26, 27)
12. Family members utilize spiritual support and guidance. (28, 29)
13. Family members report resolution of conflicts between themselves and improved communication. (3, 10, 30, 31, 32, 34)

knowledgeable about developmental disability issues.

4. Request that the family develop a list of positive, endearing, attractive qualities they see in the client.
5. Project and convey acceptance of the client to family members, professionals, teachers, and others by displaying respect, observing the client's dignity, and focusing on the client's needs and desires.
6. Explore family members' unresolved feelings of grief, blame, or guilt regarding the client's disabling condition or their lack of acceptance of his/her diagnosis.
7. Present factual data and facilitate family members' supporting each other to resolve distorted thoughts and counterproductive, destructive emotions related to the client's disability.
8. Assist family members in identifying existing support agencies for persons with developmental disabilities and the services that each offers. Coordinate contacts to create a bridge between the client and service systems.
9. Recommend that the family read books on coping with a disabled family member (e.g., *Whatever It Takes! Excellence in Family Support: When Families Experience a*

14. Family members verbalize a positive perspective about the client's developmental disabilities and the family's experiences. (10, 33)
15. Share feelings about the family tension and conflict. (34)
16. Increase the frequency of independent decision-making behaviors with support from family members. (5, 35, 36, 37)
17. Family members and the client agree on a set of rules and principles to guide them in living together in harmony. (3, 10, 38, 39)
18. Family members engage in social and recreational activities with the client as a means of keeping the relationship strong and lines of communication and indirect influence open. (10, 40, 41)
19. Siblings share their feelings and experiences related to the client. (42, 43, 44, 45)
20. Family members list ways that they can support the client in his/her parental role. (46, 47, 48, 49)
21. Family members agree on a plan for the provision of long-term care for the client. (50, 51, 52)
22. Family members and the client become active in advocacy for the rights of individuals with developmental disabilities. (53, 54, 55)

Disability [Covert]) or obtain information from Internet resources (e.g., National Parent Network on Disabilities and Family Village).

10. Encourage and monitor family members' regular attendance at and participation in a suitable support group for families and friends of individuals with developmental disabilities.
11. Act as a supportive resource for the family through quick responses to family members' needs or requests, administering satisfaction surveys and assertively pursuing the family's wishes when they do not conflict with the client's wishes.
12. Request that the family members and the client together identify their long- and short-term goals for the client's care or independence. Prompt the family to identify steps toward facilita ting the identified goals, set approximate target dates, and assign family members who will take active steps toward the goal.
13. Provide family members with feedback, support and technical assistance regarding the changes or plans they are developing. Advocate within the agency and the system to decrease barriers to the client's and family members' goals.
14. Arrange for family members to obtain needed information

__. ______________________

____

__. ______________________

____

__. ______________________

____

on medications, positioning, infection control, transport, feeding and other areas (e.g., *Meeting the Challenge of Disability or Chronic Illness: A Family Guide* [Goldfarb, Brotherson, Summers, and Turnbull] or *The Home Care Companion,* vol. 3, *Creating Healthy Home Care Conditions: Infection Control* [Karpinski]).

15. Inform family members of strategies to avoid neglect or abuse of the client (e.g., specifying minimum care requirements for the client, listing signs and symptoms of neglect and abuse, outlining possible triggers for abuse, and describing legal requirements to report abuse and neglect.
16. Encourage family members to become informed about the client's treatment and condition. With proper authorization to release information, provide information regarding pertinent areas.
17. Provide the family members with basic information regarding the client's behavior patterns and treatment. Train family members and caregivers on specific behavioral plans they are responsible for implementing.
18. Recommend that family members read *The Resourceful Caregiver: Helping Family Caregivers Help Themselves*

(National Family Caregivers Association) to generate positive coping strategies (e.g., stress management, communication strategies, identifying caregiver needs, and dealing with grief).

19. Encourage family members' venting of feelings of guilt surrounding attending to their own needs and the belief that the care recipient should come first; counter with a more rational belief that effectiveness requires that caregivers maintain their own health and well being. Give family members and caregivers permission to attend to themselves.
20. Encourage and reinforce the primary caregiver's assertiveness in requesting caregiving assistance from other family members.
21. Assign the primary caregiver to make a list of all personally pleasurable activities and events (e.g., special foods, favorite TV programs, and visiting family).
22. Request that the primary caregiver identify one or two pleasurable, relaxing activities that may be added to his/her schedule or increased in frequency; specify obstacles to accomplishment and then problem-solve resolution of those obstacles.

23. Coordinate respite services for the care of the client.
24. Request that family members identify their stressors, ranking them from most stressful to least stressful.
25. Teach stress management skills of deep muscle relaxation, positive imagery, physical exercise, deep breathing, and pleasurable activities (see *Relaxation and Stress Reduction Workbook* [Davis, Eshelman, and McKay]).
26. Help family members identify, discuss, and replace negative and distorted automatic thoughts that could be contributing to stress (e.g., Replace: "I have to stay by his side at all times" with "We both need a break from each other sometimes").
27. Refer family members with anxiety or depression to individual therapy to address their symptoms and the stress of caregiving.
28. Explore the family members' history of involvement in spiritual activities and encourage development or maintenance of spiritual activities as added support for the family.
29. Encourage family members to pray about their concerns, joys, fears, desires, and gratitudes.
30. Volunteer to mediate family disagreements regarding the

care and treatment of the client.

31. Demonstrate and encourage the use of communication techniques to promote family unity and increased family communication (e.g., assertiveness, "I" messages, specificity, and compromise).
32. Refer the parents to a class focused on teaching effective parenting skills.
33. Recommend that family members tell their stories of frustrations and failures as well as the joys and successes they have experienced in caring for the client.
34. Assist the client in identifying and expressing the feelings and issues surrounding family tensions.
35. Explore with the client the changes he/she desires in the family members that will facilitate his/her growth in independence.
36. Explore with the family members what their expectations are for the client's independence. Acknowledge health and safety concerns that the client's family may experience.
37. Acknowledge to the family members the value of allowing the client to learn from his/her errors. Support the family members as they permit the client to learn from his/her mistakes and become more independent.

38. Encourage and reinforce the family members in establishing firm behavioral expectations for the client.
39. Recommend that the family members create a written list of agreed-upon behavior guidelines and periodically review the list with the client.
40. Encourage the parents to take the initiative to engage in regularly scheduled social and recreational activities with the adult client as a way of demonstrating love, maintaining communication, and providing an indirect positive influence.
41. Assist the family members in identifying activities they could plan and initiate that would be supportive of their relationship with the client.
42. Meet with the client's siblings and discuss common joys, frustrations and sibling concerns (e.g., feelings, sibling relationships, teasing, peer acceptance, dating, and community discrimination issues).
43. Focus the siblings on personal growth and maturity that has resulted from having a sibling with developmental disabilities.
44. Encourage the adult siblings to verbalize their struggles with torn loyalties toward the client and their own families

(e.g., guardianship, genetic issues, distance, and continuing involvement).

45. Recommend that adult siblings view the video *A Family Healing: Coming to Terms with Intellectual Disabilities* (Connolly); process the content together.

46. Recommend that the family members read books on individuals with developmental disabilities as parents (e.g., *Discovering the Parent's Language of Learning: An Educational Approach to Supporting Parents with Mental Retardation* [Sweet] or *Helping Parents Parent: A Practice Guide for Supporting Families Headed by Parents with Cognitive Limitations* [Heighway]).

47. Request that the family members discuss with the client how they can best support his/her parenting efforts; facilitate a family therapy session focused on this issue.

48. Encourage the family members to develop a plan for the provision of respite, assistance, guidance and supervision relative to the client's relationship with his/her own child.

49. Provide family members with information regarding the guardianship process (for the client or the client's child). Advocate for the highest safe

level of involvement for the client with his/her own child.

50. Discuss with family members the benefit of future planning for the client and deter mine the family members' interest in long-term planning on the client's behalf (see Legal Involvement in this Planner).

51. Assist the family members in compiling a master list of all the client's identified needs, preferences, needed supports, resources, and financial information.

52. Develop specific action plans for each family member or treatment team member to achieve the family goals for the client's long-term care.

53. Encourage family members frustrated by the lack of opportunities, support, and services available for their developmentally disabled family member to become involved in relevant advocacy groups. Recommend reading on advocacy (e.g., *Don't Get Mad Get Powerful!: A Manual for Building Advocacy Skills* [Hines]).

54. Refer the client and family members to a specific advocacy organization, such as the Association for Retarded Citizens (ARC).

55. Provide opportunities for the client and family members to

become involved in the provider agency's policy monitoring and feedback procedures.

__. ____________________

____

__. ____________________

____

__. ____________________

____

DIAGNOSTIC SUGGESTIONS:

ICD-9-CM	*ICD-10-CM*	*DSM-5* Disorder, Condition, or Problem
299.00	F84.0	Autism Spectrum Disorder
301.7	F60.2	Antisocial Personality Disorder
317	F70	Intellectual Disability, Mild
319	F71	Intellectual Disability, Moderate
319	F72	Intellectual Disability, Severe
319	F73	Intellectual Disability, Profound
319	F79	Unspecified Intellectual Disability
V62.89	R41.83	Borderline Intellectual Functioning
____	____	________________
____	____	________________

FINANCIAL/SHOPPING SKILLS

BEHAVIORAL DEFINITIONS

1. Difficulties in identifying currency and its value, including counting change.
2. Lack of familiarity with and use of financial institutions and financial accounts, and of understanding of the value of banking.
3. Inability to keep adequate records of incoming and outgoing funds.
4. Difficulties in budgeting monies for future needs.
5. Lack of adherence to budget or impulsive purchasing as evidenced by deficit spending.
6. Confusion regarding the logistical or monetary aspects of paying bills.
7. Limitations in ability to make shopping lists from meal plans, comparison shop, calculate cost for items, and determine proper store for items needed.

__. ____

____

__. ____

____

__. ____

____

LONG-TERM GOALS

1. Develop and maintain financial skills that promote financial independence.
2. Understand monetary values and equivalencies.
3. Demonstrate familiarity with basic financial terms.

4. Identify different types of financial institutions, types of accounts, basic account activity, and the benefit accorded by using financial services.
5. Actively save funds on a regular basis to permit purchase of larger items.
6. Develop and adhere to a self-determined budget that delineates income, fixed costs, variable costs, and savings in order to promote financial independence.
7. Plan and shop for the ingredients necessary for nourishing, well-balanced meals.
8. Learn to be a knowledgeable consumer by utilizing shopping strategies such as preparing lists, comparing prices, and buying only necessary items.
9. Caregivers reinforce all the client's steps toward financial and shopping independence.

__. ____

____

__. ____

____

__. ____

____

SHORT-TERM OBJECTIVES

1. Participate in assessment of existing financial and consumer knowledge skills. (1, 2)
2. Cooperate with psychiatric evaluation. (3, 4)
3. Participate in training sessions to promote independence with financial and shopping skills. (5, 6)
4. List potential rewards to be used to reinforce progress in learning financial and shopping skills. (7)

THERAPEUTIC INTERVENTIONS

1. Arrange for or provide an assessment of the client's financial and shopping skills to gain insight into his/her strengths and weaknesses.
2. Identify areas in which the client requires financial management or shopping skill training, or support.
3. Arrange for psychiatric assessment to determine if concomitant Axis I disorder (e.g., Bipolar Disorder or Major Depression) may be contributing to the client's

5. Demonstrate knowledge of monetary values and coin equivalencies. (8, 9, 10, 11)
6. Define basic financial terms. (12)
7. Identify places to bank and the value of banking. (13, 14)
8. Open a bank account. (15, 16)
9. Participate in basic banking transactions. (17, 18)
10. Describe the process and value of regularly saving money. (19)
11. Demonstrate knowledge of the basic components of financial statements. (20, 21)
12. Manage money by staying within a self-determined budget. (22, 23)
13. Pay incoming bills promptly. (24)
14. Identify and purchase needed items. (25)
15. Identify a nutritious weekly food menu and generate a shopping list from the food menu. (26, 27, 28)
16. Develop ability to prudently use and handle money. (29, 30, 31)
17. Practice proper and safe storage places for items purchased. (32)
18. Demonstrate independence and initiative by making all reasonable choices in financial matters. (33)
19. Family members increase positive feedback to the client. (34, 35)

poor financial skills and whether psychotropic medication may be helpful.

4. Enlist the help of family members and caregivers to monitor the client's signs and psychiatric symptoms and provide accurate information to the psychiatrist.
5. Obtain consensus from client, family members, school officials, and caregivers regarding a referral to a suitable finance management program or other interventions that build on the client's strengths and compensate for his/her weaknesses.
6. Play the Money Skills game (Haugen) to facilitate the client's learning to manage personal finances and shopping skills.
7. Design and implement a reward system that can be used to motivate the client to improve his/her financial and shopping skills.
8. Assist the client in making flash cards with a coin and its value on one side and the name on the other to facilitate learning coin identification and corresponding values.
9. Provide the client with various amounts of real and printed coins and bills, and have him/her identify the coins and bills.

20. Family members and caregivers develop realistic expectations of the client's financial and shopping skills. (36, 37)
21. Family members increase and/or maintain involvement with the client and monitor his/her financial management progress. (34, 38, 39, 40, 41)
22. Family members and caretakers reduce the frequency of speaking for the client and/or performing activities that the client is capable of doing independently. (33, 38, 42)

—. ______________________________

____

—. ______________________________

____

—. ______________________________

____

10. Provide the client with money and request that he/she correctly count a specified amount.
11. Play a game that teaches the value of currency (e.g., Make a Buck [Redmond]).
12. Provide definitions of basic financial terms through verbal and pictorial descriptions and query the client for comprehension of terms.
13. Arrange for the client to visit different types of financial institutions to learn about the value of banking.
14. Teach the client what personal benefits (e.g., safe holding, interest earned, and convenient access to funds) he/she would realize by using a bank.
15. Provide information on savings and checking accounts and certificates of deposit to the client and request that he/she describe the different types of financial accounts.
16. Assist the client in selecting and opening an account t hat would be of personal benefit.
17. Demonstrate the proper way to fill out sample deposit and withdrawal slips and request that the client repeat until competency is obtained.
18. Set up a contrived account to demonstrate the importance of keeping track of deposits and withdrawals to facilitate

the client's comprehension of avoiding debit balances.

19. Demonstrate through a contrived savings account how an account would grow in value due to gradual accumulation and compounding interest to illustrate the value of regular, consistent saving and having money earn interest.
20. Review a financial statement with the client, educating him/her on key aspects of the statement to promote comprehension of statement basics.
21. Teach the client to identify possible bank errors that could be found on a statement and corrective steps he/she should take if such a mistake should occur.
22. Teach the client the basic components of developing a personal budget (e.g., use the Complete Budgeting System [Redmond]).
23. Using the client's relevant, personal financial facts, assist in identifying income, fixed costs, variable costs, and amount to be put into s avings for each week and month.
24. Assist the client in generating a monthly calendar of when bills are due to foster responsible bill-paying habits.
25. Request that the client identify objects he/she would be likely

to purchase and the type of store at which the items could be obtained.

26. Assist the client who has limited reading skills or knowledge of nutrition to use a color-coded system of categorizing the five different food groups in planning a list of nourishing meals for the week (e.g., use the Meal Planning Guide [Redmond]).
27. Using the client's meal plan list, teach how to generate a shopping list of needed foods and ingredients.
28. Recommend that the client regularly use a list of items to control shopping for meal preparation (e.g., the Shopping List [Redmond]).
29. Using the shopping list, assist the client in identifying an appropriate store in the community from which to purchase list items.
30. Provide the client with several similar items and each item's respective cost and have him/her identify which is the most expensive, least expensive, and the preferable buy.
31. Model and role-play the skills used in calculating cost, identifying the money required, and paying for items; have the client rehearse these skills until he/she is ready to use them *in vivo.*

32. Review the proper food and cleaner storage and have the client utilize this knowledge by properly putting away a sample of items.
33. Present situations such that the client is required to make a choice between two to three options, and reinforce independent choices.
34. Monitor the client's progress at specified intervals and give feedback to the client, family members, and caregivers.
35. Encourage family members and caregivers to provide frequent and immediate positive feedback to the client for progress in financial and consumer skills acquisition.
36. Educate family members and caregivers on expected time frames for financial and consumer skills acquisition along with potential obstacles the client may face.
37. Assist family members and caregivers in developing realistic expectations of the client's financial and consumer skills.
38. Request that the client identify what aspects of finances he/she will need assistance with, along with his/her preferences on who provides the financial assistance (e.g., family member, guardian, payee, or staff).

39. Encourage family members to maintain regular social contact with the client.
40. Encourage family members to maintain regular contact with the involved clinicians regarding the status of the client's financial and consumer skills acquisition.
41. Provide family members and caregivers with training needed to support the client's advancement in financial and consumer skills training.
42. Family members and caregivers agree to promote lifelong learning opportunities and experiences for the client in order to promote his/her choice-making, decision-making, problem-solving, and goal-setting skills and attainment, along with self-awareness and knowledge.

__. ______________________________
____

__. ______________________________
____

__. ______________________________
____

DIAGNOSTIC SUGGESTIONS:

ICD-9-CM	*ICD-10-CM*	*DSM-5* Disorder, Condition, or Problem
299.00	F84.0	Autism Spectrum Disorder
V62.89	Z60.0	Phase of Life Problem
317	F70	Intellectual Disability, Mild
319	F71	Intellectual Disability, Moderate
319	F72	Intellectual Disability, Severe
319	F73	Intellectual Disability, Profound
319	F79	Unspecified Intellectual Disability
V62.89	R41.83	Borderline Intellectual Functioning
______	______	______________________________
______	______	______________________________

HOUSEHOLD SAFETY SKILLS

BEHAVIORAL DEFINITIONS

1. Limited awareness of home safety procedures relevant to independent living.
2. Poor understanding of safe handling of poisons, household chemicals, and other dangerous substances.
3. Failure to use matches in safe manner.
4. Unsafe use of natural gas or electrical appliances and outlets.
5. Inability to adequately respond to emergency situations.
6. Lower than expected safety skills resulting from overprotection of client by caregiver.
7. History of injury due to unsafe practices around the home.

__. ____
____

__. ____
____

__. ____
____

LONG-TERM GOALS

1. Develop independence by strengthening existing household safety skills.
2. Learn and implement new household safety skills.
3. Articulate the details of appropriate responses to various emergency situations.
4. Caregivers reinforce the client's independence by encouraging acquisition of household safety skills.

5. Demonstrate skills essential to protecting self from accidental injury.

—. ____

____

—. ____

____

—. ____

____

SHORT-TERM OBJECTIVES

1. Participate in an evaluation of household safety skills. (1)
2. Adhere to recommendations from the safety skills evaluation regarding all necessary training and education interventions. (2, 3)
3. Demonstrate increased knowledge about household safety skills by enacting those skills under supervision. (4, 5, 6)
4. List potential reinforcers of rewards to earn for making progress in learning household safety skills. (7, 8, 9)
5. Demonstrate safe handling procedures for hot objects. (8, 10, 11)
6. Practice safe handling of poisons and other chemicals. (8, 11, 12, 13, 14, 16)
7. Use matches in a safe manner. (8, 11, 15, 16, 17)
8. Engage in safe use of natural gas, electrical appliances, and outlets. (8, 11, 16, 18)

THERAPEUTIC INTERVENTIONS

1. Arrange for an assessment of the client's personal safety skills (e.g., safe use of matches, appliances, dangerous liquids, and electrical cords; knowledge of procedures for fire evacuation, first aid, and emergency use of the telephone) through direct observation and reports from parents and caregivers to establish a baseline of the client's ability and to gain insight into his/her strengths and weaknesses.
2. Provide direct feedback to client, family members, and caregivers about the results of the personal safety skills evaluation.
3. Follow up on the results of the household safety skills evaluation, including recommendations for medical education, training sessions, or further assessments.

9. Safely clean up broken glass. (8, 11, 19)
10. Demonstrate use of the phone for emergency purposes. (8, 11, 20, 21, 22)
11. Identify correct response to emergency examples. (8, 23, 24, 29)
12. Describe the different types of emergency professionals and the crisis situations for which each is trained to respond. (8, 24, 25)
13. Role-play basic first-aid techniques for cuts, burns, and bites. (8, 26, 27, 28, 29)
14. Family members and caretakers monitor progress and model needed skills while in the home. (30, 31)
15. Family members and caretakers reduce the frequency of speaking for the client and/or performing activities that he/she is capable of doing independently. (30, 32, 33)

—. ______________________________
____

—. ______________________________
____

—. ______________________________
____

4. Have parents, caregivers, and teachers model household safety skills and request that the client imitate what is modeled.
5. Coordinate the client's training in a supervised, safe, supported environment.
6. Play the Safety Skills game (Haugen) in order to facilitate the client's learning of household safety skills.
7. Request that the client identify specific reinforcers he/she would like to earn for participation in safety skills training.
8. Refer the client to a behavioral specialist to design and implement a reward system to motivate the client to improve household safety skills acquisition.
9. Obtain any necessary permission for behavioral programming from the client's guardian and the agency oversight committee.
10. Instruct the client on the need to avoid hot water and hot objects. Model safe handling of hot objects.
11. Request that the client repeat modeled safety steps under the close supervision of a parent or caregiver; reinforce the implementation of safe practices.
12. Provide educational information to the client on the nature of poisons and the inherent danger of exposure to such chemicals. Obtain

informational booklets or videos from the local poison control office or fire department.

13. Model the proper handling of chemicals and poisons to ensure that the client handles dangerous objects properly.
14. Observe the client handling chemicals and poisons to ensure that he/she handles dangerous objects properly.
15. Teach the client the proper use of matches by modeling and providing verbal instruction.
16. Quiz the client to assess his/her understanding of the educational information presented to him/her.
17. Observe the client handling matches to ensure that he/she handles dangerous objects properly.
18. Teach the client the proper use of natural gas, electrical outlets, and appliances through demonstrations.
19. Demonstrate safe methods of cleaning up broken glass, explaining techniques for covering the skin (e.g., wearing gloves), gathering glass, and the proper disposal of glass.
20. Provide the client with practice dialing telephone numbers from written or pictorial prompts.

21. Provide the client with emergency telephone numbers.
22. Request that the client practice dialing emergency numbers independently under supervision.
23. Present pictorial and verbal examples of emergency situations. Request that the client correctly identify the nature of the emergency and the necessary response.
24. Ask the client what type of professional is needed for each type of emergency described.
25. Request that the client list professionals who assist with emergencies and describe the type of emergencies each serves.
26. Provide pictures of different burns, cuts, and bites and request that the client identify each injury.
27. Role-play minor injuries (e.g., use a red marker to draw on the skin) and request that the client respond appropriately to each situation.
28. Observe the client role-playing seeking assistance and utilizing basic first aid for minor injuries; reinforce his/her correct decisions and actions.
29. Review the client's previous accidents and first aid treatment obtained. Discuss the

pros and cons of the treatment delivered.

30. Encourage family members and caregivers to agree to promote lifelong learning opportunities and experiences for the client in order to promote his/her choice making, decision making, problem solving, goal setting, and attainment, along with self-awareness and knowledge.
31. Provide family members and caregivers with didactic training and encourage their modeling and verbal praise to support the client's advancement in learning household safety skills.
32. Encourage family members and caretakers to allow the client to make all possible choices and to demonstrate maximum independence in daily events.
33. Encourage and reinforce the client in making all reasonable choices in daily events.

—. ________________________________
____

—. ________________________________
____

—. ________________________________
____

DIAGNOSTIC SUGGESTIONS:

ICD-9-CM	*ICD-10-CM*	*DSM-5* Disorder, Condition, or Problem
299.00	F84.0	Autism Spectrum Disorder
319	F71	Intellectual Disability, Moderate
319	F72	Intellectual Disability, Severe
319	F73	Intellectual Disability, Profound
319	F79	Unspecified Intellectual Disability
V62.89	R41.83	Borderline Intellectual Functioning
_____	_____	______________________________
_____	_____	______________________________

LEGAL INVOLVEMENT

BEHAVIORAL DEFINITIONS

1. A pattern of illegal behaviors resulting in legal charges.
2. Incarceration for actions related to developmental disability.
3. Feelings of vulnerability while inappropriately incarcerated.
4. Parole or probation after conviction on legal charges.
5. Failure to understand Miranda rights, as evidenced by not acting in one's best legal interest.
6. Eagerness to please and cognitive deficits, resulting in false confessions or saying what others want to hear.
7. Drug and alcohol use contributing to poor judgment and impulsive behaviors.
8. Increased vulnerability to victimization due to impaired cognitive abilities, poor judgment, low adaptive skills, and physical disabilities.
9. Impaired cognitive abilities, poor judgment, maladaptive behaviors, restricted living environments, and/or health difficulties, requiring the appointment of a guardian.
10. Limited capacity to participate in specific decisions, resulting in requests from family members, physician, attorney, or court to determine abilities.

__. ____

__. ____

__. ____

LONG-TERM GOALS

1. Adhere to court-mandated consequences, punishments, or rehabilitation programs.
2. Accept responsibility for decisions and actions that resulted in arrest, arraignment, or trial.
3. Increase law-abiding behavior.
4. Abstain from alcohol and drug use.
5. Guard against abuse and victimization.
6. Accept a guardian to oversee and advocate for rights.

__. ____

__. ____

__. ____

SHORT-TERM OBJECTIVES

1. Participate in a psychological assessment of adaptive and intellectual abilities. (1, 2, 3, 4)
2. Participate in a complete forensic evaluation to assess criminal responsibility. (3, 4, 5)
3. Cooperate with a psychiatric examination in order to evaluate Axis I concerns. (2, 3, 4, 6)
4. Adhere to conditions of probation set forth by the courts. (7, 8)
5. Family members support the client through the legal system. (9, 10)

THERAPEUTIC INTERVENTIONS

1. Arrange for a comprehensive intellectual and adaptive assessment to establish the client's level of understanding of different social situations, moral reasoning, ability to generalize information, expressive and receptive language abilities, and potential for future violence or illegal activities.
2. Enlist the help of family members and caregivers to monitor the client for signs and symptoms of any psychiatric conditions in order to provide accurate information to the psychiatrist or psychologist.

6. Attend individual psychotherapy focused on resolving emotional or personality factors contributing to illegal behavior. (11)
7. Verbalize an understanding of the criminal nature of own behavior and accept responsibility for it. (12, 13)
8. Participate in rehabilitation programs, services, or other recommendations set forth by the courts. (14, 15)
9. Provide information that confirms ability to function independently. (16)
10. Increase the frequency of law-abiding behaviors. (17, 18, 19)
11. Terminate the use of mood-altering substances. (3, 20, 21, 22)
12. Verbalize acceptance of personal responsibility for all actions, including illegal acts. (23, 24, 25)
13. Verbalize an understanding of how to react within the criminal justice system. (26, 27)
14. List precautions to take to ensure safety while incarcerated. (28, 29)
15. Identify emotions or drives that underlie illegal behavior and more prosocial ways to express these feelings. (30, 31)
16. Family members and caregivers assist and support the client in his/her attempts to

3. Follow up on recommendations from evaluations (e.g., implementing behavioral programming, satisfying medical needs, or arranging specialty evaluations).
4. Provide feedback to the client, family members, school officials, and caregivers on the results of assessments along with recommendations based on those results.
5. Arrange for a forensic evaluation to determine the client's criminal responsibility and determine his/her understanding of harmful or criminal behaviors (e.g., consider using a standardized assessment tool such as the Competence Assessment for Standing Trial for Defendants with Mental Retardation [CAST-MR; Everington and Luckasson]).
6. Arrange for a psychiatric evaluation to affirm that an Axis I disorder is present and has contributed to legal difficulties, and whether psychotropic medication may be helpful.
7. Monitor and encourage the client to keep appointments with court officers; facilitate arrangements for such appointments.
8. Request that the client clearly state his/her probation requirements and how he/she plans to adhere to them. Query the client to identify

make positive behavioral changes in becoming a law-abiding citizen. (32)

17. Verbalize an understanding of community laws and customs that must be followed and the legal and/or social consequences of ignoring them. (25, 33)
18. Articulate alternative decisions that are prosocial ways to handle conflict. (34, 35)
19. Increase participation in extracurricular activities and outings. (36, 37, 38, 39)
20. Family members and caregivers advocate for the client during his/her legal involvement. (40, 41, 42)
21. Participate in training to learn skills necessary to guard against future victimization. (43, 44, 45, 46)
22. Cooperate with identifying and securing a guardian. (47, 48, 49, 50, 51)
23. Family members and caregivers plan for the client's future to ensure continuity and quality care. (52, 53, 54)

__. ________________________
____

__. ________________________
____

__. ________________________
____

challenges that would prevent his/her adherence to court-mandated conditions.

9. Assist the family in learning more about how the criminal justice system interfaces with developmentally disabled offenders by recommending readings (e.g., *People with Mental Retardation in the Criminal Justice System* [Reynolds] or "The Criminal Justice System vs. the Criminal Mentally Retarded: Is Justice Being Served?" [Goldman]).
10. Encourage and challenge the family members and caregivers to not protect the client from the legal consequences of his/her behavior if he/she has the capacity to understand the legal implications of that behavior.
11. Arrange for the client to receive individual, family, and/or group therapy to address the emotional and antisocial issues contributing to his/her legal involvement.
12. Confront statements in which the client blames others for his/her misbehavior and fails to accept responsibility for his/her actions.
13. Assist the client in making the connection between his/her criminal behavior and why behaviors are illegal through case examples and role reversal.

14. Coordinate the necessary details (e.g., work schedules and transportation) to facilitate the client's being able to follow the court's recommendations (e.g., job procurement, therapy, or skills training). Reinforce positive changes.
15. Coordinate meetings between the probation or parole office and the client. Assist the probation or parole agent in understanding the needs and abilities of the client.
16. Evaluate the client's ability to independently function using cooking skills, community access skills, vocational and financial skills, and shopping knowledge. (See Community Safety Skills, Cooking/Housekeeping Skills, Household Safety Skills, and Personal Safety Skills in this Planner.)
17. Refer the client to a behavioral specialist to develop and implement a behavioral plan that rewards prosocial behaviors and imposes consequences for antisocial behaviors. Obtain any needed approval from the client's guardian and the agency review committee.
18. Teach the client commonly accepted standards of social-sexual behavior, describing positive and negative examples. Request that the client identify his/her own examples

of acceptable and unacceptable social-sexual behaviors. (See Sexually Inappropriate Behaviors in this Planner.)

19. Identify behaviors that constitute crimes and request that the client describe why these are illegal, as well as how they differ from noncriminal behaviors. Request that the client identify his/her own examples of acceptable social-sexual behaviors and criminal behaviors.
20. Explore the client's use of addictive, mind-altering substances; process with the client the role his/her use of addictive substances has had in illegal activities.
21. Arrange for a complete substance abuse evaluation; refer the client for chemical dependence treatment, if indicated.
22. Contract with the client for his/her abstinence from alcohol and drugs as a step toward increasing self-control and taking responsibility for his/her own behavior; request that the client identify reinforcers for success and consequences for not adhering to the contract.
23. Stress the client's accountability and responsibility for his/her own behavior; reinforce steps the client takes in accepting personal

responsibility for his/her role in the illegal acts.

24. Encourage the client to engage in restitution (e.g., apologies, community service, or financial reimbursement); assist in identifying the steps involved in performing restitution (e.g., giving up purchasing cigarettes and saving the money for financial restitution).

25. Assist the client in developing an understanding of how independence and citizenship carry responsibilities. Review the rights and freedoms people have (e.g., the rights to vote, live in community, and obtain SSI benefits, medical insurance, and a driver's license) and how these rights carry the personal responsibility to abide by laws and social customs.

26. Provide information to the client about the criminal justice system.

27. Teach the client how to act in his/her own best interest in the criminal justice system (e.g., talking to the police only when a lawyer is present, or admitting he/she does not understand legal concerns). Role-play scenarios with the client to increase his/her understanding.

28. Review safety considerations with the client while he/she is in jail.

29. Advocate with the jail staff to ensure the client's right to safety and protection while incarcerated.
30. Explore with the client those feelings or desires that are problematic when they are experienced and that may precipitate illegal behavior (e.g., anger, sexual arousal, and panic).
31. Assist the client in identifying healthy ways to express feelings and desires other than acting-out (see Anger, Anxiety, and Sexually Inappropriate Behaviors in this Planner).
32. Encourage family members to provide praise and positive reinforcement for the client's progress toward law-abiding behaviors. Advise the family members or caregivers on ways to concretely display this to the client (e.g., a chart that shows the number of days without a negative target behavior).
33. Prepare the client for successful community integration by teaching social customs and laws in a concrete manner as well as the consequences for not adhering to these laws (e.g., through role-playing, pictorially, or by providing meetings with police or a tour of the local jail).
34. Provide the client with numerous opportunities to make his/her own personal decisions

regarding ways to respond to conflict.

35. Arrange for the client to learn conflict resolution skills and communication alternatives that reduce the physical expression of frustration and anger. (See Anger in this Planner.)
36. Refer the client to a recreational therapist to match his/her leisure skills to available community services.
37. Encourage the client's participation in Special Olympics or other athletic activities.
38. Assess the client's and family members' interest in faith-based activities and provide access to church ministry if indicated.
39. Refer the client to a support group for individuals with developmental disabilities.
40. Recommend books to the family members that address the issues of protecting the human and legal rights of offenders with developmental disabilities (e.g., *Disability Rights and Issues: A Consumer's Guide* [Michigan Protection and Advocacy Service] or *A Guide to Mental Illness and the Criminal Justice System: A Systems Guide for Families and Consumers* [National Alliance for the Mentally Ill]).

41. Provide family members with information about agencies that protect and advocate for the legal and human rights of persons with developmental disabilities or that provide assistance in promoting the client's equal access to legal rights (e.g., the National Association of Protection and Advocacy Systems, the Bazelon Center, and the Association for Retarded Citizens [ARC]).
42. Provide support, reassurance, guidance, and comfort to the client and family members during legal involvement. Attend legal proceedings, as needed.
43. Arrange for the client to participate in training to learn skills essential to guarding against victimization, such as safety measures, accessing immediate help, and basic self-defense (see Physical/ Emotional/ Sexual Abuse in this Planner).
44. Arrange for the client to role-play assertive responses to a variety of situations. Reinforce appropriate assertiveness (see Physical/Emotional/ Sexual Abuse in this Planner).
45. Arrange for the client to receive services from support agencies such as an adult protective services unit or a sexual assault center.

46. Align the client with community support agencies for those who have been victimized.
47. Assess the need for guardianship based on the evaluation of the client's level of intellectual disability, adaptive skills, mental status, and risk factors (e.g., restrictive residential environment, behavior treatment plans, and/or medical conditions).
48. Discuss with the client his/her understanding of guardianship and views on the necessity of guardianship. Request that the client identify his/her preference for a guardian should the court find in favor of guardianship.
49. Determine the type of guardianship best suited for the client (e.g., full, partial, limited, or temporary) and petition the probate court to secure a guardian.
50. Secure the agreement of a person who has knowledge of the client and his/her disability, medical condition, care routines, social links, interests, and communication style to be a court-appointed guardian.
51. Regularly monitor the interactions between the client and his/her guardian. Advocate for a person-centered approach to this relationship. Petition to

change guardians if the current guardian routinely fails to act in the best interests of the client.

52. Recommend that family members read *Future Planning: Guardianship and People with Mental Retardation* (Berkobien) to increase their understanding of the advantages of securing a guardian for the client.
53. Discuss with the family members the benefit of future planning for the client and determine the family members' interest in long-term planning on behalf of the client.
54. Refer family members interested in future planning through trusts and wills to *The Life Planning Workbook: A Hands-on Guide to Help Parents Provide for the Future Security and Happiness of Their Child with a Disability after Their Death* (Russell and Grant) or *Disability Rights and Issues: A Consumer's Guide* (Michigan Protection and Advocacy Service).

__. ____________________

____

__. ____________________

____

__. ____________________

____

DIAGNOSTIC SUGGESTIONS:

ICD-9-CM	*ICD-10-CM*	*DSM-5* Disorder, Condition, or Problem
295.90	F20.9	Schizophrenia
296.89	F31.81	Bipolar II Disorder
296.xx	F31.xx	Bipolar I Disorder
302.4	F65.2	Exhibitionistic Disorder (Exhibitionism)
302.81	F65.0	Fetishistic Disorder (Fitishism)
302.89	F65.81	Frotteuristic Disorder (Frotteurism)
302.84	F65.52	Sexual Sadism Disorder
302.82	F65.3	Voyeuristic Disorder (Voyeurism)
302.2	F65.4	Pedophilic Disorder
302.9	F65.9	Unspecified Paraphilic Disorder
312.30	F91.9	Unspecified Disruptive, Impulse-Control, and Conduct Disorder
303.90	F10.20	Alcohol Use Disorder, Moderate or Severe
304.30	F12.20	Cannabis Use Disorder, Moderate or Severe
304.20	F14.20	Cocaine Use Disorder, Moderate or Severe
304.00	F11.20	Opioid Use Disorder, Moderate or Severe
312.34	F63.81	Intermittent Explosive Disorder
312.32	F63.81	Kleptomania
312.9	F91.9	Unspecified Disruptive, Impulse Control, and Conduct Disorder
312.89	F91.8	Other Specified Disruptive, Impulse Control, and Conduct Disorder
V71.01	Z72.811	Adult Antisocial Behavior
301.7	F60.2	Antisocial Personality Disorder
301.9	F60.9	Unspecified Personality Disorder
317	F70	Intellectual Disability, Mild
319	F71	Intellectual Disability, Moderate
319	F72	Intellectual Disability, Severe
319	F73	Intellectual Disability, Profound
319	F79	Unspecified Intellectual Disability
V62.89	R41.83	Borderline Intellectual Functioning
______	______	______________________________
______	______	______________________________

MEDICAL CONDITION

BEHAVIORAL DEFINITIONS

1. A diagnosis of an acute, serious illness that needs attention and has an impact on daily living (e.g., high blood pressure, asthma, seizures, or diabetes).
2. A diagnosis of a chronic illness that eventually will be terminal.
3. Constant chronic pain that is debilitating and depressing.
4. Sad affect, social withdrawal, anxiety, loss of interest in activities, low energy, or suicidal ideation due to medical difficulties.
5. Denial of the seriousness of the medical condition.
6. Sensory impairments secondary to medical condition.
7. Psychological or behavioral factors that influence the course of the medical condition.
8. Refusal to cooperate with recommended medical treatments.
9. Family members and caregivers overwhelmed by care of client with little respite.
10. Family members and caregivers displaying difficulty accepting, coping with or responding appropriately to the client's medical condition.

__. ____
____

__. ____
____

__. ____
____

LONG-TERM GOALS

1. Accept the illness and adapt life to necessary changes.
2. Resolve emotional crisis and face terminal illness implications.
3. Accept emotional support from those who care without pushing them away in anger.
4. Resolve depression and find peace of mind in spite of the illness.
5. Live life to the fullest extent possible even though time may be limited.
6. Cooperate with medical treatment regimen without passive-aggressive or active resistance.
7. Become knowledgeable about the diagnosed condition and about living as normally as possible.
8. Reduce fear, anxiety, and worry associated with the medical condition.
9. Adapt to sensory deficits to the extent capable.

__. ____
____

__. ____
____

__. ____
____

SHORT-TERM OBJECTIVES

1. Describe the history, symptoms, and treatment of the medical condition. (1, 2)
2. Adhere to the medication regimen and necessary medical procedures, reporting any side effects or problems to physicians or clinicians. (3, 4)
3. Cooperate with ongoing medical treatments. (5, 6, 7)
4. Report a reduction in fear that has blocked compliance with

THERAPEUTIC INTERVENTIONS

1. Gather a history of the facts regarding the client's medical condition, including symptoms, treatment, and prognosis.
2. With the client's or guardian's informed consent, contact the treating physician and family members for additional medical information regarding the client's diagnosis, treatment, and prognosis.

medical treatment and demonstrate a concomitant increase in treatment cooperation. (8, 9)

5. Adhere to the prescribed medication regimen. (10, 11, 12, 13, 14)
6. Identify feelings, losses, or limitations associated with the medical condition. (15, 16, 17, 18)
7. Attend a support group for individuals with a chronic illness and/or developmental disability. (18)
8. Family members share with each other their feelings that are triggered by the client's medical condition. (19, 20, 21)
9. Family members attend a support group for parents and siblings of individuals who are developmentally disabled and/or chronically ill. (21)
10. Verbally identify the steps of the grieving process and the current stage in the grieving process. (17, 22, 23)
11. Family members and client verbalize factual understanding of client's medical or genetic condition. (24, 25, 26, 27)
12. Demonstrate an understanding of universal safe health care precautions. (28, 29)
13. Cooperate with the nurse's monitoring of physical and medical conditions. (12, 30)

3. Arrange appointments for the client for a periodic physical exam and recommended follow-up or specialized care.
4. Consult with the physician about the client's developmental disability and coexisting medical conditions and their expected interactions (e.g., epilepsy, diabetes, endocrine or metabolic difficulties, heart problems, neurological concerns, or respiratory deficiencies).
5. Facilitate the client's obtaining the needed medical supplies; instruct the client and caregivers on their proper use.
6. Monitor and reinforce the client's acceptance of and compliance with the medical treatment regimen.
7. Gently confront any manipulation, passive-aggressive behavior, and denial mechanisms that block the client's acceptance of and compliance with the medical regimen.
8. Provide desensitization techniques to assist the client in overcoming his/her fear of medical procedures and/or tactile defensiveness.
9. Explore and address misconceptions, fears, and situational factors that interfere with the client's acceptance of and compliance with the medical treatment.

14. Implement a stable, healthy, and appealing diet. (31, 32, 33)
15. Cooperate with dental examinations to maintain teeth and gums. (6, 34, 35, 36)
16. Implement pain management strategies to cope with chronic pain. (37, 38)
17. Implement rituals to express grief over the medical condition and its consequences. (39, 40)
18. Decrease the daily time spent focused on the negative aspects of the medical condition. (41)
19. Engage in activities supportive of spiritual faith as a source of peace and hope. (42)
20. Increase participation in enjoyable activities. (41, 43)
21. Verbalize acceptance of the reality of the medical condition and its consequences, while decreasing denial. (6, 7, 9, 44)
22. Verbally express fears about the possible deterioration of one's physical condition and death. (18, 45, 46)
23. Accept referral to a psychotherapist for evaluation and treatment. (47, 48, 49, 50)
24. Client, family members, and caregivers identify sources of emotional support. (18, 51, 52, 53)

10. Arrange for all of the client's prescriptions to be obtained from the same pharmacy.
11. Consult with the pharmacist to monitor the client's medications for interactive effects and to learn about the side effects of the client's medications.
12. Monitor the procedures for the administration of medications that have been prescribed for the client. (See Medication Management in this Planner.)
13. Assess the client's ability to properly self-administer medications; arrange for support if necessary.
14. Routinely monitor the client's expected use of medications and accurate pill counts in pill bottles.
15. Ask the client to list the changes, losses, or limitations that have resulted from his/her medical condition.
16. Help the client to identify and process the feelings generated by the medical condition.
17. Assign the client to keep a daily grief journal to be shared in therapy sessions. Process the journal material with the client.
18. Refer the client to a support group for individuals with a chronic illness and/or developmental disabilities.

25. Implement cognitive behavioral stress reduction skills to terminate tension that exacerbates the medical condition. (37, 54, 55)
26. Family members and client verbalize an understanding of managed care and its impact on the client's medical care delivery. (56)
27. Parents verbalize a reduction of fear regarding the possible death or severely disabled life of the client. (57, 58, 59)
28. Caregivers verbalize a reduction in the degree of emotional strain related to providing service to the client. (51, 57, 60, 61, 62)

—. ____________________
____

—. ____________________
____

—. ____________________
____

19. Meet with family members to facilitate clarification and sharing of their feelings associated with the client's medical condition (e.g., guilt, anger, helplessness, or sibling attention jealousy).
20. Explore how each family member is dealing with the stress and whether conflicts have developed between the family members because of differing response styles; promote support and acceptance of each other.
21. Provide the family members with information about local support groups for parents and siblings of individuals who have developmental disabilities and/or chronic illnesses.
22. Educate the client and family members on the stages of the grieving process and answer any questions.
23. Suggest that the client read (or read to the client) a book on grief and loss (e.g., *Don't Despair on Thursday* [Moser]).
24. Arrange for the client and family members to obtain accurate information regarding the symptoms, causes, treatment, and prognosis for the client's medical condition.
25. Refer the client and parents to reliable resources for medical information, including Internet material (e.g., *The*

Mayo Clinic Family Health Book [Larson] or WebMD Health).

26. Arrange for interested family members to obtain available, pertinent genetic screening or testing and counseling.
27. Provide family members with information on their rights to privacy and on how to avoid genetic discrimination.
28. Arrange for the client, family members, and caregivers to receive information on proper universal health care practices and techniques (e.g., wearing gloves, frequent hand washing, and avoiding contact with others' bodily fluids) and provide opportunities for them to practice until proficient.
29. Recommend that the client and family members view the video *The Home Care Companion,* vol. 3, *Creating Healthy Home Care Conditions: Infection Control* (Karpinski) in order to better understand personal hygiene, proper hand washing, protective barriers, how germs are spread, and waste disposal.
30. Refer the client to a nurse for ongoing monitoring of basic health, medical concerns, and medication management.

31. Refer the client to a dietician for evaluation and recommendations regarding meal planning.
32. Facilitate and monitor the client's implementation of the dietitian-approved foods and meal plan.
33. Request feedback from the client about whether the foods provided are foods that he/she enjoys; arrange for changes to meet the client's tastes within dietary constraints.
34. Arrange for the client's biannual dental examination and cleaning.
35. Monitor the client's medications for drug interactions related to oral hygiene (e.g. anticonvulsants and gingival hyperplasia.)
36. Arrange for sedation prior to appointments if the client needs extensive dental work or has a history of extreme difficulties with dental procedures; take precautions against too frequent sedation.
37. Use modeling and behavioral rehearsal to teach the client relaxation techniques such as deep breathing, progressive muscle relaxation, or positive imagery to manage pain symptoms (see *The Relaxation and Stress Reduction Workbook* [Davis, Eshelman, and McKay]).

38. Teach the client pain management strategies (e.g., see *Mastering Pain: A Twelve-Step Program for Coping with Chronic Pain* [Sternback]).

39. Provide a variety of concrete grieving rituals to help the client express his/her grief regarding the illness (e.g., letting go of a negative emotion by scattering a drawing of it to the wind; expressing anger by hitting a pillow designated to represent the illness).

40. Suggest that the client set aside a specific time-limited period each day or week to focus on mourning the medical condition. Direct that after the time period is up he/she will get on with regular daily activities, with an agreement to put off mourning thoughts until the next scheduled time. (Mourning times could include putting on dark clothing and/or sad music, etc. Clothing should be changed when the allotted time period is up.)

41. Challenge the client to focus his/her thoughts on the positive aspects of life rather than on losses associated with the medical condition; reinforce instances of such positive focus.

42. Encourage the client to rely on his/her spiritual faith's promises, activities

(e.g., prayer, meditation, worship, and music), and fellowship as sources of support.

43. With the client, generate a list of activities he/she enjoys. Identify times when participation in the identified activities is possible, and encourage initiation of such activities.
44. Contract with the client for his/her full cooperation and compliance with medical treatment procedures.
45. Explore and process with the client his/her fears associated with the deterioration of physical health, death, and dying.
46. Normalize the client's feelings of grief, sadness, or anxiety associated with the medical condition, and encourage verbal expression of these emotions.
47. Refer the client for an assessment of depression, anxiety or other Axis I disorders (see Depression and Anxiety in this Planner).
48. Refer the client for mental health treatment of Axis I disorder, including counseling and/or psychotropic medications.
49. Refer the client to a behavior specialist to design and implement a behavioral plan that reinforces coping techniques and decreases behaviors that

contribute to physical discomfort.

50. Train all family members and caregivers on the client's behavioral treatment program to ensure effective implementation and strengthening of coping techniques.
51. Refer family members and caregivers to community resources and support groups to facilitate coping with the client's medical condition (e.g., respite care, skill training, or support groups).
52. Explore and evaluate the client's and family members' sources of emotional support.
53. Encourage family members to reach out for support from church leaders, extended family, hospital social services, community support groups, and God.
54. Generate with the client a list of positive, realistic thoughts that can replace the cognitive distortions and catastrophizing regarding his/her medical condition and its treatment.
55. Use role-playing and modeling to teach the client positive self-talk and positive imagery techniques, verbally reinforcing all independent use by the client.
56. Recommend that family members read materials on

managed care to gain better insight on current health care coverage (e.g., *Managed Care and Longer-Term Services for People with Mental Retardation* [Association for Retarded Citizens (ARC)] or *Managed Care and People with Developmental Disabilities: A Guidebook* [Human Services Research Institute (HSRI) and National Association of State Directors of Developmental Disabilities Services (NASDDDS)]).

57. Draw out family members' unspoken fears about the client's possible death; empathize with their panic, helpless frustration, and anxiety. Encourage reliance on their spiritual faith for support.
58. Recommend that the family members read *Meeting the Challenge of Disability or Chronic Illness: A Family Guide* (Goldfarb, Brotherson, Summers, and Turnbull); process the content of the book as it applies to their life circumstance.
59. Refer the family members to a hospice program for support through a terminal illness.
60. Observe family members and caregivers for frustrations that may reduce their ability to interact effectively with the client. Provide opportunities for venting feelings.

61. Recommend that family members read *The Resourceful Caregiver: Helping Family Caregivers Help Themselves* (National Family Caregivers Association) to generate positive coping strategies (e.g., stress management, communication strategies, identifying caregiver needs, and dealing with grief).
62. Assess the client's and family members' interest in faith-based activities and provide access to church ministry if indicated.

__. ______________________________

____

__. ______________________________

____

__. ______________________________

____

DIAGNOSTIC SUGGESTIONS:

ICD-9-CM	*ICD-10-CM*	*DSM-5* Disorder, Condition, or Problem
300.09	F41.8	Other Specified Anxiety Disorder
300.00	F41.9	Unspecified Anxiety Disorder
309.24	F43.22	Adjustment Disorder, With Anxiety
300.29	F40.xxx	Specific Phobia
309.0	F43.21	Adjustment disorder, With Depressed Mood
310.1	F07.0	Personality Change Due to Another Medical Condition
299.00	F84.0	Autism Spectrum Disorder
317	F70	Intellectual Disability, Mild
319	F71	Intellectual Disability, Moderate
319	F72	Intellectual Disability, Severe
319	F73	Intellectual Disability, Profound
319	F79	Unspecified Intellectual Disability
V62.89	R41.83	Borderline Intellectual Functioning
____	____	________________
____	____	________________

MEDICATION MANAGEMENT

BEHAVIORAL DEFINITIONS

1. Failure to consistently take medications as prescribed.
2. Medical condition necessitating regular use of medications.
3. Verbalization of fears and dislike related to physical and/or emotional side effects of prescribed medications.
4. Lack of adherence to a prescribed medication regimen.
5. Lack of knowledge of medications, their usefulness, and potential side effects.
6. Verbalization of an unwillingness to take prescribed medications.
7. Consumption of alcohol or illicit drugs along with psychotropic medications.
8. Medication interactions causing negative side effects.

—. ____

____

—. ____

____

—. ____

____

LONG-TERM GOALS

1. Achieve regular, consistent use of prescribed medications at prescribed dosage, frequency, and duration.
2. Stabilize medical condition through medications.
3. Demonstrate increased understanding of prescribed medication dosages and side effects and the rationale for their use.
4. Report side effects on a timely basis, and minimize their severity.

5. Decrease frequency and intensity of physical and mental illness symptoms.
6. Support network of family members, clinicians, and caregivers assists client in taking prescribed medication.
7. Decrease side effects of all prescribed medication through effective, timely regulation of dosage and type of medication.
8. Attain therapeutic dosage levels, as indicated by objectively measured blood levels.

__. ______________________________

____

__. ______________________________

____

__. ______________________________

____

SHORT-TERM OBJECTIVES

1. List all medications that are currently being prescribed and consumed. (1, 2, 3, 4)
2. Cooperate with nurse's monitoring of prescribed medications. (3, 4, 5, 6)
3. Verbalize accurate information regarding reasons for, side effects of, and expected outcome of taking prescribed medications. (1, 7, 8, 9, 10)
4. Report as to medication's effectiveness and side effects. (11, 22, 23, 24)
5. Report a decrease in emotional resistance to proper medication usage. (12)
6. Cooperate with a psychological evaluation to identify

THERAPEUTIC INTERVENTIONS

1. Review with the client all currently prescribed medications, including names, times administered, and dosages.
2. Assess the client's ability to assume independent responsibility for medications.
3. Compare the client's description of medication usage with information from the client's medical chart, family members and caregivers, or personal physician or psychiatrist.
4. Refer the client for tests to measure the blood level of medications expected to be present; compare the results with the client's prescribed dosages and his/her reports as to prescription adherence.

cognitive/adaptive barriers to proper medication usage. (13)

7. Identify financial resources for payment for medication. (14, 15, 16, 17)
8. Acknowledge the intensity of suicidal ideation. (18, 19, 20)
9. Cooperate with in-depth diagnostic procedures to accurately assess symptoms and medication effectiveness. (20, 21)
10. Family members and caregivers report as to the client's medication prescription compliance, the medication's effectiveness, and any side effects. (2, 3, 22, 23, 24)
11. Modify lifestyle to minimize negative effects on medication effectiveness and side effects. (25)
12. Describe the expected positive effects of taking medications. (1, 26)
13. Take medications with assistance from caregivers. (2, 27, 28)
14. Verbalize and demonstrate correct procedures for safe medication administration. (29, 30, 31)
15. Take medications responsibly on a day-to-day basis. (2, 10, 32, 33, 34, 35)
16. Take medications responsibly on a week-to-week basis. (2, 10, 33, 34, 35, 36)

5. Refer the client to a nurse for ongoing monitoring of health, medical concerns, |and medication management.
6. Monitor the procedures that family members and caregivers use for the administration of medications that have been prescribed for the client; assess whether supervision is sufficient to guarantee prescription adherence.
7. Request that the client identify the reasons for using each medication; correct any misinformation.
8. Refer the client to a physician or other medical staff for additional information on specific medications.
9. Facilitate the involvement of a local pharmacist in providing the client with medication information and monitoring the client's filling of medication prescriptions.
10. Request that the pharmacist provide profiles of the client's medications to better understand each drug's dosage level and side effects and any interdrug effects; review this information with the client and family members.
11. Ask the client to identify the effectiveness and side effects he/she is expecting or has experienced from taking the

17. Take medications responsibly on an ongoing, permanent basis. (2, 10, 33, 34, 35, 36)
18. Accept assistance from family members, peers, and others regarding medication usage. (6, 23, 28, 37, 38, 39)
19. Express social concerns related to medication usage. (12, 40)
20. Obtain peer support regarding physical or mental illness concerns. (41)
21. Obtain a more simplified administration of medications. (42, 43)
22. Utilize a pictorial display to remind self of medication dosage and times. (44)
23. Describe the extent of use of alcohol or illicit drugs. (45)
24. Terminate substance use or abuse. (45, 46, 47)
25. Verbalize positive feelings about the improvement resulting from medication effectiveness. (11, 26, 48, 49)

—. ______________________________
____

—. ______________________________
____

—. ______________________________
____

medications; confer with the prescribing physician as to needed adjustments in medication dosage and type.

12. Request that the client describe any fears he/she may be experiencing regarding the use of medication; process these fears, correcting myths and misinformation.
13. Refer the client to a psychologist for intellectual and adaptive testing relative to his/her understanding of medication usage and ability to follow through with prescription adherence.
14. Assist the client in obtaining and maintaining employment (see Supported Employment in this Planner).
15. Refer the client to the appropriate agency to obtain assistance in gaining entitlements (e.g., Medicaid or Social Security disability).
16. Coordinate the client's access to free or low-cost medication programs through drug manufacturers or other resources.
17. Advocate for the client's use of generic drugs where appropriate.
18. Assess the client's suicidal ideation, taking into account the extent of ideation, the

presence of primary and back-up plans, past attempts, and family history.

19. Remove medication from the client's immediate access, if necessary.
20. Refer the acutely psychotic or suicidal client to a crisis residential placement or psychiatric hospital.
21. Arrange for psychiatric or psychological evaluation of the client to determine if an untreated Axis I disorder is present.
22. Monitor the client for permanent side effects of neuroleptic medications (e.g., tardive dyskinesia, muscle rigidity, and dystonia).
23. Enlist the help of family members and caregivers to monitor the signs and symptoms of the client's psychiatric condition, the effectiveness of the medication, and any side effects, in order to provide accurate information to a psychiatrist.
24. Obtain a written release from the client in order to inform his/her primary physician or other health care providers of the medications and their expected side effects, risks, and benefits.
25. Arrange for the client to receive information on lifestyle habits that can be modified to decrease the side effects of medication (e.g., tobacco use, sleep, and diet).

26. Educate the client about the expected or common symptoms of his/her physical or mental illness and how the medication is expected to ameliorate these symptoms.
27. Arrange for supervision of the client's self-administration of medications.
28. After obtaining the proper release from the client, request assistance from caregivers in administering medications to the client.
29. Demonstrate correct and safe independent medication administration for the client (e.g., following label directions, keeping medications in proper bottles, using good lighting, responding to a missed dose, and responding to a suspected overdose), and request that the client repeat what is modeled.
30. Arrange for the client to view the video *The Home Care Companion,* vol. 4, *How to Manage Medications* (Karpinski) to emphasize the need to manage medications and demonstrate safe medication practices, proper medication administration, and proper storage.
31. Verbally describe to the client the route, time, and other variables for each of the medications he/she takes.

32. Arrange for daily medication drop-offs to the client, with instructions on which dosages to take at what time of day.
33. Arrange for medications to be grouped in a multidose, compartmentalized daily medication box. Monitor the client for correct use of the pillbox.
34. Encourage the client to take medications at a specific, consistent place and time each day.
35. Monitor the client's expected use of medications, and ensure accurate pill counts in the pill bottles on a sporadic basis.
36. Coordinate all of the client's prescriptions (including nonpsychiatric medications) to be obtained from the same pharmacy.
37. Coordinate family or individual therapy to promote understanding of the client's illness and the impact of that illness on the client's and family members' needs.
38. Train family members, peers, and others in the proper use and administration of medications, and urge them to encourage or reinforce the client when he/she complies.
39. Coordinate family members to provide the client with transportation to the clinic or pharmacy.

40. Request that the client identify social concerns he/she may be experiencing regarding taking the medication (e.g., stigmatization or loss of independence); process these concerns to resolution.
41. Refer the client to a support group for individuals with mental illness and/or developmental disability concerns.
42. Advocate with the physician for less complicated dosing times for the client's medications.
43. Investigate whether longer-acting or time-release medications (e.g., depot medications) may be beneficial to the client.
44. Develop a pictorial display of the dosage schedule and the medications to be taken (i.e., size, shape, and color of each pill), and ask the client to display it prominently in his/her living area.
45. Gather a complete drug and alcohol history from the client.
46. Provide the client with information about the negative effects of substance abuse on his/her symptoms and the depotentiating effect of these substances on his/her medications.
47. Refer the client for substance abuse treatment (see

Chemical Dependence in this Planner).

48. Request that the client identify how the reduction in physical and/or mental illness symptoms has improved his/her social or family system.

49. Arrange for the client to obtain individual therapy regarding his/her adjustment to improved functioning relative to psychosis and other symptoms of mental illness.

__. ____________________

____

__. ____________________

____

__. ____________________

____

DIAGNOSTIC SUGGESTIONS:

ICD-9-CM	*ICD-10-CM*	*DSM-5* Disorder, Condition, or Problem
297.1	F22	Delusional Disorder
295.90	F20.9	Schizophrenia
295.70	F25.0	Schizoaffective Disorder, Bipolar Type
295.70	F25.1	Schizoaffective Disorder, Depressive Type
296.xx	F31.xx	Bipolar I Disorder
296.89	F31.81	Bipolar II Disorder
304.10	F13.20	Sedative, Hypnotic, or Anxiolytic Use Disorder, Moderate or Severe
304.10	F13.10	Sedative, Hypnotic, or Anxiolytic Use Disorder, Mild
V15.81	Z91.19	Nonadherence to Medical Treatment
299.00	F84.0	Autism Spectrum Disorder
317	F70	Intellectual Disability, Mild
319	F71	Intellectual Disability, Moderate
319	F72	Intellectual Disability, Severe
319	F73	Intellectual Disability, Profound
319	F79	Unspecified Intellectual Disability
V62.89	R41.83	Borderline Intellectual Functioning
_____	_____	______________________________
_____	_____	______________________________

PERSONAL SAFETY SKILLS

BEHAVIORAL DEFINITIONS

1. Personal safety jeopardized by careless, impulsive, high-risk behaviors.
2. Inability to appropriately respond to emergency situations.
3. Lack of knowledge regarding community resources available for assistance during an emergency.
4. Excessive friendliness with strangers.
5. Inability to abide by community safety signs.
6. Lower than expected safety skills resulting from overprotection of client by caregiver.

—. ____

—. ____

—. ____

LONG-TERM GOALS

1. Strengthen existing personal safety skills and develop new personal safety skills.
2. Learn the importance and key components of personal safety skills.
3. Develop increased ability to respond to emergency situations.
4. Learn skills essential to protecting self from harm.
5. Caregivers promote and reinforce the client's increased independence.

__. ____

____

__. ____

____

__. ____

____

SHORT-TERM OBJECTIVES

1. Participate in an evaluation of personal safety skills. (1, 2)
2. Adhere to recommendations made from the evaluation regarding appropriate interventions. (3)
3. Participate in training sessions designed to maximize independence via strengthening personal safety skills. (4, 5, 6)
4. Participate in developing a reward system to motivate progress in personal safety skills. (7, 8)
5. Demonstrate an understanding of which behaviors enhance personal safety. (9, 10, 11)
6. Implement personal safety skills to protect self from harm. (6, 12, 13, 14)
7. Correctly distinguish between emergency and nonemergency situations, identifying appropriate responses to the emergency situations. (6, 15)

THERAPEUTIC INTERVENTIONS

1. Arrange for an assessment of the client's personal safety skills through direct observation and/or reports from family members and caregivers to establish a baseline of ability and gain insight into the client's strengths and weaknesses.
2. Provide direct feedback to the client, family members, and caregivers on the results of the evaluation.
3. Obtain consensus from the client, family members, school officials, and caregivers regarding suitable learning programs or interventions that build on the client's strengths and compensate for his/her weaknesses.
4. Encourage parents, caregivers, and teachers to model personal safety skills and have the client imitate the modeled behavior.
5. Identify a safe training site in the community to provide the

8. Describe the different types of helping professionals and the emergency situations to which each is likely to respond. (6, 16, 17)
9. Demonstrate the correct implementation of basic first-aid techniques. (6, 18, 19, 20)
10. Identify the correct emergency response to hypothetical examples and to previously encountered emergency situations. (20, 21)
11. Demonstrate obtaining necessary emergency assistance by role-playing emergency situations. (6, 22, 23)
12. Demonstrate the ability to correctly use a telephone for emergency purposes. (6, 24, 25)
13. Family members and caregivers reduce the frequency of speaking for the client or performing activities that the client is capable of doing independently. (26, 27, 28)

__. ________________________

__. ________________________

__. ________________________

client with realistic training opportunities.

6. Direct the client in a structured repetition of identified safety skills.
7. Assist the client in identifying potential rewards or reinforcers for desired behaviors.
8. Design and implement a reward system to motivate the client to improve his/her personal safety skills.
9. Play educational games (e.g., Safety Skills: Learning to Be Careful [Haugen]) to facilitate the client's learning of safety skills.
10. Educate the client on the importance of keeping one's body safe by providing pictorial examples of safe and unsafe behaviors (e.g., handling hot objects, hazardous chemicals, and tools).
11. Query the client's comprehension of critical personal safety skills to gain insight into his/her understanding of their significance; reinforce correct comprehension.
12. Provide instructional information on basic personal safety skills (e.g., never going places with strangers, staying in groups, getting permission prior to going places, never telling others when one is home alone, practicing assertiveness if someone is

doing something one doesn't like, avoiding hitchhiking, and not giving personal information out over the phone), and request that the client identify the rationale for each.

13. Use role-playing to create learning opportunities for the client to practice using newly acquired personal safety information.
14. Test and observe the client's ability to conform his/her behavior to newly acquired knowledge of basic personal safety skills (e.g., through spontaneous role-playing, self-reports, and reports from family members and caregivers).
15. Present pictorial and verbal examples of emergency and nonemergency situations, requesting that the client correctly identify each emergency and describe an appropriate response; provide feedback on his/her successes and failures.
16. Teach the client about which professionals are needed for various types of emergencies (e.g., police, firefighters, emergency room, and poison control); test his/her understanding.
17. Request that the client list professionals who assist with emergencies and describe the types of emergencies each serves.
18. Provide pictures of different burns, cuts, and bites and

request that the client identify what response would be appropriate in each case.

19. Utilize props such as red markers, antiseptic, and Band-Aids to role-play minor injuries, and request that the client respond appropriately in applying first aid.
20. Role-play situations in which the client must display independent judgment in seeking assistance versus utilizing basic first aid for minor injuries; provide feedback on his/her successes and failures in using appropriate judgment.
21. Discuss the client's previous accidents and the treatment he/she obtained, pointing out positive and negative examples of appropriately responding to the situation.
22. Role-play serious injury situations and request that the client respond appropriately; guide and reinforce his/her decision making.
23. Monitor the client's progress through role-playing and assess his/her ability to respond independently with appropriate action.
24. Provide the client with practice at dialing phone numbers from written prompts or from memory.
25. Direct the client in practicing dialing emergency numbers independently.

26. Provide family members and caregivers with training needed to encourage and reinforce the client's advancement in personal safety skills.
27. Encourage family members and caregivers to agree to promote lifelong learning opportunities and experiences for the client in order to promote his/her choice making, decision making, problem solving, goal setting, and attainment, along with self-awareness and knowledge.
28. Urge the client to make all reasonable choices in daily events in the practice of increased independence, and reinforce him/her for doing so.

__. ____________________
____

__. ____________________
____

__. ____________________
____

DIAGNOSTIC SUGGESTIONS:

ICD-9-CM	*ICD-10-CM*	*DSM-5* Disorder, Condition, or Problem
299.00	F84.0	Autism Spectrum Disorder
317	F70	Intellectual Disability, Mild
319	F71	Intellectual Disability, Moderate

319	F72	Intellectual Disability, Severe
319	F73	Intellectual Disability, Profound
319	F79	Unspecified Intellectual Disability
V62.89	R41.83	Borderline Intellectual Functioning
_____	_____	____________________
_____	_____	____________________

PHYSICAL/EMOTIONAL/SEXUAL ABUSE

BEHAVIORAL DEFINITIONS

1. Self-reported incidents of physical, emotional, or sexual abuse.
2. Physical signs of abuse including bone fractures; skin wounds or bruises; difficulty walking; bleeding; red, swollen, or torn genitalia; torn or bloody underwear; venereal disease; and pregnancy.
3. Unexplained change in mood and social behavior with an increase in fearfulness, anxiety, distrust, depression, or anger.
4. Refusal to be alone with specific friends, family members, staff, or other residents.
5. Increase in sexualized language or behaviors (e.g., excessive masturbation, new sexualized verbalizations, or touching others inappropriately).
6. Regressive behaviors (e.g., rocking, talking to self, or incontinence).
7. Sleep disturbance, as evidenced by difficulty falling asleep, refusal to sleep, night terrors, or recurrent nightmares.
8. Attention-seeking behavior.
9. Reports by caregivers or family that the client seems unusually fearful, anxious, distressed, or guilty.
10. Reports by reliable witnesses that the client has been physically, emotionally, or sexually abused.

__. ____

____

__. ____

____

__. ____

____

LONG-TERM GOALS

1. Terminate the physical, emotional, or sexual abuse and report the incidents to the proper authorities.
2. Enjoy a safe environment where rights are fully respected.
3. Learn types of relationships and accompanying behaviors for each type of relationship.
4. Learn the skills necessary to guard against future abuse.
5. Maximize choices and preferences whenever possible.
6. Caregivers reinforce all the client's steps toward skill maintenance.
7. Process emotional sequela of abuse in a positive manner.
8. Reduce or eliminate feelings of fear, anxiety, shame, and guilt.
9. Rebuild a sense of safety and trust in others and in the environment.

—. ____

____

—. ____

____

—. ____

____

SHORT-TERM OBJECTIVES

1. Describe the abuse, including its nature, frequency, and duration. (1, 2, 3, 4)
2. Accept the need to report the abuse to the authorities. (5)
3. Obtain medical verification and documentation of the abuse and stabilize from the physical effects of the abuse. (6, 7, 8)
4. Cooperate with a psychological assessment. (9)
5. Follow recommendations as to placement in a safe environment. (10, 11, 12)

THERAPEUTIC INTERVENTIONS

1. Encourage and support the client in giving a detailed verbal account of the abuse (e.g., nature, frequency, and duration) using a structured interview (e.g., *The Sexual Abuse Interview for the Developmentally Disabled* [Valenti-Hein]).
2. Use anatomically detailed dolls to help the client tell and show how he/she was abused. Take great caution *not* to lead the client in his/her description of the events.

6. Verbalize and process negative emotions connected to the abuse. (3, 13, 14, 15)
7. Identify self as a survivor rather than a victim. (1, 16, 17)
8. Verbally identify the perpetrator as being responsible for the sexual abuse. (4, 18, 19, 20)
9. Report reduced feelings of fear, anxiety, shame, or guilt surrounding the abuse. (3, 21, 22, 23)
10. Verbalize a sense of safety and trust in others within the environment. (23, 24, 25, 26)
11. Family members demonstrate emotional support for the client. (27, 28, 29)
12. Verbalize a simple understanding of the steps in the legal process. (30, 31)
13. Utilize community resources, family members, and friends to develop a broader base of emotional support. (32, 33, 34, 35, 36)
14. Demonstrate the skills necessary to guard against future attempts at abuse. (37)
15. Identify healthy versus abusive behaviors and the appropriate reactions to each. (38, 39, 40)
16. Behaviorally demonstrate knowledge of the types of interpersonal relationships. (41, 42, 43, 44)

3. Explore the client's feelings associated with the abuse, and encourage and support him/her in verbally expressing them.
4. Encourage and support the client in identifying the perpetrator, being careful not to lead or make suggestions to the client.
5. After explaining to the client the legal requirement to report abuse, contact the proper protection agency, criminal justice officials, or medical officials.
6. Arrange for immediate medical assessment, documentation, and treatment of the client.
7. Consult with the client's physician, criminal justice officials, or the protective agency's case manager to assess the client's veracity and the extent of the abuse.
8. Consult with the client's physician, criminal justice officials, or the protective agency's case manager to develop appropriate treatment interventions.
9. Refer the client for a psychological evaluation to determine his/her emotional and cognitive status.
10. Implement the necessary steps (e.g., placing the client in a different home or providing supervision) to protect the client and others from future abuse.

17. Verbalize an understanding of the differences between assertion, aggression, and passivity. (45, 46, 47)
18. Verbalize an understanding of the right to say no, run away, and get help in abusive situations. (47, 48)
19. Implement privacy behaviors. (49)
20. Demonstrate appropriate noncompliance skills. (47, 48, 50, 51, 52)
21. Parents and caretakers list the signs and symptoms of abuse. (53, 54)

—. ______________________________
____

—. ______________________________
____

—. ______________________________
____

11. If the veracity of the charges cannot be established due to the client's cognitive impairment, assess his/her emotional status and recommend safety precautions and protections based on his/her current emotional distress, regardless of the legal resolution of the abuse charges.
12. Explore specific fears of retaliation by the perpetrator and help the client determine the probability of its actual occurrence. Assist the client, family members, and caregivers in solving problems and issues related to protection if retaliation is possible.
13. Arrange for the client to receive individual or group therapy to address emotional sequela resulting from the abuse.
14. Validate and normalize the client's emotions related to the abuse, while generating positive strategies to help process these emotions (e.g., relaxation, writing letters, attending a survivor's support group, and physical activity).
15. Refer the client for creative arts therapy to provide him/her with the opportunity to nonverbally express and work through feelings of hurt, fear, anger, anxiety, guilt, and shame.

16. Assist the client in identifying the positive and negative consequences of being a victim versus a survivor.
17. Refer the client to a survivor's group to assist him/her in realizing that he/she is not alone in having experienced abuse.
18. Request that the client role-play a speech or write a letter to the perpetrator and then process it with the clinician. Do not send the letter unless the client can thoroughly understand the ramifications of confrontation.
19. Focus on the client's feelings of guilt and responsibility; reinforce the placement of responsibility on the perpetrator.
20. Assign the client to read (or read to the client) excerpts from *The Courage to Heal: A Guide for Women Survivors of Sexual Abuse* (Bass and Davis) or, for men, *Victims No Longer* (Lew) to help process the concept that the abuse is not his/her fault.
21. Assign the client a letting-go exercise in which a symbol of the abuse is destroyed (e.g., shredding a drawing of the abuse). Process this experience.
22. Assist the client in generating a written or pictorial list of positive coping steps (e.g., relaxation exercises, a safe

person to talk to, or attending survivor's support group) that he/she can use to effectively manage difficult emotions and behaviors.

23. Encourage the client to participate in positive peer groups or extracurricular activities.
24. Utilize visual media (e.g., *Out of Harm's Way: A Safety Kit for People with Disabilities Who Feel Unsafe and Want to Do Something About It* [Ticoll]) to help the client verbally or actively identify safe people and situations. Facilitate the client's obtaining these conditions.
25. Solicit input from a third party who knows the nonverbal client as well as his/her likes and dislikes, and facilitate the client's obtaining these satisfying conditions.
26. Recommend that family members and caregivers read *It Could Never Happen Here! The Prevention and Treatment of Sexual Abuse of Adults with Learning Disabilities in Residential Settings* (Association for Retarded Citizens [ARC]).
27. Facilitate conjoint sessions to reveal the sexual abuse to key family members or caregivers.
28. Elicit and reinforce emotional support of the client by family members.

29. Assign the client's family members or caregivers to read *Sexual Assault Survivor's Handbook for People with Developmental Disabilities and Their Advocates* (Baladerian) to assist them in understanding how they can help the client.
30. Prepare the client for possible involvement in the legal process by providing a brief summary of the different steps involved and the expected time frame. Role-play possible situations in a nondirective manner.
31. Assist the client in preparing for the anxiety of talking repeatedly about the abuse by teaching him/her the use of relaxation strategies (e.g., progressive muscle relaxation, positive imagery, and slow, deep abdominal breathing).
32. Arrange for the client to receive services from support agencies such as adult protective services, child protective services, or a sexual assault center.
33. Explore the balance between the client maintaining his/her personal privacy versus gaining emotional and social support.
34. Facilitate the client's receiving physical and emotional support from close friends, family members, and advocates in community.

35. Refer the client to community support agencies involved with survivors of abuse.
36. Assess the client's and family members' interest in faith-based support and provide access to church ministry as indicated.
37. Arrange for the client to participate in training to learn skills essential in guarding against abuse, such as taking safety measures, accessing immediate help, and practicing basic self-defense.
38. Describe healthy versus abusive behaviors and then request that the client identify how the two are different.
39. Present various pictorial or descriptive scenarios of healthy versus abusive situations and request that the client correctly identify these types of situations.
40. Request that the client identify how he/she would respond to various healthy versus abusive situations.
41. Visually portray the different types of interpersonal relationships (e.g., utilize the *Circles II: Stop Abuse* curriculum [Champagne and Walker-Hirsh]).
42. Provide information on the types of behaviors associated with the different types of interpersonal relationships

and query the client's understanding by using role-playing.

43. Request that the client identify people he/she knows in his/her own life and place these people in the appropriate relationship circle.
44. Encourage the client to apply the newly learned relationship skills to his/her daily interactions with people; reinforce all efforts toward their application.
45. Model assertive, aggressive, and passive responses to the same situation and request that the client identify the most effective style.
46. Arrange for the client to role-play assertive responses to a variety of situations; reinforce appropriate assertiveness.
47. Demonstrate the right to say no, run away, and get help in abusive situations.
48. Request that the client role-play his/her response to a potentially abusive situation until he/she is comfortable with saying no forcefully, leaving the situation, and then telling a person capable of providing assistance.
49. Request that caregivers and family members model privacy behaviors (e.g., in bathing, toileting, and dressing) when around client and verbally prompt the

client to obtain privacy if he/she is not able to do so independently.

50. Teach the client about situations in which it is permissible to say no to a parent, caretaker, or supervisor, and teach him/her how to do so respectfully.
51. Model and request client to role-play appropriate noncompliance to a variety of situations.
52. Educate family members and caretakers on the importance of appropriate noncompliance and provide them with examples of when they should reinforce the client's efforts to assert noncompliance.
53. Educate family members and caretakers on the signs (e.g., bruises, bleeding, or fractures) and symptoms (e.g., changes in mood or social behaviors, fearfulness, regressive behaviors, and unusual sexualized behaviors) of abuse and the appropriate steps to take if abuse is suspected.
54. Assign family members and caregivers to read *Just Say Know! Understanding and Reducing the Risk of Sexual Victimization of People with Developmental Disabilities* (Hingsburger) or *No More Victims: Addressing the Sexual Abuse of People with a Mental Handicap: Families' and Friends' Manual* (Ticoll) to

learn ways to foster the client's development of skills to guard against abuse.

—. ____________________
____

—. ____________________
____

—. ____________________
____

DIAGNOSTIC SUGGESTIONS:

ICD-9-CM	*ICD-10-CM*	*DSM-5* Disorder, Condition, or Problem
296.xx	F32.x	Major Depressive Disorder, Single Episode
296.xx	F33.x	Major Depressive Disorder, Recurrent Episode
300.4	F34.1	Persistent Depressive Disorder
309.81	F43.10	Posttraumatic Stress Disorder
308.3	F43.0	Acute Stress Disorder
300.02	F41.1	Generalized Anxiety Disorder
995.81	Z69.11	Encounter for Mental Health Services for Victim of Spouse or Partner Violence, Physical
995.81	T74.11XA	Spouse or Partner Violence, Physical, Confirmed, Initial Encounter
995.81	T74.11XD	Spouse or Partner Violence, Physical, Confirmed, Subsequent Encounter
995.81	T74.11XA	Adult Physical Abuse by Nonspouse or Nonpartner, Confirmed, Initial Encounter
995.81	T74.11XD	Adult Physical Abuse by Nonspouse or Nonpartner, Confirmed, Subsequent Encounter
299.00	F84.0	Autism Spectrum Disorder
317	F70	Intellectual Disability, Mild
319	F71	Intellectual Disability, Moderate
319	F72	Intellectual Disability, Severe
319	F73	Intellectual Disability, Profound
319	F79	Unspecified Intellectual Disability
V62.89	R41.83	Borderline Intellectual Functioning
______	______	____________________
______	______	____________________

PSYCHOSIS

BEHAVIORAL DEFINITIONS

1. Bizarre content of thought (delusions of grandeur, persecution, reference, influence, control, somatic sensations, or infidelity).
2. Illogical forms of thought or speech (loose association of ideas or incoherence in speech; illogical thinking; vague, abstract, or repetitive speech; neologisms, preservations, or clanging).
3. Perception disturbances (hallucinations, primarily auditory but occasionally visual or olfactory).
4. Disturbed affect (blunted, none, flattened, or inappropriate).
5. Lost sense of self (loss of ego boundaries, lack of identity, or blatant confusion).
6. Diminished volition (inadequate interest, drive, or ability to follow a course of action to its logical conclusion; pronounced ambivalence or cessation of goal-directed activity).
7. Psychomotor abnormalities (marked decrease in reactivity to environment; various catatonic patterns such as stupor, rigidity, excitement, posturing, or negativism; unusual mannerisms or grimacing).
8. Withdrawal from relationships, as evidenced by decreased involvement with the external world, or preoccupation with egocentric ideas and fantasies.
9. Poor social skills, as evidenced by lack of eye contact and social recipr ocity as well as misinterpretation of the actions and motives of others.
10. Impulsivity and unpredictability, as evidenced by socially inappropriate behavior, sexual promiscuity, self-injurious behavior, or aggression.

—. ____

____

__. ____

____

__. ____

____

LONG-TERM GOALS

1. Eliminate and/or reduce psychotic symptomatology.
2. Develop control over disturbing thoughts, feelings, and impulses.
3. Develop skills and strategies to cope positively with stressors without decompensation.
4. Improve reality orientation as well as social and vocational functioning.
5. Increase social supports and activities.
6. Maximize choices and communicate preferences whenever possible.
7. Family members and caregivers reinforce all the client's steps toward managing the psychotic symptoms.

__. ____

____

__. ____

____

__. ____

____

SHORT-TERM OBJECTIVES

1. Participate in psychological assessment of psychotic symptoms. (1, 2, 3, 4, 5, 11)
2. Cooperate with physical examination to rule out medical etiologies for psychotic symptoms. (6)
3. Comply with psychiatric examination and recommendations regarding the need for

THERAPEUTIC INTERVENTIONS

1. Perform or arrange for psychological assessment of the client's psychotic symptoms, including a developmental history, family history, and previous psychiatric involvement.
2. Refer the client for a neurological exam or neuropsychological testing.

psychotropic medications. (7, 8)

4. Adhere consistently to the antipsychotic medicine regimen. (8, 9)
5. Verbalize an understanding of the psychotic disease process and its symptoms. (10, 11, 12)
6. Increase frequency of verbalizing accurate, reality-based perceptions that compete with psychotic cognitions. (13, 14, 15)
7. Verbalize a plan to obtain guidance from a respected support network on how to minimize problems between self and the environment. (16, 17, 18)
8. Report increased enjoyment of social activities. (17, 19)
9. Implement relaxation and other cognitive-behavior techniques to reduce tension in stressful situations. (20, 21)
10. Increase the frequency of reality based, nonpsychotic, nonimpulsive behaviors due to cooperation with the behavior modification program. (22, 23, 24, 25, 26)
11. Demonstrate independence and initiative by making all possible choices in daily events, as evidenced by choosing clothing, food, leisure interests, and peer group. (27, 28, 29)
12. Family members and caretakers assist and support the

3. Operationally define the frequency, stimulus control, and reinforcement and collect stimulus and reinforcement data on behaviors indicative of psychosis.
4. Assess the severity of the client's psychosis by using a rating scale such as the Diagnostic Assessment for the Severely Handicapped, Second Edition (DASH-II; Matson) or the Reiss Screen for Maladaptive Behavior, Second Edition (Reiss).
5. Train family members and caregivers to monitor signs and symptoms of the client's psychiatric condition in order to provide accurate information to the psychiatrist and psychologist.
6. Arrange for the client to obtain a complete physical to rule out any biomedical causes for his/her psychotic symptomatology (e.g., tumors, medication side effects, and substance abuse).
7. Arrange for psychiatric evaluation of the client to determine if an Axis I disorder is present and whether psychotropic medications may be helpful.
8. Coordinate or assist the client in obtaining, organizing, and administering psychotropic medications.
9. Monitor the client for compliance, effectiveness, and side effects associated with the

client in his/her attempts to make positive behavioral changes to manage the psychotic symptoms. (25, 28, 29, 30)

13. Family members and caregivers verbalize a more complete understanding of the nature, treatment, and prognosis of the client's psychotic disorder. (31, 32)

14. Increase participation in extracurricular activities and outings. (33, 34)

__. ____________________
____

__. ____________________
____

__. ____________________
____

prescribed antipsychotic medications; redirect if the client is noncompliant.

10. Arrange for the client to receive individual therapy using a therapeutic model best suited to facilitating changes in his/her feeling and thinking (e.g., cognitive-behavioral, client-centered, or behavior modification).

11. Provide support, characterized by genuine warmth, understanding, and acceptance, to reduce the client's distrust, alleviate his/her fears, and promote openness.

12. Teach the client, through education, reassurance, and feedback, that his/her psychotic symptoms are due to mental illness.

13. Encourage the client to focus on the reality of the external world as opposed to distorted fantasies.

14. Assist in restructuring the client's irrational beliefs by reviewing reality-based evidence and his/her misinterpretations (e.g., provide specific, empirical information in a matter-of-fact manner). Avoid arguing with client about his/her misperceptions.

15. Differentiate between the sources of stimuli from self-generated, internal messages and the reality of the external

world. Request that the client acknowledge or list examples of each.

16. Coordinate a mental relationship with a volunteer or peer who can assist in resolving conflicts between the client and his/her environment to promote more effective management of problems.
17. Refer the client to a support group for dually diagnosed people with developmental disabilities.
18. Encourage the client to request feedback and guidance regarding perceptions of reality and responses to it from trusted family members, friends, or peers.
19. Arrange for the client to participate in social skills training (see Social Skills in this Planner).
20. Arrange for the client to participate in a stress management program (see Anger in this Planner).
21. Teach the client stress reduction techniques to alleviate anxiety due to stressors (e.g., deep muscle relaxation, abdominal breathing, and safe-place imagery).
22. Coordinate or perform a behavioral analysis to determine the motivating variables for the client's maladaptive behaviors.
23. Identify several reinforcers that can be used to reward

behaviors that are incompatible with psychotic behaviors. Request that the client identify or endorse his/her desired reinforcers.

24. Plan for the design and implementation of a behavioral plan that reinforces desired behaviors (e.g., through verbal compliments, physical touch, or increased privileges). Add behavioral techniques to decrease or eliminate psychotic behaviors (e.g., differential reinforcement of competive behaviors or response cost).
25. Train all caregivers on the client's behavioral treatment program to ensure effective implementation and strengthening of desirable, nonpsychotic behaviors.
26. Obtain approval from the client's guardian and the agency oversight committee for any restrictive or aversive programming.
27. Present multiple choices in a variety of situations (e.g., mealtime, recreational activities, and daily routine) such that the client is able to make a selection between the options.
28. Obtain the client's consent to enlist support for increased client choice from clinicians, residential staff, family members, and vocational and educational staff.

29. Train family members and caregivers in the use of person-centered planning, self-direction, and client choice.
30. Educate family members and caregivers about the nature of the client's severe and persistent mental illness symptoms, developmental disabilities, and behavior.
31. Recommend that family members and caregivers read either *Living and Working with Schizophrenia* (Jeffries) or *The Psychiatric Tower of Babble: Understanding People with Developmental Disabilities Who Have Mental Illness* (Gabriel), or provide specific information on the client's psychotic disorder from the National Institute of Mental Health, in order to promote greater understanding of the disorder and treatment options and address common questions and concerns.
32. Provide an opportunity for the family members to view *Living with Schizophrenia: A Video Manual for Families* (Katz) in order to help them develop an understanding of the disorder and the common difficulties that families face.
33. Refer the client to a recreational therapist to determine possible leisure, social, and

community activities available to the client.

34. Encourage the client's participation in Special Olympics or other athletic events.

__. ____________________
____

__. ____________________
____

__. ____________________
____

DIAGNOSTIC SUGGESTIONS:

ICD-9-CM	*ICD-10-CM*	*DSM-5* Disorder, Condition, or Problem
295.30	F20.9	Schizophrenia
295.70	F25.0	Schizoaffective Disorder, Bipolar Type
295.70	F25.1	Schizoaffective Disorder, Depressive Type
297.1	F22	Delusional Disorder
298.8	F23	Brief Psychotic Disorder
298.9	F29	Unspecified Schizophrenia Spectrum Disorder and Other Psychotic Disorder
296.xx	F31.xx	Bipolar I Disorder
296.89	F31.81	Bipolar II Disorder
296.xx	F32.x	Major Depressive Disorder, Single Episode
296.xx	F33.x	Major Depressive Disorder, Recurrent Episode
317	F70	Intellectual Disability, Mild
319	F71	Intellectual Disability, Moderate
319	F72	Intellectual Disability, Severe
319	F73	Intellectual Disability, Profound
319	F79	Unspecified Intellectual Disability
V62.89	R41.83	Borderline Intellectual Functioning
______	______	____________________
______	______	____________________

RECREATION/LEISURE ACTIVITIES

BEHAVIORAL DEFINITIONS

1. Social isolation or maladjustment due to limited recreational opportunities.
2. Limited repertoire of leisure activity and interest, as evidenced by long periods engaged in primarily passive activities.
3. Lack of social interactions with disabled or nondisabled peer group.
4. Limited decision-making experiences or opportunities regarding recreational opportunities.
5. Lack of enjoyment with daily life due to limited activities that bring personal satisfaction or happiness.
6. Limited recreational opportunities due to physical, financial, and social barriers.
7. Lower than expected leisure activity skills resulting from overprotection of client by caregiver.
8. Limited knowledge of and experience with recreational activities.

—. ____

____

—. ____

____

—. ____

____

LONG-TERM GOALS

1. Actively select, pursue, and enjoy leisure activities.
2. Increase knowledge of and involvement in leisure activity.

3. Learn leisure activity skills that are useful in school, home, and community environments.
4. Obtain necessary accommodations or adaptations to facilitate increased participation in recreational activities.
5. Family members and caregivers provide support, encouragement, and freedom to participate in chosen leisure activities.

__. ____

__. ____

__. ____

SHORT-TERM OBJECTIVES

1. Identify past and current interest and involvement in leisure and recreational activities. (1, 2, 3)
2. Sample a wide range of leisure activities by participating in a variety of recreational activities. (4, 5, 6)
3. Identify personal preferences for recreational activities. (6, 7, 8)
4. Identify specific leisure activities that are available within the home. (2, 7, 8, 9)
5. Research leisure activities available within the community and list those that are of interest. (10, 11, 12)
6. Identify personal resources or accommodations that will be necessary to participate in leisure activities. (13, 14)

THERAPEUTIC INTERVENTIONS

1. Review with the client his/her interests in various types of recreational activities. Elicit stories about his/her favorite recreational experiences.
2. Assess the client's existing leisure activity patterns (e.g., home-based or community-based activities), barriers to leisure activity, and personal characteristics impacting his/her leisure patterns (e.g., use the TRAIL Leisure Assessment Battery [TLAB; Dattilo and Hoge] for people with cognitive impairments).
3. Refer the client to an activity and recreation therapist to assess his/her interests and abilities in available recreational activities.

7. Cooperate with learning new leisure activity skills through meetings with a leisure educator. (15, 16)
8. Consent to the utilization of the necessary adaptations to allow safe participation in leisure activities. (14, 17, 18, 19)
9. Demonstrate the physical skills necessary to participate in desired leisure activities. (20, 21, 22, 23)
10. Demonstrate the social skills necessary for participation in many recreational activities. (24, 25, 26)
11. Make and initiate the implementation of personal choices regarding specific leisure pursuits. (27, 28, 29, 30)
12. Family members and caregivers encourage and reinforce the client's independent selection of and participation in his/her preferred leisure activities. (30, 31, 32, 33)
13. Initiate the selection of recreational activities during free time. (3, 7, 34, 35, 36)
14. Accept volunteers to aid in recreational and leisure activities. (15, 37, 38)
15. Engage in physical fitness activities to increase ability to participate in other leisure activities. (18, 39, 40, 41)
16. Increase the frequency of social interaction and the

4. Arrange for the client to experience a wide array of recreational and leisure activities to foster his/her ability to develop preferences. Schedule activities with a variety of individuals and settings.
5. Assign the client community-based experiences to introduce him/her to new free-time interests (e.g., volunteering at the animal shelter, attending free community musical concerts, or exploring a YMCA membership). Discuss these resources with the client, focusing on increasing his/her awareness of the available options.
6. Explore the client's culturally or ethnically diverse interests that may influence the enjoyment of leisure activities (e.g., with respect to music, jazz, rap, or rock). Probe for his/her preferences.
7. Encourage the client to identify specific recreational activities of personal interest by choosing from a wide range of age-appropriate leisure and recreational activities (e.g., hobbies, sports, crafts, table games, music, cultural activities, and social or community activities).
8. Arrange to have a person who knows the client well discern the client's nonverbal indications of preferences

building of friendships. (41, 42, 43)

17. Implement coping strategies to manage stress. (44, 45)
18. Identify financial resources available for recreational pursuits. (46, 47)

__. __________________________

__. __________________________

__. __________________________

for or interest in leisure activities.

9. Compare the results from the assessment of the client's leisure patterns and interests to the opportunities for leisure activities available in the client's home.
10. Request that the client generate a list of community activities from newspapers, community calendars, brochures, and/or the phone book.
11. Assist the client in gathering additional information on available community resources that correspond to his/her interests. Obtain information from community agencies, camps, facilities, advocacy groups, and entertainment businesses.
12. Verbally reinforce the client's interest in activities that promote community inclusion.
13. Assist the client in identifying the personal resources needed for his/her participation in identified leisure activities (e.g., free time, money, transportation, education, or adaptations).
14. Maximize the probability of client's success in initiating leisure activities within the community by facilitating accommodations for his/her intellectual or physical disabilities through education (e.g.,

community education classes) or adaptations (e.g., braces or prostheses).

15. Refer the client to a suitable leisure educator (e.g., certified therapeutic recreation specialist, family member, or volunteer). Provide the client with multiple choices of who to select as a leisure educator, if possible.
16. Facilitate the client's involvement in leisure education. Provide support and encouragement as the client learns new leisure activity skills.
17. Discuss with the client the degree of adaptation required for his/her leisure activity (e.g., materials used or environmental or instructional strategies). Facilitate the necessary adaptation.
18. Refer the client to a recreational therapist or nurse to assess his/her limitations due to health and safety issues.
19. Meet with family members and caregivers regarding their health and safety concerns for the client as new leisure activities are selected.
20. Model leisure activity skills for the client, providing many opportunities for repetition and practice of the newly acquired skills. Reinforce all imitative behavior.

21. Develop (or refer the client to a psychologist for) a behavior modification program to shape and reinforce the client's attending behaviors in order to increase his/her duration and interaction during leisure activity.
22. Perform (or refer the client to an activity therapist for) a task component analysis of complex activities to aid the client in learning small components of his/her desired recreational activities.
23. Provide leisure activity instructional prompts tailored to the client's learning style (e.g., verbal, environmental, visual, or kinesthetic).
24. Select a series of activities and games that the client has identified as being enjoyable to promote the practice of social skills, such as taking turns, following rules, being a good winner/loser, and cooperation (see Social Skills in this Planner).
25. Utilize role-playing, behavioral rehearsal, modeling, and role-reversal techniques to help the client acquire interpersonal skills.
26. Teach family members and caregivers to utilize specific games or activities to teach skills to the client (e.g., basic card games to teach taking turns; team sports to emphasize cooperation).

27. Assist the client in developing a specific plan for participation in identified leisure pursuits. Include logistic details (e.g., when and where), social details (e.g., who to socialize with), and financial concerns (e.g., how to pay for the activities).
28. Refer the client for or administer assertiveness training appropriate to his/her intellectual level and communication style. Encourage and reinforce the use of assertiveness techniques to persist in personal choices for leisure activities.
29. Reinforce the client's reports of success in implementing assertiveness, social contacts, or recreational involvement.
30. Encourage family members and caregivers to honor all of the client's reasonable decisions in order to foster his/her assertiveness and ability to make independent decisions.
31. Encourage family members and caregivers to be involved in the client's pleasurable activities to foster positive interaction within the home.
32. Meet with the client, family members, and caregivers to help them identify and vent emotions or concerns about the client's increased independence.

33. Advocate for the client when family members, caregivers, or other clinicians attempt to arbitrarily decrease the client's freedom to pursue personal recreational interests. Work with advocacy groups or client rights monitors to promote the client's desires.
34. Provide the client with a written and/or pictorial list of free-time activities to choose from. Encourage the client, family members, and caregivers to utilize the list to make leisure activity decisions during free times.
35. Verbally reinforce all the client's self-initiated independent filling of free time with mental-age-appropriate recreational activities.
36. Describe, list, and demonstrate free-time cues in the client's home, school, or vocational environment (e.g., break times, after chores are completed, and holidays) that could trigger a leisure activity.
37. Ask the client to identify individuals (or characteristics of such individuals) that he/she would like to have as volunteers to provide support in leisure pursuits.
38. Coordinate volunteers, family members, and others in supporting the client in his/her preferred leisure activities.

39. Refer the client for a physical evaluation of his/her ability to engage in physical fitness opportunities.
40. Verbally encourage physical activity as a healthy behavior that promotes physical fitness.
41. Coordinate the client's involvement in Special Olympics.
42. Provide information to the client's nondisabled peers on how to be a companion for a disabled person in order to ensure cooperative, friendly interactions (e.g., treat the client as an equal, take turns, and make positive statements).
43. Facilitate opportunities for the client to develop and maintain social relationships in his/her community (e.g., access to telephone, transportation, and social support groups).
44. Teach the client to self-initiate activities that have a calming effect on him/her. Provide the client with a list of identified activities to refer to as needed.
45. Assist the client in creating a master list of his/her anxious and angry responses and identified prosocial alternate responses. Encourage the client to keep the list nearby for easy reference (see Anger and Anxiety in this Planner).

46. Assist the client or guardian in developing a budget of his/her resources in order to provide needed funds for the client's recreational activities.
47. Link the client or guardian to resources within the community to assist in paying for the client's recreational pursuits (e.g., advocacy groups, businesses, civic organizations, or charities).

__. ____________________

__. ____________________

__. ____________________

DIAGNOSTIC SUGGESTIONS:

ICD-9-CM	*ICD-10-CM*	*DSM-5* Disorder, Condition, or Problem
299.00	F84.0	Autism Spectrum Disorder
317	F70	Intellectual Disability, Mild
319	F71	Intellectual Disability, Moderate
319	F72	Intellectual Disability, Severe
319	F73	Intellectual Disability, Profound
319	F79	Unspecified Intellectual Disability
V62.89	R41.83	Borderline Intellectual Functioning
____	____	__________
____	____	__________

RESIDENTIAL OPTIONS

BEHAVIORAL DEFINITIONS

1. Inability to maintain household because of physical and/or cognitive deficits.
2. Inadequate funds to meet housekeeping expenses and/or rent deposit.
3. History of residential placements and/or roommates dictated by convenient availability rather than client's preferences or needs.
4. Lack of necessary family support system to allow for semiindependent living options.
5. Loneliness and social isolation due to current residential constraints (e.g., rural setting, house rules, or limited transportation).
6. Lack of knowledge regarding community-supported supervised housing options.
7. Residential placement jeopardized and/or terminated with short notice due to increasing behavior problems or medical issues.

—. ____
____

—. ____
____

—. ____
____

LONG-TERM GOALS

1. Locate residential placement congruent with physical, emotional, and cognitive needs, preferences, and abilities.
2. Create own home based on personal values, lifestyle, and routines.
3. Acknowledge that personal assistance and support are needed to maintain semi-independent living.
4. Reside in clean, safe, and accessible housing that is blended into the community.
5. Secure adequate socialization opportunities in and outside of the home.
6. Identify and utilize creative financing options.

__. ____
____

__. ____
____

__. ____
____

SHORT-TERM OBJECTIVES

1. Identify personal needs and supervision requirements for residential placement. (1, 2)
2. Identify personal preferences, values, and lifestyle desired. (1, 3, 4)
3. Read agreement with family members regarding the amount and nature of support family members can provide for the housing situation. (2, 5)
4. Locate and select support staff outside of the family. (6, 7, 8, 9)

THERAPEUTIC INTERVENTIONS

1. Explore the client's feelings and preferences regarding all relevant variables pertaining to housing needs (e.g., physical and mental health, safety, existing relationships, finances, home maintenance, social activities, mobility, and transportation).
2. Discuss with the client and family members the amount of supervision and support needed by the client for medical issues, safety concerns, and housing support; facilitate unanimously agreeable

5. Family members and caregivers review the client's financial information in order to prepare a financial plan to meet the client's housing needs and abilities. (10, 11, 12)
6. Family members and caregivers develop a master list of the client's personal needs, support staff, financial resources, and identified residential needs and preferences, matching them with available housing options. (13, 14, 15)
7. Family members, caregivers, and client decide on an appropriate residence for the client. (16, 17)
8. Move into a new residential setting following short-notice termination of current residential setting. (18, 19)
9. Agree to a financial supervision plan. (20)
10. Process emotions pertaining to a change in residence. (21, 22)
11. Use a calendar to remind self of important dates in maintaining the residence. (23)
12. Obtain needed household items for the residence. (19, 24, 25, 26)
13. Support workers clearly state their responsibilities and duties. (27, 28)
14. Request needed training in those skills necessary to foster

or compromised supervision parameters.

3. Assess the client's strengths and weaknesses in self-determination (see the ARC's Self-Determination Scale [Wehmeyer]) and use the results to promote the client's involvement in his/her future residential planning.
4. Make a list with the client describing his/her ideal housing situation. Provide feedback on parameters that are currently available and those that are not currently available (e.g., barrier-free apartment, access to public transportation, or rent within budget).
5. Facilitate a discussion between the client and family members regarding the amount and nature of support desired by the client and what support the family is capable of providing (e.g., paying bills, coordinating paid supports, helping with household maintenance).
6. Assist the client in locating sources of support (e.g., family, friends, paid support, or volunteers) available to permit his/her success in a residential setting.
7. Assist the client in selecting support and back-up providers he/she feels comfortable with, and monitor and coordinate the client's support system.

increasingly independent living. (29, 30, 31)

15. Continue or increase social and recreational activities. (32, 33)
16. Family members and caregivers reinforce all the client's steps toward desired residential options. (34, 35, 36)
17. Client and family members address discrimination and rights violations. (37, 38, 39)

__. ____________________
____

__. ____________________
____

__. ____________________
____

8. Advise the client and family members on their option to request a background check on potential support providers to minimize the chances of the client experiencing abuse or neglect. Refer interested family members to the local law enforcement agency for details.
9. Coordinate paid support staff in receiving necessary training or in-service sessions to adequately guide and supervise the client (e.g., transfers, medications, first aid, or other client-specific issues).
10. Assist family members in organizing or personally compile the client's financial information to determine the monthly budget and financing options available to the client. Compare this information with the costs of different living arrangement options and determine the best strategy for planning for his/her residential needs.
11. Explain to the client and family members the different financial options available for individuals with developmental disabilities who desire and are capable of independent living (e.g., rental certificates, housing vouchers, housing cooperatives, or state and local rent subsidy programs).

12. Examine ways to reduce housing financing costs (e.g., housing finance agencies, HUD's Section 202 direct loan program, or community development block grants) and secure the program best suited to the client.
13. Assist the family members in compiling a master list of all the client's identified needs, preferences, needed supports, resources, and financial information.
14. Assist the client and family members in obtaining information on housing and support organizations in order to secure a residence most suitable to the client's identified needs (e.g., *Housing, Support, and Community: Choices and Strategies for Adults with Disabilities* [Racino, Walker, O'Connor, and Taylor] lists numerous housing and support organizations).
15. Refer the client and family members to community and faith-based resources for additional sources of information pertaining to residential opportunities (e.g., Association for Retarded Citizens [ARC] agencies, center for independent living, or church-based agencies).
16. Help the client and family members determine which residential setting, support

staff, and/or financial options best blend to provide the desired housing.

17. Assist the client in implementing the necessary steps to complete the residential plan (e.g., putting the lease and utilities in the client's name; opening checking and savings accounts).
18. Secure an alterative housing arrangement for the client that is suited to his/her needs.
19. Arrange for the client's possessions to be moved, change of address forms for the new residence to be filed, and assistance in getting settled in the new residence to be provided.
20. Request that the client identify what aspects of finances he/she will need assistance with, along with his/her preferences on who provides assistance with financial matters (e.g., family member, guardian, payee, or agency staff).
21. Explore the mixture of emotions (e.g., excitement, fear, apprehension, ambivalence, and reluctance) the client experiences associated with obtaining a new residence, and validate the normalcy of these feelings.
22. Encourage the client to process his/her emotions with an identified person and/or to keep a journal of his/her

emotions in order to prevent emotions from becoming problematic and interfering with the success of the new residential setting.

23. Use a calendar to identify important dates to prepare the client for the lengthy time frames involved in meeting the responsibilities of an independent residence.
24. Arrange for the client to obtain any necessary adaptive equipment needed in his/her residential environment (e.g., toilet or shower chair, positioners, or eating utensils).
25. Assist the client in making a list of all needed household items (e.g., dishes, appliances, and furniture), and identify places to obtain household items (e.g., yard sales, Goodwill, or Salvation Army).
26. Facilitate the client's opportunity to select and purchase needed household items.
27. Provide the support staff with a delineation of their responsibilities to the client, including the nature of personal care, household instructions, and day-to-day household management responsibilities.
28. Create a master list containing schedules, the household budget, medical information,

and a list of contacts as a reference for the support staff.

29. Arrange for the client to receive education of interest to him/her on needed home-living skills (see Cooking / Housekeeping Skills in this Planner).
30. Arrange for the client to receive education of interest to him/her regarding money management skills (see Financial/Shopping Skills in this Planner).
31. Arrange for the client to receive education of interest to him/her regarding household safety skills (see Household Safety Skills in this Planner).
32. Refer the client to a recreational therapist to determine possible leisure, social, and community activities available to the client.
33. Encourage the client's participation in Special Olympics or other athletic events.
34. Assist family members in becoming comfortable with choices the client has made. Facilitate this through discussions and recommend that family members read "Letting Go, Moving On: A Parent's Thoughts" (Chapter 8 in *Housing, Support, and Community: Choices and Strategies for Adults with Disabilities* [Racino, Walker, O'Connor, and Taylor]), *Home at Last: How Two*

Young Women with Profound Intellectual and Multiple Disabilities Achieved Their Own Home (Fitton, O'Brien, and Willson), or "Momanddad, i can reed nd rite" (Chapter 11 in *Parables of Hope* [Hoogewind]).

35. Encourage family members to permit the client to learn from his/her mistakes and have them verbally acknowledge the value of this experience in learning to be increasingly independent.
36. Advise family members and guardians who are opposed to and unsupportive of the client's realistic residential plan that the courts can be petitioned to have the guardianship removed and/or reassigned to another party.
37. Encourage family members and support staff to become familiar with current residential trends by providing sources of information (e.g., information published by the Center for Independent Living or *Disability Rights and Issues: A Consumer's Guide* [Michigan Protection and Advocacy Service]).
38. Recommend that family members read *Fair Housing for People with Disabilities: Legal Protections, Remedies, and Practical Strategies* (Stokes and Luker) to better understand how to deal with

discriminatory housing denials and evictions.

39. Report any violations of the Fair Housing Amendments Act (FHAA) or the Americans with Disabilities Act (ADA) to a recipient rights officer.

__. ____________________________
____

__. ____________________________
____

__. ____________________________
____

DIAGNOSTIC SUGGESTIONS:

ICD-9-CM	*ICD-10-CM*	*DSM-5* Disorder, Condition, or Problem
295.90	F20.9	Schizophrenia
296.xx	F32.x	Major Depressive Disorder, Single Episode
296.xx	F33.x	Major Depressive Disorder, Recurrent Episode
296.89	F31.81	Bipolar II Disorder
296.xx	F31.xx	Bipolar I Disorder
299.00	F84.0	Autism Spectrum Disorder
317	F70	Intellectual Disability, Mild
319	F71	Intellectual Disability, Moderate
319	F72	Intellectual Disability, Severe
319	F73	Intellectual Disability, Profound
319	F79	Unspecified Intellectual Disability
V62.89	R41.83	Borderline Intellectual Functioning
______	______	______________________________
______	______	______________________________

SELF-DETERMINATION

BEHAVIORAL DEFINITIONS

1. Lack of choice in daily life, school, residence, or vocation.
2. Limited experience with making decisions.
3. Poor planning for near and distant future resulting in difficult transitions.
4. Decreased responsibilities and opportunities due to mental impairments.
5. Limited freedom of choice due to agencies dictating the options and services that have been available.
6. Lack of skills necessary for living independently.
7. Vocational and/or residential placement failures due to lack of appropriate decision-making skills and inability to adjust to changing situations.
8. Lack of assertiveness and decision-making and problem-solving skills resulting from overprotection of the client by caregivers.
9. Client's choice of services and providers blocked by treatment agency structure.
10. Lack of knowledge or training in the concepts of self-determination on the part of client, family members, caregivers, and clinicians.

__. ____

____

__. ____

____

__. ____

____

LONG-TERM GOALS

1. Maximize available choices in all aspects of life.
2. Assertively advocate for own needs and preferences.
3. Increase understanding and identification of own needs and preferences.
4. Increase belief in self-worth and in ability to pursue own needs and desires.
5. Develop planning and goal-setting skills.
6. Caregivers consistently encourage and reinforce all of the client's movements toward his/her own decision making.
7. Develop and maintain lasting relationships with handicapped and nonhandicapped peers.
8. Plan for future needs to prepare for life-span transition periods.
9. Treatment agency revises structure to enhance the client's attempts to become more independent.
10. Caregivers, client, family members, and clinicians display a clear understanding of the intent and mechanics of self-determination.

__. ____
____

__. ____
____

__. ____
____

SHORT-TERM OBJECTIVES

1. Verbalize an understanding of the process of person-centered planning or self-determination. (1, 2, 3)
2. Clinician, caregivers, and family members verbalize an understanding of the process and spirit of person-centered planning and self-determination. (2, 3, 4, 5)
3. Participate in an assessment of skills that will facilitate

THERAPEUTIC INTERVENTIONS

1. Assess the client's understanding of self-determination or person-centered planning ideas.
2. Provide the opportunity for the client, caregivers, and family members to read literature (e.g., *Ten Steps to Independence: Promoting Self-Determination in the Home* [Davis]) and/or view videos (e.g., *Fred's Story* [Kranz] and

self-determination. (6, 7)

4. Develop a plan for a person-centered planning meeting. (8, 9, 10, 11, 12)
5. Prepare for the person-centered planning meeting by clarifying own goals and barriers to those goals. (13, 14, 15, 16)
6. Participate in a person-centered planning meeting. (17, 18, 19)
7. Identify short- and long-term hopes, dreams and desires. (20, 21)
8. Increase involvement in chosen recreational, social, employment, financial, and residential activities. (22, 23)
9. Demonstrate the ability to make choices that are safe, responsible, informed, and not harmful to self or others. (22, 24, 25, 26)
10. Choose service providers based on own preferences, needs, and financial resources. (27, 28, 29)
11. Service providers verbalize a recognition that the client has a choice of providers and must be given respectful, service-oriented treatment. (2, 4, 30)
12. Advocate for self, representing own best interest and exercising choices. (31, 32, 33)
13. Implement problem-solving techniques to resolve daily life issues. (34, 35)

the *Whose Decision Is It Anyway?* series, *Young Adults Working on Self-Determination* and *Parents Prompting Self-Determination* [Thorin]) on the topic of self-determination.

3. Help the client, family members, and caregivers identify examples of self-determination in their own lives as well as others'. Give personal examples of how one experiences self-determination. Provide factual information to the client as needed.
4. Invite the client, family members, and caregivers to agency training sessions on person-centered planning and self-determination.
5. Encourage the client, family members, and caregivers to discuss the use of self-determination principles relative to the client's treatment, dreams and desires.
6. Assess the client's strengths and weaknesses in self-determination (e.g., assess the degree of the client's autonomy, self-regulation, psychological empowerment, and self-realization) using a structured interview and/or an objective instrument (e.g., ARC's Self-Determination Scale [Wehmeyer]). Use the results to promote the client's involvement in planning

14. Express preferences and choices in all aspects of personal life. (32, 36, 37, 38, 39)
15. Review own behavior and assess whether it is focused on goal attainment. (40, 41)
16. Develop cooperative relationships with peers with and without developmental disabilities. (42, 43, 44, 45)
17. Increase participation in community-based opportunities for social, recreation, and vocational activities. (46, 47, 48)
18. Family members support and reinforce the client in making his/her own decisions. (49, 50, 51, 52, 53)
19. Client and family members advocate for greater self-determination within the agency and the mental health and welfare systems. (54, 55)

__. ______________________________

____

__. ______________________________

____

__. ______________________________

____

future goals with the support of family members.

7. Share the findings from the client's self-determination assessment with the client, family members, and caregivers, emphasizing the client's strengths.
8. Facilitate the client's developing an agenda for a person-centered planning meeting (e.g., listing the goals the client would like to achieve); pursue the client's leadership in identifying what should be accomplished at the meeting.
9. Assist the client in inviting all individuals he/she would like to be present during the person-centered planning meeting (e.g., clinicians, family members, peers, advocates, and friends). Allow the client to choose the members, as well as how they are invited and where the meeting is held.
10. Review with the client the people he/she would prefer not to have at the meeting, and the procedure he/she wishes to use if a person on that list indicates an interest in coming. Review the implications of not inviting a specific individual.
11. Request that the client choose a facilitator for the person-centered planning meeting. Emphasize that this

does not have to be a clinical person.

12. Allow the client to identify off-limits topics (e.g., topics he/she does not wish to be brought up at the person-centered planning meeting). Prompt the client to identify a setting in which he/she would be willing to discuss those topics.
13. Taking direction from the client, use a written personal planning workbook such as PATH (Pearpoint) to review the client's dreams and desires for his/her life.
14. Assist the client in describing his/her current daily life, relationships, personal history, preferences, dreams, hopes and fears, community choices, and issues related to home, career, and health.
15. Request that the client identify barriers that interfere with his/her stated desires; assist in identifying the kinds of support needed to attain future goals and dreams.
16. Request that the client identify areas he/she would like to improve (e.g., living situation, work setting, or relationships).
17. Have the facilitator or the client call the person-centered planning meeting to order, focusing the

participants on the client and his/her desires and needs.

18. Ask the participants in the person-centered planning meeting to direct their comments to the client, rather than to the clinician or the facilitator.
19. Pose questions such as "Who is ______?"; "What are ______'s strengths and problems?"; "What supports, accommodations, or barriers exist?"; and "What shall we put in the action plan for goals and objectives?" Ask the client to answer first, then the rest of the participants.
20. Assist the client in making a list of his/her short- and long-term goals. Request that the client identify his/her favorite three. Ensure that continuity exists between short-term and long-term goals and that those goals are objectively observable and attainable in a reasonable amount of time.
21. Assist the client in identifying and creating conditions that will facilitate the realization of his/her goals and desires (e.g., expand and deepen friendships, increase community participation, exercise more control and choice in life, and develop competencies). Identify creative solutions for breaking

existing barriers to the identified goals.

22. Explore the client's desires to participate in a wide range of possible activities (e.g., social contacts, independent living, volunteer or work placement, service groups, and church or recreational events) that promote community integration and the development of self-determination skills.
23. Arrange for all significant people in the client's life (e.g., family members, advocates, community members, staff, and agency personnel) to brainstorm creative options for the expansion of the client's personal choices and to commit to assisting the client in attaining the identified goals.
24. Assess the client's potential for making adverse choices. Help determine the risk of the choices resulting in physical and/or mental harm by talking with the client, family members, and professionals, as well as by direct observation.
25. Weigh the assessed level of risk of harm against the client's right to make his/her own choices. Factor in the likelihood of short- or long-term harm, physical or psychological harm, direct or indirect harm, and predictable or unpredictable

harm to the client or others. Use these findings to determine the degree of freedom of choice best suited for the client (e.g., total independence with unrestricted choice or limited independence with restricted options available from which to choose).

26. Obtain a consensus from the client, family members, and support staff regarding the level of risk that is tolerable and the degree of freedom of choice that is the client's right.
27. Remind the client or guardian that he/she has a choice about the services provided, who provides them, and where he/she receives these services.
28. Develop a listing or network of providers for the client or guardian to choose from, which may include the clinician's own services.
29. List the costs of all the currently provided services. Provide the client with the cost of each individual service and provider that is available and appropriate for meeting his/her needs. Allow the client or guardian to choose whatever services and providers they see fit within their financial resources or the agency funds allotted for that client.
30. Focus the service providers on the need to provide

customer service and emphasize that the client has a choice of providers available. (Help the provider adopt a "We need them!" philosophy rather than "They need us.")

31. Help the client identify actual examples from his/her life when he/she has used decision-making skills such as gathering information, weighing pros and cons, and consulting with others.

32. Teach the client techniques for assertive self-advocacy, such as those listed in *The Self-Advocacy Manual for Consumers* (Michigan Protection and Advocacy Service) or *The Self-Advocacy Workbook* (Gardner). Promote self-advocacy and leadership by providing practice opportunities whenever possible (e.g., with counselors, personal care support personnel, and residential supervisors).

33. Teach the client the difference between passive, assertive, and aggressive behaviors. Model assertive, aggressive, and passive responses to the same situation, and request that the client identify the most effective style.

34. Teach the client problem-solving techniques such as those in *Thinking It Through: Teaching a Problem-Solving Strategy for Community Living*

(Foxx and Bittle). Use role-playing and modeling to reinforce the techniques.

35. Encourage the client to keep a problem-solving log of his/her conflicts to prompt regular use of problem-solving techniques. Review problem-solving logs with the client.
36. Assess the client's responses to various activities and situations to better understand his/her preferences (e.g., approach, verbalizations, gestures, and affect).
37. Provide opportunities for the client to choose in all areas of his/her life (e.g., leisure, shopping, mealtime, lifestyle, or employment).
38. Stress with family members, caregivers, and support staff the importance of the client being able to express his/her own choices and preferences and have them honored.
39. Plan for the client's self-determination skills generalization by providing many learning opportunities, expanding the range of situations the client responds to, and ensuring similarity between the learning stimuli and the client's natural environment.
40. Review the client's decisions with him/her, and encourage the client to evaluate his/her

own behavior to determine if it is compatible with the identified goals. Assist the client in changing his/her behavior as needed to obtain goals.

41. Request that the client identify reinforcers he/she desires that can be attained as rewards for achieving his/her own predetermined target behaviors.

42. Teach the client social skills through didactic presentation and role-playing (e.g., basic conversational skills, self-assertion, honesty, truthfulness, and how to handle teasing; see Social Skills in this Planner).

43. Arrange for the client to utilize social skills in situations he/she has identified as being desirable.

44. Urge the client to take risks in participating in social situations with people who have a disability and those who do not, and reinforce him/her for doing so.

45. With proper authorization to release information, provide feedback to family members and peers who do not have developmental disabilities about how to best approach the client and his/her needs (e.g., with equality, respect, and reciprocity of friendship).

46. Teach the client about the availability and use of

community resources (see Recreation/Leisure Activities in this Planner).

47. Teach the client community access skills (see Community Access in this Planner).
48. Assist the client in obtaining employment via a supported employment referral or by assisting with the preparation of a resume, and job applications. (See Supported Employment in this Planner.)
49. Encourage family members and caregivers to identify a plan of supporting lifelong learning opportunities and experiences for the client. Assist in identifying specific steps to promote the client's decision making, problem solving, goal setting, and attainment, as well as self-awareness and knowledge in the home.
50. Demonstrate to family members the many opportunities throughout the day that the client can use for exerting choices and preferences (e.g., meal choices, schedule for the day, and clothing choices).
51. Encourage family members to foster independence by helping only when needed, permitting the client to maximize his/her abilities.
52. Recommend that family members read *Ten Steps to Independence: Promoting*

Self-Determination in the Home (Davis).

53. Emphasize with the family members that freedom to make choices, even harmful ones, is a freedom most people value. Encourage family members to allow the client to assume responsibility for his/her own actions and the natural consequences, both positive and negative, which result.

54. Encourage family members and the client to be involved in positions of leadership, advocacy, or advisorship within the agency.

55. Support and encourage the family's efforts in petitioning, lobbying, writing letters to legislators, and/or meeting with legislators to advocate for the right of self-determination for people with mental illnesses. *Making Your Case* (Minnesota Governor's Planning Council on Developmental Disabilities) provides helpful information for families embarking on making policy changes.

__. ____________________________

____

__. ____________________________

____

__. ____________________________

____

DIAGNOSTIC SUGGESTIONS:

ICD-9-CM	*ICD-10-CM*	*DSM-5* Disorder, Condition, or Problem
299.00	F84.0	Autism Spectrum Disorder
317	F70	Intellectual Disability, Mild
319	F71	Intellectual Disability, Moderate
319	F72	Intellectual Disability, Severe
319	F73	Intellectual Disability, Profound
319	F79	Unspecified Intellectual Disability
V62.89	R41.83	Borderline Intellectual Functioning
______	______	______________________________
______	______	______________________________

SEXUALLY INAPPROPRIATE BEHAVIORS

BEHAVIORAL DEFINITIONS

1. Unfamiliarity with common social-sexual behaviors.
2. Lack of understanding of appropriate public and private behavior, as evidenced by displaying sexualized behavior in public places.
3. Inappropriate initiation of sexual activity toward others.
4. Difficulties identifying sexual and other body parts.
5. Lack of understanding of basic human sexuality.
6. Sexualized behavior that is motivated by attention seeking, boredom, or escape and avoidance variables.
7. Initiation of harmful or criminal sexual behavior.
8. Repetitive masturbatory behavior, most often without reaching orgasm.

—. ____
____

—. ____
____

—. ____
____

LONG-TERM GOALS

1. Learn common social-sexual behaviors.
2. Utilize healthy sexual behaviors only in appropriate places and at appropriate times.
3. Identify sexual and other body parts.
4. Gain knowledge about basic sexuality.
5. Identify differences between public and private sexual behaviors.
6. Terminate harmful and criminal sexual behavior.

—. ____

____

—. ____

____

—. ____

____

SHORT-TERM OBJECTIVES

1. Describe areas of question and concern regarding sexuality. (1)
2. Verbalize accurate information on sexual functioning, using appropriate terms for sexually related body parts. (2, 3, 4, 5, 6)
3. Discuss sexual attitudes learned throughout life. (7, 8, 9)
4. Verbalize accepted standards of social-sexual behavior. (10, 11, 12, 13)
5. Verbalize the potential negative consequences of inappropriate sexual behavior. (5, 6, 14, 15)
6. Verbalize the rights and responsibilities associated with sexual behavior. (16, 17, 18, 19)
7. Identify harmful and dangerous sexual behavior. (20, 21, 22, 23)
8. Identify sexual behaviors that are criminal. (24, 25)
9. Educate family members and caregivers on appropriate responses to the client's sexual expression. (5, 26, 27, 28)

THERAPEUTIC INTERVENTIONS

1. Solicit information from the client, family members, and caregivers to determine if the client has any questions, misperceptions, or fears about topics related to sexuality.
2. Provide education on body parts and their function and request that the client identify the differences between males and females.
3. Desensitize and educate the client by talking freely and respectfully regarding sexual body parts, sexual feelings, and sexual behaviors.
4. Obtain a curriculum to teach sexuality at an appropriate education level and present it to the client.
5. Affirm the client's rights to controlled and appropriate sexual expression by advocating with family members, caregivers, and other professionals.
6. Validate the normalcy and universality of sexual urges while pointing out the need

10. Express familiarity with the agency's policy on sexuality. (29)
11. Cooperate with assessment of sexual behaviors to determine if further treatment is indicated. (30, 31, 32)
12. Cooperate with medical and pharmacological consultations to assess impact on sexual functioning. (33, 34)
13. Participate in enjoyable leisure activities to prevent boredom and reduce frequency of public masturbation. (32, 35, 36, 37)
14. Request attention from caregivers in a socially acceptable fashion. (32, 37)
15. Practice sexually expressive behaviors in the proper place and time. (38, 39)
16. Parent or guardian and agency consent to the client receiving masturbation training. (40)
17. Participate in prescriptive guidelines for masturbation training. (41)

__. ____________________________

____

__. ____________________________

____

__. ____________________________

____

for control, respect, and privacy.

7. Request that the client identify moral values related to sexuality.
8. Explore the role of family members and others in influencing the client's attitudes regarding sexuality.
9. Request that family members identify their moral values related to sexuality.
10. Teach the client commonly accepted standards of social-sexual behavior, describing positive and negative examples.
11. Present an opportunity for the client to view educational slides and hear accurate information regarding sexuality among persons with severe developmental disabilities (e.g., examples of male/female anatomy, appropriate male/female sexual behavior and appropriate male/female social behavior).
12. Query the client on his/her understanding of positive (e.g., holding hands, arms across shoulders, and brief kisses) and negative (e.g., long, full body embraces, sitting on laps, and extended kisses) examples of social-sexual behavior; reinforce appropriate judgment.
13. Assist the client in identifying acceptable circumstances under which sexual behavior can occur.

14. Teach the client that sexual behavior needs to conform to societal standards of respect for others and the need for privacy.
15. Discuss the potential negative consequences (e.g., offending the other person, being arrested for sexual assault or exposing self, unwanted pregnancy, and embarrassing self and others) of sexually inappropriate behavior.
16. Teach the client the importance of mutual consent in all sexual activity with a partner.
17. Teach the client how appropriateness of physical contact depends on the specific situation (e.g., at work, at school, or at home alone).
18. Discuss potentially difficult situations the client may encounter as a sexual person (e.g., locating private places, family and societal values, birth control, and lack of understanding of client's sexuality) to assist him her in making good decisions.
19. Teach the client that he/she has the right to stop at any point in sexual activity and a partner must respect that right.
20. List harmful sexual behaviors that could result in physical or psychological harm (e.g., rape, HIV, intravenous drug use), and have the client identify why each behavior is harmful.

21. Assist the client in identifying what steps he/she should take (e.g., assertively and forcefully saying no, using barrier contraceptives, and avoiding drugs) to prevent harmful behaviors from occurring to him/her.
22. Assist the client in identifying how to avoid engaging in harmful or dangerous sexual behavior.
23. Recommend that the client read (or read to the client) *Learn to Be Safe* (Association for Retarded Citizens [ARC]) to promote understanding about AIDS and safer sex. Process with the client the different behaviors he/she can engage in to reduce the risk of contracting HIV (e.g., abstinence, monogamy, and safer sex).
24. Identify behaviors that constitute sex crimes and have the client describe why these are illegal, as well as how they differ from noncriminal sexualized behaviors.
25. Assess the client's understanding of harmful and criminal sexual behaviors.
26. Educate family members by having them read *I Contact* (Hingsburger) and view *Person to Person* (Carmody, Lieberman, and Pacale) to promote the reality of individuals with developmental disabilities as sexual human beings.

27. Educate family members and caregivers on how to deal with sexual behavior by having them watch the video *Objectively Dealing with Sexual Behavior* (McGwin and Born) or read *Shared Feelings: A Parent Guide to Sexuality Education for Children, Adolescents, and Adults Who Have a Mental Hadicap* (Maksym).
28. Recommend that family members read *HIV and AIDS Prevention Guide for Parents* (Lerro) in order to better understand pertinent information that should be taught to the client on how to protect himself/herself and to gain an understanding of the ARC's position on sexuality for those with developmental disabilities.
29. Review the agency's policy on sexuality for mental health consumers with the client, family members, and caregivers. (To review an exemplary agency policy, see *Human Sexuality Handbook: Guiding People toward Positive Expressions of Sexuality* [Brown, Carney, Cortis, Metz, and Petrie].)
30. Assess the frequency and severity of the client's public or ineffective sexual behavior from staff reports.
31. Gather information or collect data from caregivers for 2 weeks to establish a baseline on the precursor conditions,

frequency, and topography of the client's sexual behavior.

32. Assess the role of boredom or attention-seeking behavior as the motivating variable for the client's masturbatory behavior.
33. Assess the possible role that substance abuse, diabetes, hypertension, or thyroid disease may have on the client's sexual functioning.
34. Review medications taken by the client with regard to their possible negative side effects on sexual functioning (e.g., diuretics, anorexants, narcotic analgesics, muscle relaxants, antidepressants, and antipsychotic agents).
35. Assess whether redirecting the client to other leisure activities overcomes boredom that may trigger his/her public masturbation.
36. Present the client with a variety of his/her preferred leisure activities to prevent boredom.
37. Teach the client to perform a specific replacement or incompatible behavior to get the staff's attention besides public masturbation.
38. Confront the client's inappropriate behavior by describing why it is unacceptable.
39. Verbally prompt the client to relocate from a public location to a private location as a place to engage in sexual gratification behavior. If verbal prompts are not effective,

physically guide him/her to a designated private location.

40. Obtain the guardian's and agency's consent to offer masturbatory training to the client.
41. Refer the client to a professional knowledgable in human sexuality in people with developmental disabilities to assess the client's ineffective sexualized behaviors and need for masturbation training.

__. ______________________________

____

__. ______________________________

____

__. ______________________________

____

DIAGNOSTIC SUGGESTIONS:

ICD-9-CM	*ICD-10-CM*	*DSM-5* Disorder, Condition, or Problem
299.00	F84.0	Autism Spectrum Disorder
302.4	F65.2	Exhibitionistic Disorder (Exhibitionism)
302.81	F65.0	Fetishistic Disorder (Fitishism)
302.89	F65.81	Frotteuristic Disorder (Frotteurism)
302.84	F65.52	Sexual Sadism Disorder
302.82	F65.3	Voyeuristic Disorder (Voyeurism)
302.2	F65.4	Pedophilic Disorder
302.9	F65.9	Unspecified Paraphilic Disorder
312.30	F91.9	Unspecified Disruptive, Impulse-Control, and Conduct Disorder
302.73	F52.31	Female Orgasmic Disorder
302.74	F52.32	Delayed Ejaculation

317	F70	Intellectual Disability, Mild
319	F71	Intellectual Disability, Moderate
319	F72	Intellectual Disability, Severe
319	F73	Intellectual Disability, Profound
319	F79	Unspecified Intellectual Disability
V62.89	R41.83	Borderline Intellectual Functioning
______	______	______________________________
______	______	______________________________

SLEEP DISTURBANCE

BEHAVIORAL DEFINITIONS

1. Difficulty in going to sleep, staying asleep, and/or returning to sleep.
2. Chronic daytime sleepiness regardless of amount of nighttime sleep.
3. Poor functioning as evidenced by slower reaction time, distortions in perception, low energy levels, and/or poor attention or memory capabilities.
4. Sleep disturbance interfering with community integration, vocational, and habilitative activities.
5. Medical problems such as sleep apnea, restless leg syndrome, or circadian rhythm interruption contributing to sleep disturbance.
6. Medical conditions such as migraines, heart conditions, respiratory disorders, and gastroesophageal reflux contributing to insomnia.
7. Sleep-related bruxism.
8. Severity of sleep problem inversely related to level of intellectual disability.
9. Psychiatric condition contributing to and/or exacerbated by sleep disturbance.

—. ____
____

—. ____
____

—. ____
____

LONG-TERM GOALS

1. Develop consistent sleep/wake schedule with an adequate amount of restful, refreshing sleep.
2. Improve performance in daily activities.
3. Address medical concerns contributing to sleep disturbance.
4. Address psychological issues contributing to sleep disturbance.

__. ____

____

__. ____

____

__. ____

____

SHORT-TERM OBJECTIVES

1. Participate in assessment of sleep history and habits. (1, 2, 3)
2. Cooperate with medical examination to rule out biomedical etiologies for the sleep disturbance. (4, 5)
3. Make lifestyle choices that support an improved sleep pattern. (6)
4. Implement a consistent sleep induction routine. (6, 7)
5. Create a bedroom environment conducive to sleep. (8)
6. Terminate daytime naps beyond one for 30 minutes or less. (9)
7. Take natural supplements to aide in sleep induction. (10)
8. Utilize the bed as a place for sleep only. (11, 12)

THERAPEUTIC INTERVENTIONS

1. Arrange for or conduct an assessment of the client's sleep history and consumption habits (e.g., food, caffeine, or alcohol) in order to determine the impact on his/her sleep disturbance.
2. Provide the client, family members, or caregivers with a form to collect data on the client's sleep patterns during several 24-hour periods in order to establish his/her pattern of disturbance.
3. Arrange for or conduct an assessment of and treatment for depression, anxiety, or life stressors as causal factors in the client's disruptive sleep habits.
4. Arrange for the client to obtain a complete physical to rule out any biomedical

9. Get up at a consistent time each morning. (13)
10. Retire to bed on a gradually later basis until the desired time is reached for a consistent sleep/wake cycle. (14)
11. Exercise on a regular basis. (15)
12. Utilize stress management steps to deal constructively with life's conflicts. (16, 17)
13. Utilize deep muscle relaxation procedures to aid in sleep induction. (17)
14. Take prescribed medication to regulate sleep pattern. (18)

—. ______________________________
____

—. ______________________________
____

—. ______________________________
____

explanations for his/her sleep disturbance.

5. Consult with a physician or pharmacist regarding medications the client takes that may have a negative impact on his/her sleep.
6. Advise the client regarding changes in his/her food or liquid consumption (e.g., avoiding caffeine, alcohol, and late or spicy meals) or lifestyle habits (e.g., avoiding late-night exercising and emotional or cognitive stimulation) which would promote restful sleep.
7. Solicit input from the client or a party who knows the client's preferences to develop a consistent nighttime routine (e.g., a relaxing bath, low stimulation, a movie or reading, and listening to soothing music), and get his/her committment to implement such activities.
8. Assist the client in creating a bedroom environment conducive to sleep (e.g., a quiet, dark room with a comfortable bed and pillow).
9. Contract with the client, family members, or caregivers to eliminate daytime naps or schedule one short nap (30 minutes or less) early in the afternoon.
10. Discuss with the client, family members, and caregivers different vitamins, minerals, and herbs which, under a physician's direction, may

assist in promoting sleep (e.g., niacin, folic acid, ma gnesium, calcium, and lime blossom or primrose teas).

11. Educate the client, family members, and caregivers on the importance of using the bed only for sleeping or sexual activity and of getting up if unable to fall asleep within 15 minutes.
12. Instruct the client to stay up (or have family members or caregivers assist the client in staying up) until he/she feels sleepy.
13. Contract with the client for a consistent morning wake-and-arise time regardless of the time he/she falls asleep.
14. Gradually move the client's bedtime closer to the desired bedtime in order to reset his/her circadian cycle (chronotherapy).
15. Work with the client to identify an enjoyable, practical, and consistent exercise pattern.
16. Teach the client stress mana gement exercises (e.g., problem solving and assertiveness) by modeling positive and negative examples. Request that he/she repeat modeled skills (see Anger in this Planner).
17. Teach the client relaxation exercises (e.g., deep breathing, progressive muscle relaxation, or imagery).
18. Consult with or refer the client to a physician for

pharmacological options to promote consistent sleep patterns.

__. ____________________

____

__. ____________________

____

__. ____________________

____

DIAGNOSTIC SUGGESTIONS:

ICD-9-CM	*ICD-10-CM*	*DSM-5* Disorder, Condition, or Problem
307.42	F51.01	Insomnia
347.00	G47.419	Narcolepsy without Cataplexy but with Hypocretin Deficiency
347.01	G47.411	Narcolepsy with Cataplexy but without Hypocretin Deficiency
327.23	G47.33	Obstructive Sleep Apnea Hypopnea
307.44	F51.11	Hypersomnolence Disorder
307.45	G47.xx	Circadian Rhythm Sleep-Wake Disorder
307.47	F51.5	Nightmare Disorder
307.46	F51.4	Non-Rapid Eye Movement Sleep Arousal Disorder, Sleep Terror Type
307.46	F51.3	Non-Rapid Eye Movement Sleep Arousal Disorder, Sleepwalking Type
317	F70	Intellectual Disability, Mild
319	F71	Intellectual Disability, Moderate
319	F72	Intellectual Disability, Severe
319	F73	Intellectual Disability, Profound
319	F79	Unspecified Intellectual Disability
V62.89	R41.83	Borderline Intellectual Functioning
______	______	____________________
______	______	____________________

SOCIAL SKILLS

BEHAVIORAL DEFINITIONS

1. Difficulty initiating, maintaining, or joining in conversations with others, as evidenced by awkward social interactions.
2. Strained interpersonal relationships resulting from inappropriate or exaggerated emotional responses.
3. Inflexibility and a lack of personal responsibility in social relationships.
4. Limitations in problem-solving skills, resulting in overdependence upon others for assistance.
5. Lack of honesty and forthrightness, negatively impacting relationships with others.
6. Limited cooperation with others, as evidenced by a lack of volunteering, offering assistance, or following directions, as well as an increased tendency to go along with group consensus.
7. Lack of skills to be assertive in making peer choices to avoid problem social situations.
8. Lack of understanding of the different types of social relationships.
9. Lower than expected social skills resulting from overprotection of client by caregiver.

—. ____
____

—. ____
____

—. ____
____

LONG-TERM GOALS

1. Exhibit basic conversational skills, as evidenced by maintaining interactions with others, appropriate to cognitive level.
2. Improve quality of interpersonal relationships with family, friends, and coworkers.
3. Routinely follow reasonable directions and requests from others.
4. Accept responsibility for own choices.
5. Learn and implement social skills that allow for controlled, appropriate expression of emotions.
6. Display problem-solving skills in situations that promote self-sufficiency.
7. Prioritize and practice honesty and truthfulness in daily activities.
8. Demonstrate cooperative skills to enhance interpersonal relationships.
9. Assert self in peer-pressure situations to make healthy, independent choices.

—. ____

____

—. ____

____

—. ____

____

SHORT-TERM OBJECTIVES

1. Participate in an assessment of social skills. (1, 2, 3)
2. Adhere to training recommendations made from social skills evaluation. (4)
3. Maximize social skills acquisition by participating in social skills training exercises. (5, 6)
4. List potential reinforcers or rewards to be earned following progress with social skills. (7)

THERAPEUTIC INTERVENTIONS

1. Arrange for an assessment of the client's social skills to establish a baseline of the client's ability and to gain insight into his/her strengths and weaknesses.
2. Ask family members or caregivers to complete the Social Performance Survey Schedule (Matson, Helsel, Bellack, and Senatore) prior to and after treatment.

5. Cooperate with psychiatric evaluation and take prescribed psychotropic medications to reduce social skills deficits. (8, 9)
6. Implement basic social interaction skills. (10, 11, 12)
7. Participate in activities between sessions that will foster social skills development (e.g., role-playing, supervised interactions, and question-and-answer sessions). (7, 13, 14, 15)
8. Utilize social skills in group and one-on-one situations directed by the counselor. (7, 16, 17, 18, 19)
9. Generalize learned social skills from training situations to relevant, diversified environments. (7, 20)
10. Identify labels for and trigger events of strong emotions. (21, 22)
11. Demonstrate the ability to control and express strong emotions in a socially acceptable manner. (7, 23, 24)
12. Independently solve problems of daily living situations. (7, 25)
13. Utilize knowledge of the types of interpersonal relationships by increasing functioning in each type of relationship. (7, 26, 27, 28)
14. Family members and caregivers reduce the frequency of handling social matters for the client that he/she is capable of dealing with

3. Provide direct feedback to the client, family members, and caregivers on the results of an assessment.
4. Obtain consensus from the client, family members, school officials, and caregivers regarding suitable social skills training programs or interventions that build on the client's strengths and compensate for his/her weaknesses; make referral to the selected program.
5. Encourage parents, caregivers, and teachers to model social skills that the client can imitate.
6. Develop a specific plan regarding social skills to be taught, modalities to be used, and the number of sessions needed.
7. Assist the client in listing potential rewards that can be used to reinforce behavioral progress in social skills training.
8. Arrange for a psychiatric evaluation to determine if a concomitant Axis I disorder may be contributing to the client's poor social skills and whether psychotropic medication may be helpful.
9. Enlist the help of family members and caregivers to monitor the signs and symptoms of the client's psychiatric condition in order

independently. (5, 29, 30, 31, 32, 33)

15. Increase participation in extracurricular activities and outings. (34, 35, 36, 37)

__. ____________________________
____

__. ____________________________
____

__. ____________________________
____

to provide accurate information to the psychiatrist.

10. Present social skills of benefit to the client (e.g., basic conversational skills, self-assertion, honesty, truthfulness, and how to handle teasing), identifying critical components, while providing positive and negative role-playing to the client for each skill. Reward progress using a predetermined schedule of reinforcement.

11. Assess the client's comprehension of presented skills b y requesting that he/she verbalize or role-play social skills.

12. Assess the client's ability to conform his/her behavior to acquired knowledge of social skills through spontaneous role-playing, self-reports, and reports from caregivers or supervisors.

13. Provide homework (e.g., initiating a conversation with a stranger, inviting a friend to participate in an activity, or ignoring teasing) to the client in order to promote skills acquisition between sessions.

14. Arrange for family members and caregivers to be informed about the skills worked on in each session, and encourage them to model skills for the client and provide positive reinforcement to him/her for

utilizing the newly acquired skills.

15. Arrange for the client to practice social skills in contrived and *in vivo* social situations.
16. Utilize recreational activities such as board games, directed drawing or worksheets, treasure hunts, or arts and crafts projects to promote good listening skills and create opportunities to teach and role-play relevant interactional skills.
17. Design cooperative tasks for a group to work on such as a large mural, games requiring teamwork, and group problems to solve.
18. Provide fun, cooperative, interactive activities to foster development of the client's social skills (e.g., see *Social Skills Activities* [Mannix]).
19. Arrange for the client to play educational games to facilitate learning social skills (e.g., Stacking the Deck: A Social Skills Game for Adults with Developmental Disabilities [Foxx and McMorrow]).
20. Plan for social skills generalization by providing many learning opportunities, expanding the range of stimuli the client responds to, and providing similarity between learning stimuli

and the client's natural environment.

21. Teach the client about the different emotions and how to identify the triggering event of an emotion (e.g., "I am angry because I was not considered for a job").
22. Request that the client identify his/her own problematic emotions and the situations that elicit those problematic emotions.
23. Assist the client in identifying healthy ways to control and express problematic emotions, role-playing his/her identified strategies. Utilize role-reversal techniques to teach the impact of his/her negative behavior on others.
24. Provide the client with a written or pictorial form of his/her problematic emotions, triggers, and healthy responses so this can be referred to in the future.
25. Teach the client problem-solving techniques (e.g., using *Thinking It Through: Teaching a Problem-Solving Strategy for Community Living* [Foxx and Bittle]).
26. Visibly portray the different types of interpersonal relationships (e.g., with coworkers, acquaintances, friends, or close friends and family; see *Circles I: Relationships and Relationship Building* [Champagne and Walker-Hirsh]).

27. Request that the client identify people he/she knows in his/her own life and then place these people in the appropriate relationship circle.
28. Provide information on the types of behaviors (e.g., polite hellos, handshakes, or hugs for greetings) associated with the different types of interpersonal relationships and query the client's understanding by using role-playing.
29. Provide family members and caregivers with the training needed to support the client's advancement in social skills acquisition (e.g., reading materials, information from social skills training, or educational videos).
30. Urge family members and caregiver to provide the client with a variety of activities to promote social skills development in order to foster the client's social skills acquisition.
31. Encourage family members and caregivers to promote the client's independence in social situations by permitting him/her to handle problematic situations.
32. Encourage family members and caregivers to agree to promote lifelong learning opportunities and experiences for the client in order to promote his/her choice making, decision making, problem solving, goal setting, and attainment,

along with self-awareness and knowledge.

33. Urge the client to take risks in using new skills in social situations in the practice of increased and improved socialization, and reinforce him/her for doing so.
34. Refer the client to a recreational therapist to determine possible leisure and community activities available to the client.
35. Encourage the client's participation in Special Olympics or other athletic events.
36. Assess the client's and/or family members' interest in faith-based activities and provide access to church ministry.
37. Refer family members and caregivers to *Dimensions of Faith and Congregational Ministries with Persons with Developmental Disabilities and their Families* (Gavanta) to obtain information on many different faith-based books, videos, and programs available for persons with developmental disabilities and their families.

__. ______________________________

____

__. ______________________________

____

__. ______________________________

____

DIAGNOSTIC SUGGESTIONS:

ICD-9-CM	*ICD-10-CM*	*DSM-5* Disorder, Condition, or Problem
299.00	F84.0	Autism Spectrum Disorder
317	F70	Intellectual Disability, Mild
319	F71	Intellectual Disability, Moderate
319	F72	Intellectual Disability, Severe
319	F73	Intellectual Disability, Profound
319	F79	Unspecified Intellectual Disability
V62.89	R41.83	Borderline Intellectual Functioning
_____	_____	______________________
_____	_____	______________________

STEREOTYPIC MOVEMENT DISORDER

BEHAVIORAL DEFINITIONS

1. Repetitive, nonfunctional behavior, as evidenced by rocking, mouthing objects, skin picking, or self-injurious behavior (SIB).
2. Significant tissue damage resulting from SIB, as evidenced by amputation, bruising, open wounds, and/or loss of vision.
3. Behaviors interfering with adaptive, vocational, emotional, and social growth.
4. High level of motor tension such as restlessness, tiredness, shakiness, or muscle tension.

—. ____

____

—. ____

____

—. ____

____

LONG-TERM GOALS

1. Reduce or eliminate the frequency and intensity of stereotypic motor behavior.
2. Resolve conditions that are antecedent and maintaining variables for stereotypic motor behavior.
3. Improve health status by permitting damaged tissue to heal.
4. Increase participation in habilitative, vocational, and leisure activities.
5. Maximize choices and communicate preferences whenever possible.

6. Family members and caregivers reinforce all of the client's steps toward managing stereotypic behaviors.

—. ______________________________
____

—. ______________________________
____

—. ______________________________
____

SHORT-TERM OBJECTIVES

1. Participate in a behavioral assessment of stereotypic behaviors. (1, 2, 3, 4)
2. Cooperate with medical examination to rule out biomedical etiologies for self-injurious symptoms. (5, 6)
3. Cooperate with psychiatric examination and recommendations regarding the need for psychotropic medications. (6, 7, 8)
4. Cooperate with physical and occupational therapy assessment to facilitate sensory integration as well as skills acquisition of functional activities that are incompatible with stereotypic motor behavior. (9, 10, 11, 12)
5. Increase the frequency of calm, nonrepetitive, functional behaviors. (13, 14, 15, 16, 17)
6. Family members, caregivers, and client interrupt the early stages of tension, frustration, or agitation by engaging in

THERAPEUTIC INTERVENTIONS

1. Arrange for an assessment of the client's stereotypic behavior to identify antecedent conditions, topography of behavior, and conditions maintaining behavior.
2. Operationally define and collect stimulus and reinforcement data on the client's stereotypic behaviors.
3. Assess the severity of the client's stereotypic behavior by using a rating scale (e.g., the Diagnostic Assessment for the Severely Handicapped, Second Edition [DASH-II; Matson] or the Reiss Screen for Maladaptive Behavior, Second Edition [Reiss]).
4. Train family members and caregivers to monitor the signs and symptoms of the client's stereotypic behaviors in order to provide accurate information to the psychiatrist and psychologist.

noninjurious physical activity that is adaptive. (18, 19)

7. Family members and caregivers modify the environment to establish a less stimulating, quieter, more stable routine. (20, 21, 22)
8. Demonstrate functional communication skills that reduce the frequency of stereotypic motor behavior engaged in as a substitute for communication. (23, 24)
9. Demonstrate prosocial methods of dealing with and expressing anger and frustration in interactions with others. (25, 26, 27)
10. Implement self-management steps to reduce stereotypic behaviors. (28, 29, 30)
11. Use relaxation techniques to reduce negative emotions that stimulate stereotypic behavior. (31, 32)
12. Demonstrate independence and initiative by making all possible choices in daily events, as evidenced by choosing clothing, food, leisure interests, and peer group. (33, 34)
13. Family members and caretakers assist and support the client in his/her attempts to make positive behavioral changes to manage stereotypic symptoms. (35, 36, 37)

5. Arrange for the client to obtain a complete physical examination to rule out any biomedical explanations for his/her stereotypic behaviors (e.g., Lesch-Nyhan syndrome, phenylketonuria [PKU], Cornelia de Lange's syndrome, drug withdrawal, ear infection, toothache, headaches, or other physical illness).
6. Follow up on recommendations from the client's physical examination, including suggestions for further lab work, new medications, or specialty assessments.
7. Arrange for a psychiatric evaluation of the client to determine whether psychotropic medications may be helpful.
8. Monitor the client for compliance, effectiveness, and side effects associated with the prescribed psychotropic medications.
9. Refer the client to a physical or occupational therapist to determine if ongoing physical therapy or occupational therapy services are needed to improve integration of sensory stimuli.
10. Arrange for the client to receive recommended occupation and/or physical therapy services.
11. Provide opportunities for the client to engage in alternative nonharmful activities that

14. Increase participation in extracurricular activities and outings. (38, 39, 40)

__. ____________________________
____

__. ____________________________
____

__. ____________________________

approximate the type of sensory stimulation received from the stereotypic movement (e.g., swinging, rocking in a rocking chair, sitting by a fan, or watching colorful, rapid-moving objects).

12. Arrange for the client to participate in a wide variety of enjoyable activities and exercise on a daily basis.
13. Identify several reinforcers that can be used to reward prosocial behaviors that are incompatible with the client's stereotypic behaviors.
14. Refer the client to a behavioral specialist to design and implement a behavioral plan that reinforces desired behaviors coupled with behavioral techniques (e.g., reinforcing low frequency of behavior incidents, reinforcing incompatible behaviors, extinction, response cost, and overcorrection) to decrease or eliminate stereotypic behaviors.
15. Arrange for the client to have a pictorial schedule of when reinforcers can be obtained (e.g., at hourly intervals or with naturally occurring events during the day) and what reinforcers are available to him/her.
16. Train all caregivers on the client's behavioral treatment program to ensure consistent,

effective implementation and strengthening of desirable nonrepetitive behaviors.

17. Obtain approval from the client's guardian and the agency oversight committee for any use of restrictive or aversive programming.
18. Teach the client to recognize the early signs of negative emotions and then self-initiate alternative activities that will reduce agitation expressed as self-injurious behavior (e.g., working, going for a walk, or other predetermined incompatible behavior).
19. Provide training and in-service sessions to family members and caregivers to promote their identification of early signs of the client's agitation. Instruct caregivers to redirect the client's behavior at early, low levels of agitation to reduce the likelihood of the client injuring himself/herself.
20. Modify the client's environment to remove physical, psychological, and antecedent conditions not conducive to healthy behaviors (e.g., noisy conditions, hunger, and bright sunlight). Replace with conditions that prompt appropriate prosocial behaviors.
21. Recommend that family members and caregivers read *Parent Survival Manual*

(Schopler) for examples of how to modify the client's environment to decrease the need for acting-out behaviors.

22. Provide education to family members and caregivers (e.g., counseling, training, and/or in-service sessions) regarding the importance of providing positive stimulation and a positive physical and psychological environment for the client.
23. Refer the client to a speech and language therapist to learn functional communication skills in order to avoid stereotypic behavior in communication.
24. Use modeling and training to teach family members and caregivers to listen for the client's direct and indirect communication and to reinforce the client when he/she cooperates with reasonable, routine requests.
25. Refer the client for anger management treatment to develop the requisite skills needed to effectively manage anger and frustration. (See Anger in this Planner.)
26. Coordinate a mentor relationship with a volunteer or peer who can assist in resolving conflicts between the client and his/her environment in order to promote more

effective self-management of the client's problems.

27. Arrange for the client to participate in social skills training (see Social Skills in this Planner).
28. Teach the client to discriminate between stereotypic behavior and appropriate behavior by requesting that he/she identify random video, pictorial, or modeled presentations of stereotypic and appropriate behavior. Reinforce correct responses.
29. Provide the client with a videotape of himself/herself and request that he/she identify his/her own stereotypic and appropriate behavior. Reinforce correct identification and praise appropriate behavioral control.
30. Teach the client to monitor his/her own behavior and to record time intervals of controlled, appropriate behavior on a form. Reinforce consistent self-monitoring behavior.
31. Arrange for the client to participate in a stress management program (see Anger in this Planner).
32. Teach the client stress reduction techniques to alleviate stressors encountered (e.g., deep muscle relaxation, abdominal breathing, and safe-place imagery).

33. Frequently present situations such that the client is required to make choices between two to three options, and reinforce his/her independent choices.
34. Encourage family members to allow the client to make all possible choices and to demonstrate maximum independence in daily events.
35. Arrange with family members and caregivers to spend time with the client doing only what the client expresses an interest in (e.g., planning a meal, playing a game, or doing a puzzle) in order to promote unconditional, nondemanding interactions while the family members and caregivers provide verbal attention to the client's activities.
36. Encourage family members and caregivers to increase their frequency of positive interactions with the client while modeling desirable behaviors, positive demeanors, and helpful attitudes.
37. Teach family members and caregivers how the client's Axis I diagnosis contributes to his/her self-injurious behavior.
38. Refer the client to a recreational therapist to determine possible leisure and community activities available to the client.

39. Arrange for the client to participate in activities that promote enjoyment for him/her.
40. Encourage the client's participation in Special Olympics or other athletic organizations.

__. ________________________
____

__. ________________________
____

__. ________________________
____

DIAGNOSTIC SUGGESTIONS:

ICD-9-CM	*ICD-10-CM*	*DSM-5* Disorder, Condition, or Problem
307.3	F98.4	Stereotypic Movement Disorder
300.3	F42	Obsessive-Compulsive Disorder
299.00	F84.0	Autism Spectrum Disorder
312.39	F63.2	Trichotillomania
312.34	F63.81	Intermittent Explosive Disorder
300.00	F41.9	Unspecified Anxiety Disorder
317	F70	Intellectual Disability, Mild
319	F71	Intellectual Disability, Moderate
319	F72	Intellectual Disability, Severe
319	F73	Intellectual Disability, Profound
319	F79	Unspecified Intellectual Disability
V62.89	R41.83	Borderline Intellectual Functioning
______	______	________________________
______	______	________________________

SUPPORTED EMPLOYMENT

BEHAVIORAL DEFINITIONS

1. Limited vocational opportunities due to social skills deficits.
2. Limited vocational opportunities due to emotional lability.
3. Difficulty learning and remembering rules.
4. Movement, visual, or hearing deficits that require accommodation in vocational setting.
5. History of limited vocational opportunities.
6. No experience in working independently.

__. ____

____

__. ____

____

__. ____

____

LONG-TERM GOALS

1. Manage symptoms adequately such that employment can be maintained.
2. Identify, secure, and maintain a desired job.
3. Utilize vocational opportunities that maximize integration into the local community.
4. Take advantage of opportunity to perform relatively independent, meaningful, and functional work.
5. Take advantage of opportunity to experience a sense of value and make a meaningful contribution to the community.
6. Develop meaningful relationships with other people within the work environment.

__. ____
____

__. ____
____

__. ____
____

SHORT-TERM OBJECTIVES

1. Participate in assessment of vocational skills to develop career plan. (1, 2)
2. Verbalize own legal rights and the financial effects of gaining employment. (3, 4)
3. Utilize community resources to assist in vocational placement. (5)
4. Family members verbalize their goals, fears, and concerns regarding the client being employed. (6, 7, 8)
5. Family members verbalize support for the client's identified career decisions. (9)
6. Choose which employment option to pursue. (10, 11, 12)
7. Implement a plan to overcome perceived barriers to employment. (13, 14)
8. List potential rewards to be used to reinforce progress in learning vocational skills. (15)
9. Participate in training sessions to develop and strengthen vocational skills. (16, 17)

THERAPEUTIC INTERVENTIONS

1. Arrange for an employment specialist to perform an assessment of the client's a ptitudes, employment preferences, work history, dislikes, and special interests to develop a personal profile that will be used as the foundation of his/her career planning process.
2. Provide direct feedback to the client and family members on the results of the assessment and the client's personal profile.
3. Provide the client and family members with information about the client's legal rights related to employment, as explained in *Know Your Rights! Working and the Americans with Disabilities Act* (Hall and Harris) or *The Americans with Disabilities Act (ADA) and Working* (Association for Retarded Citizens [ARC]).
4. Determine how employment will impact Medicaid and supplemental security income

10. Demonstrate an understanding of job interviews. (18, 19, 20)
11. Increase productivity in the work setting. (21, 22)
12. Decrease the frequency of maladaptive behavior. (23, 24, 25, 26, 27)
13. Increase job skills through self-instruction. (28)
14. Generalize newly learned skills to other similar situations. (29, 30)
15. Demonstrate ability to navigate through environment and care for personal needs while in the work setting. (31, 32)
16. Identify and utilize transportation services to get to and from the job. (33)
17. Identify negative behaviors that could lead to employment termination. (34, 35, 36)
18. Implement social skills behaviors that improve work relationships. (37)
19. Demonstrate an understanding of the safety skills needed in vocational settings. (38, 39)
20. Utilize assistance for any special physical or medical needs. (40, 41, 42)

__. ______________________________
____

__. ______________________________
____

__. ______________________________
____

(SSI) or supplemental security disability income (SSDI) checks the client receives before he/she accepts a job by utilizing information from booklets such as *Disability Benefits* (Social Security Administration).

5. Refer the client to state employment and job-training agencies for evaluation, training, and job placement or referral.
6. Elicit and address concerns the client's family members may have regarding the client's employment, assuring them that measures will be taken to ensure that the client will be in a safe, dignified environment, performing meaningful, functional, independent activities.
7. Become familiar with family members' goals and wishes for the client, communicating understanding of the goals and of the fears they may have.
8. Discuss with family members the level of communication they feel is appro-priate for staying involved in the client's employment progress.
9. Encourage family members to read and follow steps outlined in *Parents Guide to Career Development* (Schutt, O'Donnell, and Saura) in order to actively demonstrate their support of the client's career decisions.

10. Identify the type of vocational setting most suitable for the client based on his/her vocational level (e.g., entry-level competitive job placement, small enterprise, mobile work crew, or enclave).
11. Determine vocational options that are available and are congruent with the client's identified career plan, and present the options to the client for his/her consideration.
12. Facilitate the client's making a personal choice about where he/she will work.
13. Identify potential and real challenges that impede the client's achievement of his/her desired work option, and brainstorm solutions to these challenges.
14. Formulate a plan specifying the steps to overcome the client's challenges; identify a responsible party who will assist him/her in the implementation of each step.
15. Assist the client in identifying reinforcers and then design and implement a reward system that can be used to motivate the client to improve his/her vocational skills.
16. Identify the type of antecedent conditions (e.g., prompts, sequential prompts, or time-delay procedures), consequence conditions (e.g., positive reinforcement, error correction, or modifying tasks) and job cues

(e.g., chaining of tasks, color coding, job jogs, or modifying the environment or the complexity of tasks) most appropriate for improving the client's performance in a vocational setting.

17. Complete a task analysis of the client's duties and develop a training protocol that best fits his/her learning style (e.g., physical demonstrations, auditory training, color-coding information, and checklists).
18. Arrange for the client to view a job interview, either by role-playing or on video (e.g., see *Winning the Job Interview with Personal Presentation Skills* [Chandler, Ginther, and Mountrose]), in order to gain first-hand knowledge of the experience prior to an actual interview.
19. Teach the basic elements of a job interview to the client (e.g., good eye contact, neat appearance, honesty, openness, friendliness, and cooperation), and request that he/she describe why these qualities are important.
20. Provide an opportunity for the client to role-play a job interview with someone who is a stranger to him/her and who will conduct a realistic interview.

21. Identify and provide job aids for the client that will maximize his/her productivity and independence in the workplace (e.g., color coding, jigs, and checklists).
22. Review the use of natural and social cues and prompts that direct an employee's productivity; request that the client identify these in his/her work setting.
23. Assess the ecological factors contributing to the client's maintenance of maladaptive behaviors.
24. Identify internal states (e.g., medical problems, hunger, thirst, fatigue, or side effects from medications) and environmental conditions (e.g., crowding, noise, temperature, or poorly trained staff) that contribute to the client's maladaptive behavior.
25. Refer the client to a behavioral specialist to design and implement a behavioral plan that reinforces desired behaviors coupled with behavioral techniques (e.g., reinforcing low levels, reinforcing other behaviors, extinction, response cost, and overcorrection) to decrease or eliminate the client's stereotypic behaviors.
26. Train all staff and family members regarding the client's behavioral treatment program to ensure effective and consistent implementation.

27. Obtain approval from the client's guardian and the agency oversight committee for any use of restrictive or aversive programming.
28. Teach self-instructional strategies by developing the client's necessary discriminatory skills (e.g., see *Innovations: How to Teach Self-Instruction of Job Skills* [Agran and Moore]).
29. Plan for vocational skills generalization by providing the client with training that uses work skills across different settings, materials, and/or instructors; ensure similarity between the learning stimuli and the client's natural environment.
30. Assess the client's skill generalization to ensure his/her maximum independence, and provide booster-training sessions as indicated.
31. Tour the work place with the client to ensure that he/she is able to independently find bathrooms, break room, exits, entrances, and snack machines.
32. Teach the client how to independently operate vending machines by physical demonstrations; request that he/she repeat demonstrations.
33. Assist the client in arranging transportation to and from work and observe him/her independently arranging

transportation following an instructional demonstration.

34. Assist the client in identifying negative behaviors that could lead to being fired (e.g., stealing, lying, insubordination, and unsafe work behaviors), and request that the client identify why these are not tolerated in work environments.
35. Provide the opportunity for the client to view a video to learn skills essential to maintaining employment (e.g., *How to Get Fired and What to Do Instead* [Stanfield]).
36. Play educational games with the client to develop his/her sense of what makes a good or bad employee (e.g., You're The Boss [Rubenstein] or *Workplace Skills Program* [Haugen]).
37. Teach the client necessary job-related social skills by giving direct information, role-plays, and role reversals on relevant social skills including asking permission, accepting criticism, following directions (see Social Skills Deficits in this Planner).
38. Describe behaviors essential to the client's safety on the job and request that he/she identify positive and negative examples of safe behaviors in the workplace.
39. Provide the opportunity for the client to view a video on job safety (e.g., *How to Get*

Hurt and What to Do Instead [Stanfield]).

40. Ensure that the client's employer is equipped with the proper knowledge and supplies to handle any expected medical needs.
41. Refer the client to an occupational or physical therapist to identify the maximal positioning, lifting, and transfer techniques to use while working.
42. Coordinate and train individuals to properly assist the client with any special eating, toileting, or lifting and transferring needs he/she may experience.

__. ____________________
____

__. ____________________
____

__. ____________________
____

DIAGNOSTIC SUGGESTIONS:

ICD-9-CM	*ICD-10-CM*	*DSM-5* Disorder, Condition, or Problem
299.00	F84.0	Autism Spectrum Disorder
317	F70	Intellectual Disability, Mild
319	F71	Intellectual Disability, Moderate
319	F72	Intellectual Disability, Severe
319	F73	Intellectual Disability, Profound

319	F79	Unspecified Intellectual Disability
V62.89	R41.83	Borderline Intellectual Functioning
____	____	________________
____	____	________________

Appendix A

BIBLIOTHERAPY SUGGESTIONS

Activities of Daily Living (ADL)

Gavanta, W., ed. (1998). *Dimensions of Faith and Congregational Ministries with Persons with Developmental Disabilities and Their Families.* Princeton, NJ: Religion Division, American Association on Mental Retardation.

National Family Caregivers Association (1996). *The Resourceful Caregiver: Helping Family Caregivers Help Themselves.* St. Louis, MO: Mosby Lifeline.

Sweeny, W. (1998). *The Special Need Reading List.* Bethesda MD: Woodbine House.

Anger

Bilodeau, L. (1997). *The Anger Workbook.* New York: MJF Books.

Bloomquist, M. L. (1996). *Skills Training for Children with Behavioral Disorders: A Parent and Therapist Workbook.* New York: Guilford Press.

Davis, M., E. R. Eshelman, and M. McKay (1988). *The Relaxation and Stress Reduction Workbook.* Oakland, CA: New Harbinger.

Foxx, R., and R. Bittle (1989). *Thinking It Through: Teaching a Problem-Solving Strategy for Community Living.* Champaign, IL: Research Press.

Johnston, M. (1996). *Dealing with Anger.* New York: Rosen Publishing Group.

Moser, A. (1988). *Don't Pop Your Cork on Mondays!* Kansas City, MO: Landmark Editions.

Moser, A. (1992). *Don't Pop Your Cork on Mondays!* Videotape. Evanston IL: Altschul Group.

Moser, A. (1994). *Don't Rant and Rave on Wednesdays!* Kansas City, MO: Landmark Editions.

Anxiety

Bloomquist, M. L. (1996). *Skills Training for Children with Behavioral Disorders: A Parent and Therapist Workbook.* New York: Guilford Press.

Bourne, E. J. (1995). *Anxiety and Phobia Workbook.* Oakland, CA: New Harbinger.

Clark, L. (1998). *SOS: Help for Emotions: Managing Anxiety, Anger, and Depression.* Bowling Green, KY: Parents Press.

Dalrymple, N. J. (1998). *Helping People with Autism Manage Their Behavior.* Bloomington, IN: Institute for the Study of Developmental Disabilities.

Gabriel, S. (1996). *The Psychiatric Tower of Babble: Understanding People with Developmental Disabilities Who Have Mental Illness.* Quebec, Canada: Diversity Press.

Lark, S. (1996). *Anxiety and Stress Self Help Book.* Berkeley, CA: Celestial Arts.

National Institute of Mental Health. Information available includes mental health facts and a listing of Axis I disorders. (301) 443-5158. www.nimh.nih.gov.

Schopler, E. (1995). *Parent Survival Manual: A Guide to Crisis Resolution in Autism and Related Developmental Disorders.* New York: Plenum Press.

Chemical Dependence

American Institute for Learning (1998). *Addiction and Recovery Series.* Videotape. Verona, WI: Attainment Company.

Discover Films Video (1999). *Gateway Drugs: Binge Drinking Blowout.* Videotape. Verona, WI: Attainment Company.

Discover Films Video (1999). *Gateway Drugs: Marijuana: The Gateway Drug.* Videotape. Verona, WI: Attainment Company.

Discover Films Video (1999). *Gateway Drugs: Tobacco X-Files.* Videotape. Verona, WI: Attainment Company.

Fanning, P., and J. T. O'Neill (1996). *The Addictions Workbook: A Step-by-Step Guide to Quitting Alcohol and Drugs.* Oakland, CA: New Harbinger.

Fleming, M. (1992). *101 Support Group Activities: For Teenagers Recovering from Chemical Dependence.* Minneapolis, MN: Johnson Institute-QVS.

Visions Video Productions (1998). *H.A.L.T.: A Relapse Prevention Guide.* Videotape. Evanston, IL: Altschul Group.

Cognitive/Emotional Decompensation

Association for Retarded Citizens (ARC) (1995). *Alzheimers Disease and People with Mental Retardation.* Arlington, TX: Author.

Gavanta, W., ed. (1998). *Dimensions of Faith and Congregational Ministries with Persons with Developmental Disabilities and Their Families.* Princeton, NJ: Religion Division, American Association on Mental Retardation.

Gray-Davidson, F. G. (1993). *The Alzheimer's Sourcebook for Caregivers: A Practical Guide for Getting through the Day.* Los Angeles: Lowell House.

Kopp, D. (1990). *Aging People with Mental Retardation.* Videotape. Watertown, WI: Bethesda Lutheran Homes and Services.

Mace, N. L., and P. V. Rabings (1991). *The Thirty-six Hour Day: A Family Guide to Caring for Persons with Alzheimer's Disease, Related Dementing Illnesses and Memory Loss in Later Life.* Baltimore: Johns Hopkins University Press.

National Family Caregivers Association (1996). *The Resourceful Caregiver: Helping Family Caregivers Help Themselves.* St. Louis, MO: Mosby Lifeline.

Roberto, K. A., ed. (1993). *The Elderly Caregiver: Caring for Adults with Developmental Disabilities.* Newbury Park, CA: Sage.

Roberts, J. D. (1991). *Taking Care of Caregivers: For Families and Others Who Care for People with Alzheimer's Disease and Other Forms of Dementia.* Palo Alto, CA: Bull.

Russell, L. M., and A. E. Grant (1995). *The Life Planning Workbook: A Hands-on Guide to Help Parents Provide for the Future Security and Happiness of Their Child with a Disability after Their Death.* Evanston, IL: American.

Teri, L. (1990). *ABC's.* Videotape. Seattle, WA: Alzheimer's Disease Research Center, University of Washington.

Teri, L. (1990). *Managing Aggressive Behaviors.* Videotape. Seattle, WA: Alzheimer's Disease Research Center, University of Washington.

Teri, L. (1990). *Managing Psychotic Behaviors.* Videotape. Seattle, WA: Alzheimer's Disease Research Center, University of Washington.

Visser, F. E., A. P. Aldenkamp, and A. C. Van Huffelen (1997). "Prospective Study of the Prevalence of Alzheimer-Type Dementia in Institutionalized Individuals with Down Syndrome." *American Journal on Mental Retardation,* 101(4): 400–412.

Community Access

Gavanta, W., ed. (1998). *Dimensions of Faith and Congregational Ministries with Persons with Developmental Disabilities and Their Families.* Princeton, NJ: Religion Division, American Association on Mental Retardation.

Cooking/Housekeeping Skills

National Family Caregivers Association (1996). *The Resourceful Caregiver: Helping Family Caregivers Help Themselves.* St. Louis, MO: Mosby Lifeline.

Redmond, R. (1982). *The Housekeeping/Grooming Checklist.* Holland, MI: Association for Retarded Citizens (ARC).

Redmond, R. (1982). *101 Pictures Cookbook.* Holland, MI: Association for Retarded Citizens (ARC).

Depression

Bloomquist, M. L. (1996). *Skills Training for Children with Behavioral Disorders: A Parent and Therapist Workbook.* New York: Guilford Press.

Greenlee, S. (1992). *When Someone Dies.* Atlanta, GA: Peachtree.

Simon, N. (1992). *The Saddest Time.* Norton Grove, IL: Albert Whitman.

Eating Disorder

Bloomquist, M. L. (1996). *Skills Training for Children with Behavioral Disorders: A Parent and Therapist Workbook.* New York: Guilford Press.

Enuresis/Encopresis

Bloomquist, M. L. (1996). *Skills Training for Children with Behavioral Disorders: A Parent and Therapist Workbook.* New York: Guilford Press.

Family Conflict

Connolly, M. (1996). *A Family Healing: Coming to Terms with Intellectual Disabilities.* Syracuse, NY: Program Development Associates.

Covert, S. B. (1995). *Whatever It Takes! Excellence in Family Support: When Families Experience a Disability.* St. Augustine, FL: Training Resource Network.

Davis, M., E. R. Eshelman, and M. McKay (1988). *The Relaxation and Stress Reduction Workbook.* Oakland, CA: New Harbinger.

Family Village: A Global Community of Disability-Related Resources. Resource information available at www.familyvillage.wisc.edu/jpkf.

Goldfarb, L., M. J. Brotherson, J. A. Summers, and A. P. Turnbull (1986). *Meeting the Challenge of Disability or Chronic Illness: A Family Guide.* Baltimore: Paul H. Brookes.

Heighway, S. (1992). *Helping Parents Parent: A Practice Guide for Supporting Families Headed by Parents with Cognitive Limitations.* Madison, WI: Wisconsin Council on Developmental Disabilities.

Hines, M. L. (1987). *Don't Get Mad Get Powerful!: A Manual for Building Advocacy Skills.* Lansing, MI: Michigan Protection and Advocacy Service. www.mpas.org.

Karpinski, M. (1988). *The Home Care Companion.* Vol. 3: *Creating Healthy Home Care Conditions: Infection Control.* Videotape. Medford, OR: Healing Arts Communication.

National Family Caregivers Association. (1996). *The Resourceful Caregiver: Helping Family Caregivers Help Themselves.* St. Louis, MO: Mosby Lifeline.

National Parent Network on Disabilities. Resource information available at www.npnd.org.

Sweet, M. (1990). *Discovering The Parent's Language of Learning: An Educational Approach to Supporting Parents with Mental Retardation.* Madison, WI: Wisconsin Council on Developmental Disabilities.

Financial/Shopping Skills

Haugen, J. (1998). Money Skills: Learning to Manage Your Money Game. San Antonio, TX: PCI.

Redmond, R. (1982). Complete Budgeting System. Holland, MI: Advocacy Resource Center.

Redmond, R. (1982). Make a Buck. Holland, MI: Advocacy Resource Center.

Redmond, R. (1982). Meal Planning Guide. Holland, MI: Advocacy Resource Center.

Redmond, R. (1982). Shopping List. Holland, MI: Advocacy Resource Center.

Household Safety Skills

Haugen, J. (1993). Safety Skills: Learning to Be Careful. Game set. San Antonio, TX: PCI.

Legal Involvement

Association for Retarded Citizens (ARC). Resource information available from national headquarters, 500 E. Border St., S-300, Arlington, TX 76010. (817) 261-6003.

Bazelon Center for Mental Health Law. Resource information available from 1101 15th St. NW, Suite 1212, Washington, DC 20005-5002. www.bazelon.org.

Berkobien, R. (1997). *Future Planning: Guardianship and People with Mental Retardation.* Arlington, TX: Association for Retarded Citizens (ARC).

Goldman, M. (1997). "The Criminal Justice System vs. the Criminal Mentally Retarded: Is Justice Being Served?" *NADD Newsletter,* 14(6): 236–240.

Michigan Protection and Advocacy Service (1998). *Disability Rights and Issues: A Consumer's Guide.* Lansing, MI: Author. www.mpas.org.

National Alliance for the Mentally Ill (1998). *A Guide to Mental Illness and the Criminal Justice System: A Systems Guide for Families and Consumers.* Arlington, VA: Author.

National Association of Protection and Advocacy Systems, Inc. Resource information available from 900 Second St. NE, Suite 211, Washington, DC 20002. (202) 408-9514. www.protectionandadvocacy.com.

Reynolds, L. A. (1995). *People with Mental Retardation in the Criminal Justice System.* Arlington, TX: Association for Retarded Citizens (ARC).

Russell, L. M., and A. E. Grant (1995). *The Life Planning Workbook: A Hands-on Guide to Help Parents Provide for the Future Security and Happiness of Their Child with a Disability after Their Death.* Evanston, IL: American.

Medical Condition

Association for Retarded Citizens (ARC) (1999). *Managed Care and Longer-Term Services for People with Mental Retardation.* Arlington, TX: Author.

Davis, M., E. R. Eshelman, and M. McKay (1988). *The Relaxation and Stress Reduction Workbook.* Oakland, CA: New Harbinger.

Goldfarb, L. M. J. Brotherson, J. A. Summers, and A. P. Turnbull (1986). *Meeting the Challenge of Disability or Chronic Illness: A Family Guide.* Baltimore: Paul H. Brookes.

Human Services Research Institute (HSRI) and National Association of State Directors of Developmental Disabilities Services (NASDDDS) (1995). *Managed Care and People with Developmental Disabilities: A Guidebook.* Alexandria, VA: National Association of State Directors of Developmental Disabilities Services.

Karpinski, M. (1998). *The Home Care Companion.* Vol. 3: *Creating Healthy Home Care Conditions: Infection Control.* Videotape. Medford, OR: Healing Arts Communications.

Larson, D., ed. (1992). *Mayo Clinic Family Health Book: The Ultimate Illustrated Home Medical Reference.* New York: William Morrow.

Moser, A. (1996). *Don't Despair on Thursday.* Kansas City, MO: Landmark Editions.

National Family Caregivers Association (1996). *The Resourceful Caregiver: Helping Family Caregivers Help Themselves.* St. Louis, MO: Mosby Lifeline.

Sternbach, R. (1988). *Mastering Pain: A Twelve-Step Program for Coping with Chronic Pain.* New York: Ballantine.

WebMD Health. Medical resource information available at www.WebMD.com.

Medication Management

Karpinski, M. (1998). *The Home Care Companion.* Vol. 4: *How to Manage Medications.* Videotape. Medford, OR: Healing Arts Communications.

Personal Safety Skill Deficits

Haugen, J. (1993). Safety Skills: Learning to Be Careful. Game set. San Antionio, TX: PCI.

Physical/Emotional/Sexual Abuse

Association for Retarded Citizens (ARC) (1993). *It Could Never Happen Here: The Prevention and Treatment of Sexual Abuse of Adults with Learning Disabilities In Residential Settings.* Chesterfield, England: Author.

Baladerian, N. J. (1991). *Sexual Assault Survivor's Handbook for People with Developmental Disabilities and Their Advocates.* Saratoga, CA: R & E.

Bass, E., and L. Davis (1992). *The Courage to Heal: A Guide for Women Survivors of Sexual Abuse.* New York: HarperPerennial.

Champagne, M. P., and L. Walker-Hirsch (1993). *Circles II: Stop Abuse.* Santa Barbara, CA: James Stanfield.

Hingsburger, D. (1995). *Just Say Know! Understanding and Reducing the Risk of Sexual Victimization of People with Developmental Disabilities.* Eastman, Quebec: Diversity Press.

Lew, M. (1992). *Victims No Longer.* New York: HarperCollins.

Ticoll, M. (1992). *No More Victims: Addressing the Sexual Abuse of People with a Mental Handicap: Families' and Friends' Manual.* North York, Ontario: Roeher Institute.

Ticoll, M. (1997). *Out of Harm's Way: A Safety Kit for People with Disabilities Who Feel Unsafe and Want to Do Something About It.* North York, Ontario: Roeher Institute.

Psychosis

Gabriel, S. (1996). *The Psychiatric Tower of Babble: Understanding People with Developmental Disabilities who have Mental Illness.* Quebec, Canada: Diversity Press.

Jeffries, J. J., E. Plummer, M. V. Seeman, and J. F. Thornton (1990). *Living and Working with Schizophrenia.* Toronto, Ontario: University of Toronto Press.

Katz, D. (1990). *Living with Schizophrenia: A Video Manual for Families.* Videotape. St. Louis, MO: Washington University.

National Institute of Mental Health. Information available includes mental health facts and a listing of Axis I disorders. (301) 443-5159. www.nimh.nih.gov.

Residential Options

Center for Independent Living. Resource information available from 2536 Telegraph Ave., Berkeley, CA 94704. (510) 841-4776.

Fitton, P., C. O'Brien, and J. Willson (1995). *Home at Last: How Two Young Women with Profound Intellectual and Multiple Disabilities Achieved Their Own Home.* London: Jessica Kingsley.

Hoogewind, A. J. (1998). *Parables of Hope: Inspiring Truths from People with Disabilities.* Grand Rapids, MI: Zondervan.

Michigan Protection and Advocacy Service (1998). *Disability Rights and Issues: A Consumer's Guide.* Lansing, MI: Author. www.mpas.org.

Racino, J. A., P. Walker, S. O'Connor, and S. Taylor (1993). *Housing, Support, and Community: Choices and Strategies for Adults with Disabilities.* Baltimore: Paul H. Brookes Publishing.

Stokes, D. M., and C. A. Luker, eds. (1994). *Fair Housing for People with Disabilities: Legal Protections, Remedies, and Practical Strategies.* Lansing, MI: Service.

Self-Determination

Davis, S. (1999). *Ten Steps to Independence: Promoting Self-Determination in the Home.* Arlington, TX: Association for Retarded Citizens (ARC).

Foxx, R., and R. Bittle (1989). *Thinking It Through: Teaching a Problem-Solving Strategy for Community Living.* Champaign, IL: Research Press.

Gardner, N. (1996). *The Self-Advocacy Workbook.* Lawrence, KS: Kansas University.

Kranz, C. (1996). *Fred's Story.* Videotape. Gilman, CT: Pennycorner Press.

Michigan Protection and Advocacy Service (1998). *The Self-Advocacy Manual for Consumers.* Lansing, MI: Author. www.mpas.org.

Minnesota Governor's Planning Council on Developmental Disabilities (1994). *Making Your Case.* St. Paul, MN: Author.

Pearpoint, J. (1993). *PATH: A Workbook for Planning Positive Possible Futures.* Toronto, Ontario: Inclusion Press.

Thorin, E. (1997). *Whose Decision Is It Anyway?: Parents Prompting Self-Determination.* Videotape. Syracuse, NY: Program Development Associates.

Thorin, E. (1997). *Whose Decision Is It Anyway?: Young Adults Working on Self-Determination.* Videotape. Syracuse, NY: Program Development Associates.

Sexually Inappropriate Behaviors

Association for Retarded Citizens (ARC) (1993). *Learn to Be Safe.* Arlington, TX: Author.

Brown, G. T., P. Carney, J. Cortis, L. L. Metz, and A. M. Petrie (1994). *Human Sexuality Handbook: Guiding People toward Positive Expressions of Sexuality.* Springfield, IL: Association for Community Living.

Carmody, M. (1991). *Person to Person.* Silver Spring, MD: American Film and Video.

Hingsburger, D. (1991). *I Contact.* Mountville, PA: VIDA.

Lerro, M. (1990). *HIV And AIDS Prevention Guide for Parents.* Arlington TX: The ARC.

Maksym, D. (1990). *Shared Feelings: A Parent Guide to Sexuality Education for Children, Adolescents, and Adults Who Have a Mental Handicap.* North York, Ontario: Roeher Institute.

McGwin, K., and G. Born (1989). *Objectively Dealing with Sexual Behavior.* Videotape. Watertown, WI: Bethesda Lutheran Home.

Social Skills

Champagne, M., and L. Walker-Hirsh (1993). *Circles I: Relationships and Relationship Building.* Santa Barbara, CA: James Stanfield.

Gavanta, W., ed. (1998). *Dimensions of Faith and Congregational Ministries with Persons with Developmental Disabilities and Their Families.* Princeton, NJ: Religion Division, American Association on Mental Retardation.

Foxx, R., and M. McMorrow (1983). Stacking the Deck: A Social Skills Game for Adults with Developmental Disabilities. Champaign, IL: Research Press.

Foxx, R., and R. Bittle (1989). *Thinking It Through: Teaching a Problem-Solving Strategy for Community Living.* Champaign, IL: Research Press.

Mannix, D. (1998). *Social Skills Activities.* San Antonio, TX: PCI.

Stereotypic Movement Disorder

Schopler, E. (1995). *Parent Survival Manual: A Guide to Crisis Resolution in Autism and Related Developmental Disorders.* New York: Plenum Press.

Supported Employment

Agran, M., and S. Moore (1994). *Innovations: How to Teach Self-Instruction of Job Skills.* Washington, D.C.: American Association on Mental Retardation.

Association for Retarded Citizens (ARC) (1993). *The Americans with Disabilities Act (ADA) and Working—An Easy to Read Book for People with Disabilities.* Arlington, TX: Author.

Chandler, C., B. Ginther, and P. Mountrose (1995). *Winning the Job Interview with Personal Presentation Skills.* Videotape. Santa Barbara, CA: James Stanfield.

Hall, M., and P. Harris (1997). *Know Your Rights! Working and the Americans with Disabilities Act.* Syracuse, NY: ARC Center on Human Policy.

Haugen, J. (1992). *Workplace Skills Program.* San Antonio, TX: PCI.

Schutt, D., M. O'Donnell, and K. Saura. (1996). *Parents Guide to Career Development.* Madison, WI: Wisconsin Career Information System.

Social Security Administration (1991). *Disability Benefits.* Booklet. Washington, D.C.: Author.

Stanfield, J. (1997). *How to Get Fired and What to Do Instead.* Videotape. Santa Barbara, CA: James Stanfield.

Stanfield, J. (1997). *How to Get Hurt and What to Do Instead.* Videotape. Santa Barbara, CA: James Stanfield.

Rubenstein, F. (1996). You're The Boss. Game set. Westport, CT: Franklin Learning Systems.

Appendix B

RECOVERY MODEL OBJECTIVES AND INTERVENTIONS

The Objectives and Interventions that follow are created around the 10 core principles developed by a multidisciplinary panel at the 2004 National Consensus Conference on Mental Health Recovery and Mental Health Systems Transformation, convened by the Substance Abuse and Mental Health Services Administration (SAMHSA, 2004):

1. **Self-direction:** Consumers lead, control, exercise choice over, and determine their own path of recovery by optimizing autonomy, independence, and control of resources to achieve a self-determined life. By definition, the recovery process must be self-directed by the individual, who defines his or her own life goals and designs a unique path toward those goals.
2. **Individualized and person-centered:** There are multiple pathways to recovery based on an individual's unique strengths and resiliencies as well as his or her needs, preferences, experiences (including past trauma), and cultural background in all of its diverse representations. Individuals also identify recovery as being an ongoing journey and an end result as well as an overall paradigm for achieving wellness and optimal mental health.
3. **Empowerment:** Consumers have the authority to choose from a range of options and to participate in all decisions—including the allocation of resources—that will affect their lives, and are educated and supported in so doing. They have the ability to join with other consumers to collectively and effectively speak for themselves about their needs, wants, desires, and aspirations. Through empowerment, an individual gains control of his or her own destiny and influences the organizational and societal structures in his or her life.
4. **Holistic:** Recovery encompasses an individual's whole life, including mind, body, spirit, and community. Recovery embraces all aspects of life, including housing, employment, education, mental health and healthcare treatment and services, complementary and naturalistic services, addictions treatment, spirituality, creativity, social networks, community participation, and family supports as determined by the person. Families,

providers, organizations, systems, communities, and society play crucial roles in creating and maintaining meaningful opportunities for consumer access to these supports.

5. **Nonlinear:** Recovery is not a step-by-step process but one based on continual growth, occasional setbacks, and learning from experience. Recovery begins with an initial stage of awareness in which a person recognizes that positive change is possible. This awareness enables the consumer to move on to fully engage in the work of recovery.
6. **Strengths-based:** Recovery focuses on valuing and building on the multiple capacities, resiliencies, talents, coping abilities, and inherent worth of individuals. By building on these strengths, consumers leave stymied life roles behind and engage in new life roles (e.g., partner, caregiver, friend, student, employee). The process of recovery moves forward through interaction with others in supportive, trust-based relationships.
7. **Peer support:** Mutual support—including the sharing of experiential knowledge and skills and social learning—plays an invaluable role in recovery. Consumers encourage and engage other consumers in recovery and provide each other with a sense of belonging, supportive relationships, valued roles, and community.
8. **Respect:** Community, systems, and societal acceptance and appreciation of consumers—including protecting their rights and eliminating discrimination and stigma—are crucial in achieving recovery. Self-acceptance and regaining belief in one's self are particularly vital. Respect ensures the inclusion and full participation of consumers in all aspects of their lives.
9. **Responsibility:** Consumers have a personal responsibility for their own self-care and journeys of recovery. Taking steps toward their goals may require great courage. Consumers must strive to understand and give meaning to their experiences and identify coping strategies and healing processes to promote their own wellness.
10. **Hope:** Recovery provides the essential and motivating message of a better future—that people can overcome the barriers and obstacles that confront them. Hope is internalized, but can be fostered by peers, families, friends, providers, and others. Hope is the catalyst of the recovery process. Mental health recovery not only benefits individuals with mental health disabilities by focusing on their abilities to live, work, learn, and fully participate in our society, but also enriches the texture of American community life. America reaps the benefits of the contributions individuals with mental disabilities can make, ultimately becoming a stronger and healthier Nation.[1]

---

[1]From: Substance Abuse and Mental Health Services Administration's (SAMHSA) National Mental Health Information Center: Center for Mental Health Services (2004). *National consensus statement on mental health recovery.* Washington, DC: Author. Available from http://mentalhealth.samhsa.gov/publications/allpubs/sma05-4129/

The numbers used for Objectives in the treatment plan that follows correspond to the numbers for the 10 core principles. Each of the 10 Objectives was written to capture the essential theme of the like-numbered core principle. The numbers in parentheses after the Objectives denote the Interventions designed to assist the client in attaining each respective Objective. The clinician may select any or all of the Objectives and Intervention statements to include in the client's treatment plan.

One generic Long-Term Goal statement is offered should the clinician desire to emphasize a recovery model orientation in the client's treatment plan.

LONG-TERM GOAL

1. To live a meaningful life in a self-selected community while striving to achieve full potential during the journey of healing and transformation.

SHORT-TERM OBJECTIVES

1. Make it clear to therapist, family, and friends what path to recovery is preferred. (1, 2, 3, 4)

THERAPEUTIC INTERVENTIONS

1. Explore the client's thoughts, needs, and preferences regarding his/her desired pathway to recovery (from depression, bipolar disorder, posttraumatic stress disorder [PTSD], etc.).
2. Discuss with the client the alternative treatment interventions and community support resources that might facilitate his/her recovery.
3. Solicit from the client his/her preferences regarding the direction treatment will take; allow for these preferences to be communicated to family and significant others.
4. Discuss and process with the client the possible outcomes that may result from his/her decisions.

2. Specify any unique needs and cultural preferences that must be taken under consideration during the treatment process. (5, 6)

5. Explore with the client any cultural considerations, experiences, or other needs that must be considered in formulating a mutually agreed-upon treatment plan.

6. Modify treatment planning to accommodate the client's cultural and experiential background and preferences.

3. Verbalize an understanding that decision making throughout the treatment process is self-controlled. (7, 8)

7. Clarify with the client that he/she has the right to choose and select among options and participate in all decisions that affect him/her during treatment.

8. Continuously offer and explain options to the client as treatment progresses in support of his/her sense of empowerment, encouraging and reinforcing the client's participation in treatment decision making.

4. Express mental, physical, spiritual, and community needs and desires that should be integrated into the treatment process. (9, 10)

9. Assess the client's personal, interpersonal, medical, spiritual, and community strengths and weaknesses.

10. Maintain a holistic approach to treatment planning by integrating the client's unique mental, physical, spiritual, and community needs and assets into the plan; arrive at an agreement with the client as to how these integrations will be made.

5. Verbalize an understanding that during the treatment process there will be successes and failures, progress and setbacks. (11, 12)

11. Facilitate realistic expectations and hope in the client that positive change is possible, but

does not occur in a linear process of straight-line successes; emphasize a recovery process involving growth, learning from advances as well as setbacks, and staying this course toward recovery.

12. Convey to the client that you will stay the course with him/her through the difficult times of lapses and setbacks.

6. Cooperate with an assessment of personal strengths and assets brought to the treatment process. (13, 14, 15)

13. Administer to the client the *Behavioral and Emotional Rating Scale (BERS): A Strength-Based Approach to Assessment* (Epstein).

14. Identify the client's strengths through a thorough assessment involving social, cognitive, relational, and spiritual aspects of the client's life; assist the client in identifying what coping skills have worked well in the past to overcome problems and what talents and abilities characterize his/her daily life.

15. Provide feedback to the client of his/her identified strengths and how these strengths can be integrated into short-term and long-term recovery planning.

7. Verbalize an understanding of the benefits of peer support during the recovery process. (16, 17, 18)

16. Discuss with the client the benefits of peer support (e.g., sharing common problems, receiving advice regarding successful coping skills, getting encouragement, learning of helpful community

resources, etc.) toward the client's agreement to engage in peer activity.

17. Refer the client to peer support groups of his/her choice in the community and process his/her experience with follow-through.

18. Build and reinforce the client's sense of belonging, supportive relationship building, social value, and community integration by processing the gains and problem-solving the obstacles encountered through the client's social activities.

8. Agree to reveal when any occasion arises that respect is not felt from the treatment staff, family, self, or the community. (19, 20, 21)

19. Discuss with the client the crucial role that respect plays in recovery, reviewing subtle and obvious ways in which disrespect may be shown to or experienced by the client.

20. Review ways in which the client has felt disrespected in the past, identifying sources of that disrespect.

21. Encourage and reinforce the client's self-concept as a person deserving of respect; advocate for the client to increase incidents of respectful treatment within the community and/or family system.

9. Verbalize acceptance of responsibility for self-care and participation in decisions during the treatment process. (22)

22. Develop, encourage, support, and reinforce the client's role as the person in control of his/her treatment and responsible for its application to his/her daily life; adopt a supportive role as a resource

person to assist in the recovery process.

10. Express hope that better functioning in the future can be attained. (23, 24)

23. Discuss with the client potential role models who have achieved a more satisfying life by using their personal strengths, skills, and social support to live, work, learn, and fully participate in society toward building hope and incentive motivation.

24. Discuss and enhance internalization of the client's self-concept as a person capable of overcoming obstacles and achieving satisfaction in living; continuously build and reinforce this self-concept using past and present examples supporting it.

Appendix C

ASSESSMENT INSTRUMENTS

The ARC's Self-Determination Scale. M. L. Wehmeyer (1995). Arlington, TX: Association for Retarded Citizens (ARC).

Beck Depression Inventory, Second Edition (BDI-II). A. Beck, R. A. Steer, and G. Brown (1996). New York: Psychological Corporation.

Competence Assessment for Standing Trial for Defendants with Mental Retardation (CAST-MR). C. Everington and R. Luckasson (1992). Worthington, OH: International Diagnostic Services.

Dementia Rating Scale for Mentally Retarded Adults (DMR). H. M. Evenhuis, M. M. F. Kengen, and H. A. L. Eurlings (1990). Zwammerdam, The Netherlands: Institute for Mentally Retarded People. Available from HoogeBurch, P.O. Box 2027, 2470 AA Zwammerdam, The Netherlands.

Dementia Scale for Down Syndrome. A. Gedye (1995). Vancouver, British Columbia: Canga.

Diagnostic Assessment for the Severely Handicapped Scale, Second Edition (DASH-II). J. L. Matson (1995). Baton Rouge, LA: Scientific.

Reiss Screen for Maladaptive Behavior Test Manual. 2d ed. S. A. Reiss (1994). Overland Park, IL: International Diagnostics Systems.

The Sexual Abuse Interview for the Developmentally Disabled. D. Valenti-Hein, (1993). Sacramento, CA: James Stanfield.

"Social Performance Survey Schedule–Revised for Mentally Retarded Adults—Informant Report (SPSS-I)." J. L. Matson, W. J. Helsel, A. S. Bellack, and V. Senatore (1983). *Applied Research in Mental Retardation,* 4(4): 399–407.

State-Trait Anger Expression Inventory: Professional Manual. Rev. ed. C. D. Spielberger (1996). Odessa, FL: Psychological Assessment Resources.

TRAIL Leisure Assessment Battery for People with Cognitive Impairments (TLAB). J. Dattilo and G. Hoge (1993). Athens, GA: University of Georgia.

BIBLIOGRAPHY

Agran, M., and S. Moore (1994). *Innovations: How to Teach Self-Instruction of Job Skills.* Washington, DC: American Association on Mental Retardation.

Aman, M. G. (1991). *Assessing Psychopathology and Behavior Problems in Persons with Mental Retardation: A Review of Available Instruments.* Rockville, MD: U.S. Department of Health and Human Services.

American Psychiatric Association (1994). *Diagnostic and Statistical Manual of Mental Disorders.* 4th ed. Washington, DC: Author.

Belfoire, P. J., and W. Toro-Zambrana (1994). *Innovations: Recognizing Choices in Community Settings by People with Significant Disabilities.* Washington, DC: American Association on Mental Retardation.

Blotzer, M. A., and R. Ruth (1995). *Sometimes You Just Want to Feel Like a Human Being: Case Studies of Empowering Psychotherapy with People with Disabilities.* Baltimore: Paul H. Brookes.

Bradley, V. J., J. Knoll, and J. M. Agosta (1992). *Emerging Issues in Family Support.* Washington, DC: American Association on Mental Retardation.

Brown, G. T., P. Carney, J. Cortis, L. L. Metz, and A. M. Petrie (1994). *Human Sexuality Handbook: Guiding People toward Positive Expressions of Sexuality.* Springfield, IL: Association for Community Living.

Conley, R. W., R. Luckasson, and G. N. Bouthilet (1992). *The Criminal Justice System and Mental Retardation.* Baltimore: Paul H. Brookes.

Dattilo, J. (1994). *Inclusive Leisure Services: Responding to the Rights of People with Disabilities.* State College, PA: Venture.

Dattilo, J., and K. Bemisderfer (1996). *Leisure Education Curriculum Introduction.* Athens, GA: University of Georgia.

Davis, S. (1999). *Ten Steps to Independence: Promoting Self-Determination in the Home.* Arlington, TX: Association for Retarded Citizens (ARC).

Dosen, A., and F. J. Menolascino (1990). *Depression in Mentally Retarded Children and Adults.* Leiden, the Netherlands: Logon Publications.

Dunst, C. J., C. M. Trivette, and A. C. Deal (1994). *Supporting and Strengthening Families: Methods, Strategies, and Practices.* Cambridge, MA: Brookline Books.

Durand, M. (1998). *Sleep Better: A Guide to Improving Sleep for Children with Special Needs.* Baltimore: Paul H. Brookes.

Field, S., and A. Hoffman (1996). *Steps to Self-Determination: Instructors Guide.* Austin, TX: PRO-ED.

Finley, J., and B. Lenz (1999). *The Chemical Dependence Treatment Homework Planner.* New York: John Wiley & Sons.

Fletcher, R. J., ed. (1998). *Effective Therapy Approaches with Persons who Have Mental Retardation.* Kingston, NY: National Association for Dual Diagnosis.

Fletcher, R. J., and A. Dosen (1993). *Mental Health Aspects of Mental Retardation: Progress in Assessment and Treatments.* New York: Lexington Books.

Fox, R. M., and N. H. Azrin (1973). *Toilet Training the Retarded.* Champaign IL: Research Press.

Gorski, T. (1986). *Staying Sober: A Guide for Relapse Prevention.* Independence, MO: Independence Press.

Gorski, T. (1991). *Understanding the Twelve Steps: An Interpretation and Guide for Recovering People.* New York. Prentice Hall/Parkside.

Jacobson, J. W., S. N. Burchard, and P. J. Carling (1992). *Community Living for People with Developmental and Psychiatric Disabilities.* Baltimore: Johns Hopkins University Press.

Kaye, A., E. N. Sulllivan, M. A. Benedict, J. Knoll, and D. Skowyra (1994). *Aging and Developmental Disabilities Project in Michigan: A Curriculum Resource Packet.* Lansing, MI: Lansing Community College.

Kedesdy, J. H., and K. S. Budd (1998). *Childhood Feeding Disorders: Biobehavioral Assessment and Intervention.* Baltimore: Paul H. Brookes.

Kindig, M. N., and M. Carnes (1993). *Coping with Alzheimers Disease and Other Dementing Illnesses.* San Diego, CA: Singulare Publishing Group.

Levy, R. M., and L. S. Rubenstein (1996). *The Rights of People with Mental Disabilities: The Authoritative ACLU Guide to the Rights of People with Mental Illness and Mental Retardation.* Carbondale, IL: Southern Illinois University Press.

Little, J. (1997). *A Guide to Fair Housing: Creating Options for People with Disabilities.* Chicago: Chicago's Mayor's Office for People with Disabilities.

Lowman, D. K. (1999). *The Educator's Guide to Feeding Kids with Disabilities.* Baltimore: Paul H. Brookes.

McLoughlin, C. S., J. B. Garner, and M. Callahan (1987). *Getting Employed, Staying Employed.* Baltimore: Paul H. Brookes.

Moon, S., K. Inge., P. Wehman, V. Brooke, and M. Barcus (1990). *Helping Persons with Severe Mental Retardation Get and Keep Employment.* Baltimore: Paul H. Brookes.

Nezu, C. M., A. M. Nezu, and M. J. Gill-Weiss (1992). *Psychopathology in Persons with Mental Retardation.* Champaign, IL: Research Press.

Paine, R. (1992). *Handbook for Developing Community Based Employment.* Tucson, AZ: RPM Press.

Perkinson, R. R., and A. E. Jongsma (1998). *The Chemical Dependence Treatment Planner.* New York: John Wiley & Sons.

Poindexter, A. (1996). *Assessment and Treatment of Anxiety Disorders in Persons with Mental Retardation.* Kingston, NY: National Association for Dual Diagnosis.

Racino, J. A., P. Walker, S. O'Connor, and S. Taylor (1993). *Housing, Support, and Community: Choices and Strategies for Adults with Disabilities.* Baltimore: Paul H. Brookes.

Rappaport, S. R., S. A. Burkhardt, and A. F. Rotatori (1997). *Child Sexual Abuse Curriculum for the Developmentally Disabled.* Springfield, IL: Charles C. Thomas.

Reiss, S., and M. G. Aman (1998). *Psychotropic Medications and Developmental Disabilities: The International Consensus Handbook.* Columbus, OH: Nisonger Center, Ohio State University.

Sands, D. J., and M. L. Wehmeyer (1996). *Self-Determination across the Life Span.* Baltimore: Paul H. Brookes.

Schleien, S. J., L. H. Meyer, L. A. Heyne, and B. B. Brandt (1995). *Lifelong Leisure Skills and Lifestyles for Persons with Developmental Disabilities.* Baltimore: Paul H. Brookes.

Smith, G. H., C. D. Coles, M. K. Poulsen, and C. Cole (1995). *Children, Families, and Substance Abuse: Challenges for Changing Educational and Social Outcomes.* Baltimore: Paul H. Brookes.

Sobsey, D., S. Gray, D. Wells, D. Pyper, and B. Reimer-Heck (1991). *Disability, Sexuality, and Abuse: An Annotated Bibliography.* Baltimore: Paul H. Brookes.

Sqroi, S. (1989). *Sexual Abuse Treatment for Children, Adult Survivors, Offenders, and Persons with Mental Retardation.* Lexington, MA: Lexington Books.

Strumbo, N. J., and S. R. Thompson, eds. (1986). *Leisure Education: A Manual of Activities and Resources.* Peoria, IL: Central Illinois Center for Independent Living and Easter Seal Center.

Turnbull, A. P., J. M. Patterson, S. K. Behr, D. L. Murphy, J. G. Marquis, and M. J. Blue-Banning (1993). *Cognitive Coping, Families, and Disability.* Baltimore: Paul H. Brookes.

Visser, F. E., A. P. Aldenkamp, and A. C. Van Huffelen (1997). "Prospective Study of the Prevalence of Alzheimer-Type Dementia in Institutionalized Individuals with Down Syndrome." *American Journal on Mental Retardation,* 101(4): 400–412.

Wehmeyer, M. L. (1995) *Whose Future Is It Anyway? A Student-Directed Transition Planning Process.* Arlington TX: Association for Retarded Citizens (ARC).

Wehmeyer, M. L., M. Agran, and C. Hughes (1998). *Teaching Self-Determination to Students with Disabilities.* Baltimore: Paul H. Brookes.

Wehmeyer, M. L., and D. J. Sands (1998). *Making It Happen: Student Involvement in Education Planning, Decision Making, and Instruction.* Baltimore: Paul H. Brookes.

ABOUT THE DISK*

TheraScribe® 3.0 and 3.5 Library Module Installation

The enclosed disk contains files to upgrade your TheraScribe® 3.0 or 3.5 program to include the behavioral definitions, goals, objectives, and interventions from ***The Intellectual and Developmental Disability Treatment Planner.***

Note: You must have TheraScribe® 3.0 or 3.5 for Windows installed on your computer in order to use ***The Intellectual and Developmental Disability Treatment Planner*** library module.

To install the library module, please follow these steps:

1. Place the library module disk in your floppy drive.
2. Log in to TheraScribe® 3.0 or 3.5 as the Administrator using the name "Admin" and your administrator password.
3. On the Main Menu, press the "GoTo" button, and choose the Options menu item.
4. Press the "Import Library" button.
5. On the Import Library Module screen, choose your floppy disk drive a:\ from the list and press "Go." Note: It may take a few minutes to import the data from the floppy disk to your computer's hard disk.
6. When the installation is complete, the library module data will be available in your TheraScribe® 3.0 or 3.5 program.

Note: If you have a network version of TheraScribe® 3.0 or 3.5 installed, you should import the library module one time only. After importing the data, the library module data will be available to all network users.

User Assistance

If you need assistance using this TheraScribe® 3.0 or 3.5 add-on module, contact Wiley Technical Support at:

Phone: 212-850-6753
Fax: 212-850-6800 (Attention: Wiley Technical Support)
E-mail: techhelp@wiley.com

*Note: This section applies only to the book with disk edition, ISBN 0-471-38252-3.

Bib. # 943672

616. 858 SLA

For information on how to install disk, refer to the **About the Disk** section on page 311.

CUSTOMER NOTE:* IF THIS BOOK IS ACCOMPANIED BY SOFTWARE, PLEASE READ THE FOLLOWING BEFORE OPENING THE PACKAGE.

This software contains files to help you utilize the models described in the accompanying book. By opening the package, you are agreeing to be bound by the following agreement:

This software product is protected by copyright and all rights are reserved by the author, John Wiley & Sons, Inc., or their licensors. You are licensed to use this software on a single computer. Copying the software to another medium or format for use on a single computer does not violate the U.S. Copyright Law. Copying the software for any other purpose is a violation of the U.S. Copyright Law.

This software product is sold as is without warranty of any kind, either express or implied, including but not limited to the implied warranty of merchantability and fitness for a particular purpose. Neither Wiley nor its dealers or distributors assumes any liability for any alleged or actual damages arising from the use of or the inability to use this software. (Some states do not allow the exclusion of implied warranties, so the exclusion may not apply to you.)

WILEY

*Note: This section applies only to the book with disk edition, ISBN 0-471-38252-3.